Making Money

Making Money

The Philosophy of Crisis Capitalism

Ole Bjerg

VERSO
London • New York

FOUNDATION BOOKS

FOUNDATION
BOOKS

Foundation Books is an imprint of Cambridge University Press, India.

Cambridge House, 4381/4 Ansari Road, Daryaganj, New Delhi 110 002

www.cambridgeindia.org

First published by Verso 2014
First South Asia edition 2015

Printed in India at Shree Maitrey Printech Pvt. Ltd., Noida

ISBN 978-93-84463-48-9 Paperback

For Simon

Contents

PART THREE: THE AGE OF POST-CREDIT MONEY

Introduction: *Seinsvergessenheit* and Money

This is a book about how to make money. The phrase 'making money' has a double meaning. The first and most immediate meaning refers to the circulation and distribution of money in the world. When someone starts a working day with the declaration: 'Let's make some money!', it typically means: 'Let's appropriate a portion of the existing pool of money already in circulation in the economy'. But, if we take the phrase literally, making money has another meaning that refers to the procedure whereby new money comes into being and is introduced into the economy.

In the first interpretation, making money is something that a lot of people think about a lot of the time. 'How can I make some money?' This is a question that most people have to ask themselves from time to time. For some, the question is a matter of survival. They need to make some money in order to put food on the table and pay their bills. For others, it is an existential question defining who they are and how they fit into the social order. And, for most people, the question probably hinges on a combination of both survival and identity.

In the second and more literal interpretation, making money is something few people think about. 'Where does money come from? How does money come into the world? Who makes the money that we use in our everyday economic interactions?' These kinds of questions seem to receive relatively little attention considering the scope of our preoccupation with money in contemporary capitalism. According to Martin Heidegger, the most difficult things to think about and understand are often the ones that are closest to us, the things we take for granted. Our familiarity with a particular thing seems to stand in the way of the reflection and speculation that is necessary to reach a deeper understanding of the thing. This applies, for instance, to language. Language is such a natural part of our being that even small children know how to use it. Nevertheless, few if any people can claim to have a full understanding of what language actually is. The same paradox applies to money. We use money every day. It is a key component in many of our interactions with other people and in our perceptions of the things surrounding us. Nevertheless, the fundamental nature of money remains for the most part taken for granted.

This fact plays out not only in individual people's everyday dealings with money, but also in our collective political imagination. The critical economic situation that came about in 2007–8 as an increasing number of defaults among American homeowners strained banks and financial institutions, eventually causing the collapse of Bear Stearns and Lehman Brothers, was immediately named a 'financial crisis'. While this naming may have seemed to merely register the fact that alarming events were indeed unfolding in financial markets and major financial institutions, the term 'financial crisis' created a particular framing of the situation, preconditioning certain interpretations and solutions. First of all, the term 'financial' suggested that the critical situation that came about was a result of the way that activities and assets in the economy were priced and the way that capital was allocated to fund them. Secondly, the term 'crisis' suggested that the situation was an exceptional deviation from a normal state. Crises may be overcome, allowing us to return to normality.

Understanding the situation as a financial crisis invites the explanation that the problem lies in the way that individuals and institutions *make money* in financial markets. Bankers are greedy and immoral, financial models are out of sync with economic realities, regulators are naive, corrupt or both, and the combination of these three factors leads to the exploitation of ordinary people, who in turn lack the ability to restrain their desire for excessive consumption funded by cheap credit. Invoking this type of explanation, we think in terms of the first meaning of the phrase 'making money'. While such explanations do indeed hold true to an extent, they tend to divert our attention away from the second meaning of the phrase, which has to do with the more fundamental issue of the way money comes into being in contemporary capitalism.

Heidegger may provide us with the concepts to make a philosophical distinction between the two meanings of 'making money'. At the heart of his thinking we find the ontological difference between beings (*Seiende*) and Being (*Sein*). When something is investigated as a being it is approached as an individual entity among other entities. The purpose of the investigation is to map out the properties distinguishing it from other beings and to explore its relations to other beings. Investigations of particular beings are structured around questions of the form 'What is X?' Such questions might include: What is Man? (Is it rational, is it animal, is it moral?, etc.); or, What is the world? (Is it real, is it an idea, is it knowable?, etc.).

In contrast to this kind of questioning, investigations of Being are concerned with the implications of the fact that something *is*; they are concerned with the meaning of 'to be'. Investigations of this type do not pose questions in the form 'What is X?' but rather 'How is X?' In *Being and Time* the 'X' in question is Man, but in order to avoid treating Man merely as a being, Heidegger instead uses the term *Dasein*, as the designation of Man's 'to be' (Dasein means simply 'being-there', but the term is not normally translated from the original German).[1] When Heidegger thus inquires into the Being of Dasein, it is crucial to note that the emphasis is on Being, not on Dasein. The focus of the investigation is the implication of 'to be'. Heidegger's is an investigation of the constitution of the Being of Dasein.

When we ask questions like 'How can I make some money?', 'How can this company make some money?', or even 'How can this country make some money?', we think of money merely as a being. Our concern is to intervene in the circulation of monetary entities in order to cause a redistribution of the money in a way that benefits us. But once we move beyond this immediate understanding of the phrase 'making money' and start questioning the way money comes into being in the first place, we enter into the investigation of the very Being of money. In *The Principle of Reason*, Heidegger provides us with a method for reversing our questioning in a way that opens up this kind of investigation. Heidegger takes as his point of departure Leibniz's Principle of Reason: 'Nothing is without reason' *nihil est sine ratione*. But rather than reading the sentence as '*nothing* is *without* reason', which simply means that there is a reason for everything in the world, Heidegger shifts the emphasis by reading the sentence 'nothing *is* without *reason*'. In this way, the sentence comes to be a statement about the way that nothing 'is', a statement about the very Being of Nothingness. This shift of emphasis turns the sentence into an answer to the ontological question: How *is* Nothingness? Heidegger himself explains the method: 'Behind the shift in tonality is concealed

1 Heidegger, *Being and Time*. (As with all citations in this book, full publication details are provided in the bibliography.)

a leap of thinking'.[2] The further metaphysical implications of Heidegger's analysis of Nothingness point beyond the scope of our current investigation. However, the shift in emphasis is highly relevant to our analysis of money. Rather than falling into the intellectual traps of the question 'What is money?' or even implicitly accepting existing answers to this question, our investigation is concerned with the question 'How is it that money exists?', or simply 'How *is* money?'

In his sweeping critique of Western metaphysics, Heidegger coins the beautiful word *Seinsvergessenheit*, which translates into something like 'forgetfulness of Being'. He claims that philosophy since even before Plato and Aristotle has been preoccupied only with the investigation of the world of beings, thus systematically neglecting the fundamental question of Being. Leaving aside the validity of Heidegger's claim vis-à-vis the history of philosophy for more than 2,000 years, we may apply his thinking to the status of the question of money in contemporary capitalism.

> Do we in our time have an answer to the question of what we really mean by the word 'money'? Not at all. So it is fitting that we should raise anew *the question of the meaning of the Being of money*. But are we nowadays even perplexed at our inability to understand the expression 'money'? Not at all. So first of all we must reawaken an understanding for the meaning of this question.[3]

This is a paraphrase of Heidegger's preamble to *Being and Time*. In the passage, I have taken the liberty of substituting the word 'Being' with 'money' and with 'Being of money'. With these alterations, the passage makes two points about the *Seinsvergessenheit* of money today. Not only do we lack a proper understanding of the phenomenon of money. We are not even perplexed at this lack of understanding. For the most part, we are perfectly content to use money without understanding or even questioning its functioning, or we uncritically accept popular shorthand accounts of the origins and nature of money.

Given the amount of economic research and education today, and the lofty status of the discipline of economics in politics as well as popular discourse, it would be erroneous to claim that we do not have

2 Heidegger, *The Principle of Reason*, 53.
3 Heidegger, *Being and Time*, 1.

enough knowledge about money. The question is, rather, whether we have the proper kind of knowledge about money. According to Heidegger, *Seinsvergessenheit* is not an error occurring at some point in the course of thinking about a specific matter. *Seinsvergessenheit* sets in at the very beginning, at the very moment when we set out to think about and investigate a matter, if we are not careful to pose our questions in the proper fashion. I want to argue that much of the thinking about economic issues in mainstream economics as well as in popular political discourse suffers from *Seinsvergessenheit*.

To see how the difference between beings and Being applies to money and how *Seinsvergessenheit* plays out in the field of economics, we shall look at the opening pages of an introductory textbook on economics. This beginning of a beginning reads:

> On the evening news you have just heard that the Federal Reserve is raising the federal funds rate by ½ of a percentage point. What effect might this have on the interest rate of an automobile loan when you finance your purchase of a sleek new sports car? Does it mean that a house will be more or less affordable in the future? Will it make it easier or harder for you to get a job next year? This book provides answers to these and other questions by examining how financial markets (such as those for bonds, stocks, and foreign exchange) and financial institutions (banks, insurance companies, mutual funds, and other institutions) work and by exploring the role of money in the economy.[4]

Even though this quote is more or less arbitrarily chosen, it serves as an illustration of the way mainstream economists think about money. It's worth noting that besides having outstanding academic credentials, the author of the book, Frederic Mishkin, has held prominent positions with the US Federal Reserve Bank, including as a member of its Board of Governors between 2006 and 2008. The questions raised in the passage regard correlations between different monetary measures: between the federal funds rate and the interest rate on consumer loans, between interest rate and real estate prices, and between interest rate and employment rate. In Heidegger's terms, these are all *ontic* as opposed to *ontological* questions. They concern

4 Mishkin, *The Economics of Money, Banking, and Financial Markets*, 3.

the way money functions as a particular being in relation to other beings, leaving the fundamental 'to be' of money unexamined.

The scientific discipline of economics has been extremely successful in producing sophisticated formulas and models to map the interrelations between such economic measures in society. Few scientific disciplines have had as much success in influencing the way we think about, talk about and organize society. Given this success, it is indeed difficult to raise objections to the way economics deals with money. Even if we grant that economics as a discipline has neglected to pose the question of the Being of money, has it not done very well without having to deal with this question? It can even be argued that the reason for the relative success of economics is exactly that the discipline has not been caught up in philosophical sophistry. Economics is very quick to get down to business. This is in contrast to, say, philosophy, which seems to have been stuck on the same questions for more than 2,000 years.

What is lost, however, in neglecting the question of the Being of money is an awareness of the contingency and changeability of the contemporary forms of money. Markets evolve and the distribution of value and money in society constantly changes. This is what economics is able to track in great detail. Yet, for economic models to achieve the impressive level of accuracy and precision that makes them applicable to the practical affairs of business and government, certain components of the models must be kept constant and unquestioned. This includes the nature and constitution of money. When actual politics are guided by mainstream economics, the constancy of money is presupposed and the monetary imagination is severely narrowed. This is how ideology operates with regard to the question of money. At work is the mechanism that Slavoj Žižek refers to as 'ideological naturalization':

> In contemporary global capitalism, ideological naturalization has reached an unprecedented level: rare are those who dare even to *dream* utopian dreams about possible alternatives . . . Far from proving that the era of ideological utopias is behind us, this uncontested hegemony of capitalism is sustained by the properly utopian core of capitalist ideology. Utopias of alternative worlds have been exorcized by the utopia in power, masking itself as pragmatic realism.[5]

5 Žižek, *First as Tragedy, Then as Farce*, 77.

As the contemporary form of money is naturalized, it becomes difficult to discuss or even imagine other forms of money as solutions to contemporary economic and social problems. Political discussions in the aftermath of the financial meltdown of 2008 were soon directed towards the narrow question of whether and how state governments should intervene and support major private financial institutions to prevent a total collapse of the markets. The extraordinary capacity of capitalism to 'naturalize' itself, not just as the dominant but as the *only* thinkable system for the production and distribution of value today, was manifested in the curious paradox that the most radical ideas in the debate came from the most inveterate proponents of free-market capitalism, who suggested that the state stay out and let the forces of the market take their 'natural' course. The difference of opinion in today's political landscape is measured not by *whether* you are for or against capitalism, but by *how* you are for capitalism.

The political reaction to the financial crisis of 2008 is comparable to the reaction to the destruction of the World Trade Center on September 11, 2001. Just as the financial crisis could have been an occasion to rethink and revise contemporary capitalism, the attack on 9/11 could have been an occasion to debate the role of the US as the hegemonic world power and to reconsider the relationship between the so-called developed and developing countries of the world. The event was a tragedy, but at the same time it opened a political window of opportunity to possibly change the basic coordinates of our political system. As we know, however, this window was shut almost immediately when the collapse of the three towers was used to launch the War on Terror.

The solution to the financial crisis adopted by most Western states was to bail out the financially distressed banks. The rationale behind government intervention in financial markets went like this: 'Under normal circumstances, financial markets find their own equilibrium, which provides the optimal conditions for the production and distribution of value and money in society. The current situation, however, is exceptional. It falls outside the spectrum of normality and thus calls for exceptional measures. We, the government, will therefore make an exceptional intervention in the markets in order to restore a state of normality so that the markets can again be trusted to function in a way that requires no further government interference.'

The approach to government intervention in financial markets is structurally homologous to the reasoning applied to the issue of torture (and the suspension of various civil rights) following 9/11. The rationale behind the use of torture on 'enemy combatants' suspected of terror-related activities by the US and its allies went like this: 'Under normal circumstances, we as democratic governments believe in the sanctity of human rights and condemn the use of torture. The current situation, however, is exceptional. It falls outside the spectrum of normality and thus calls for exceptional measures. We, democratic governments, will therefore make exceptional use of torture in order to eliminate an immediate threat to our societies and restore a state of normality so that democracy can again be trusted to function and survive in a way that requires no further use of undemocratic measures of force such as torture'.

In both cases – 9/11 and the financial crisis – the closing of the window of opportunity meant fundamental questions about the social order were excluded from debate. In the context of the financial crisis, many crucial questions about the constitution of money were not raised, such as: Do we want private banks at all? Do we want an economy based on money created out of debt? Should we allow financial markets to determine the conditions for economic policy? Is it an absolute duty for debtors to pay their debts? Do we want an economy based on perpetual growth? It would be an overstatement to say that the question of the nature of money is completely absent from mainstream economics. Nevertheless, the question is typically treated in a way that evades the ontological constitution of money. The standard reply to the question 'What is money?' is to list what are believed to be the four defining functions of money: 1) medium of exchange; 2) unit of account; 3) store of value; and 4) standard of deferred payment. This fourfold definition of money can even be summed up in a neat rhyme: 'Money is a matter of functions four / A medium, a measure, a standard, a store'.

It is crucial to note that in this account, the original question of what money *is* is answered by a description of what money *does*; the fourfold list enumerates the *functions performed by money*. By no means can we claim this account is wrong. The answer provided amounts to replying to the question 'What is a hammer?' by saying 'It is a thing used to knock nails into wood'. However, the account implies the naturalization of money in at least two ways.

First, we might ask whether this list of functions is exhaustive. Money certainly performs these four functions, but money also seems to do a lot more than this. Is money not also a means of controlling other people, a standardization of desire, a mechanism for the concentration of wealth in the hands of a minority of people, and a cause for the grievances of a majority of people? The listing of the four aforementioned functions implies that these are the necessary capacities of money, whereas all other functions are merely accidental. This is analogous to saying that the capacity for hammering nails is a necessary property of a hammer, whereas the capacity for hammering thumbs is merely an accidental property. In the case of a hammer, such a definition is perhaps unproblematic, but in the case of money, it is certainly not. Defining money in terms of the four functions is as misleading as answering the question 'What is a gun?' by saying, 'A gun is a thing that promotes peace by protecting innocent people'.

Second, defining money in terms of the functions performed by money presents money as merely a practical solution to a practical problem. This point can be further elaborated if we take a look at another passage from the introductory economics textbook. The following passage, which comes from a chapter entitled 'What Is Money?', tries to explain the function of money as a medium of exchange:

> The use of money as a medium of exchange promotes economic efficiency by minimizing the time spent in exchanging goods and services. To see why, let's look at a barter economy, one without money, in which goods and services are exchanged directly for other goods and services.
>
> Take the case of Ellen the Economics Professor, who can do just one thing well: give brilliant economics lectures. In a barter economy, if Ellen wants to eat, she must find a farmer who not only produces the food she likes but also wants to learn economics. As you might expect, this search will be difficult and time-consuming, and Ellen might spend more time looking for such an economics-hungry farmer than she will teaching. It is even possible that she will have to quit lecturing and go into farming herself. Even so, she may still starve to death.
>
> The time spent trying to exchange goods or services is called a transaction cost. In a barter economy, transaction costs are high

> because people have to satisfy a 'double coincidence of wants'—they have to find someone who has a good or service they want and who also wants the good or service they have to offer.
>
> Let's see what happens if we introduce money into Ellen the Economics Professor's world. Ellen can teach anyone who is willing to pay money to hear her lecture. She can then go to any farmer (or his representative at the supermarket) and buy the food she needs with the money she has been paid. The problem of the double coincidence of wants is avoided, and Ellen saves a lot of time, which she may spend doing what she does best: teaching.[6]

The scenario in the passage is indeed imaginary. Nevertheless, it provides a number of key insights into the way money is conceived in mainstream economics. Given the imaginary nature of the scenario, we might treat the passage much in the same way as psychoanalysts treat dreams, i.e. as a scenario revealing the underlying fantasies of the economist.

The scenario presents the genesis of money as a practical solution to a practical problem. There is a professor with services (teaching economics) and a farmer with goods (produce), and the problem is how to make them enter into a relation of exchange. Money is then introduced into the equation and the problem is solved. In this exposition, the problem solved by money is naturalized. Lurking in the background of this exposition is a variation on Heidegger's enigmatic question: 'Why are there beings at all instead of nothing?'[7] This variation is of course: Why is there money at all instead of no money? But while Heidegger's question is retained as a metaphysical enigma, the purpose of which is to perpetuate radical metaphysical thinking, the textbook exposition of the question of money is, on the contrary, rendered as a banality for which there is a simple conclusive answer.

There is, furthermore, a curious paradox built into the textbook scenario: the presence of an economist in a barter economy. We might argue that in a barter economy there would be no economists, since the problems economists work to solve emerge only with the introduction of money. To even imagine a farmer in a barter economy who would be interested in lectures on economics veils the fact that the

6 Mishkin, *The Economics of Money, Banking, and Financial Markets*, 45.
7 Heidegger, *Introduction to Metaphysics*, 1.

problems that would make economics relevant to the farmer emerge only in a money economy. In this sense, the image of an economist in a barter economy obscures the dual role of money as problem-solver and problem-creator. The presence of an economist in a barter economy elevates economics from being not only the science of the problems and questions posed by the evolution of money, but even the science of pre-monetary Man. In other words, the economist is a philosopher. Is this not indicative of the position of economic science and economists in the political landscape today? In contemporary post-ideological capitalism, economics functions as the science of life itself.

The image of money as a practical solution to a practical problem obscures the ideological dimensions of money. We can discuss who should get more or less money and who should be forced to pay more or less money, and indeed these issues are readily debated in contemporary political fora. Yet, these debates operate largely within the boundaries marked out by the existing form of the monetary system. It is taken for granted that the contemporary forms of money provide the most optimal solutions to a set of economic problems considered to be merely the extension of human nature. The political challenges of today are reduced to administering the current economic and monetary systems in a way that optimizes the functioning of these systems, as measured by a set of parameters already defined by the systems themselves.

Making Money is a philosophical analysis of money in contemporary capitalism. Besides reaching a deeper understanding of money, the purpose of the analysis is to politicize money. If there is an intrinsic tendency in mainstream economics towards a naturalization of the current form of money, the ambition of this book is to utilize philosophy to disturb this naturalization. The scope of our collective political imagination should not be limited to different models for what we can do with the money we have. It should be opened up to include speculation about the potential for creating new and different kinds of monetary systems, new and different kinds of money.

We should be careful not to exaggerate the extent to which the ontological question of money has been completely forgotten by all forms of thinking about economic matters. Introducing mainstream economics as the initial *Prügelknabe* of the discussion is in some sense picking an easy target. Thinking about money takes place in other fields of knowledge as well, where there tends to be more reflection about the nature of money. First, we should realize that economics is not identical to mainstream economics. In recent years there has been a growing interest in so-called heterodox economics; especially after the onset of the 2008 financial crisis, this field of research has gained momentum.[8] Heterodox economics is not in itself a unitary paradigm, but rather an umbrella term covering a range of different approaches to the study of economic matters, including post-Keynesianism, Marxism, Austrian economics, social economics, etc. What holds these diverse perspectives together is not an inner consistency around fundamental assumptions but rather their common opposition to orthodox or mainstream economics. Heterodox economics is, in other words, united in agreement over its disagreement with orthodox economics. Over the course of the book I shall draw on insights from heterodox economists, as they do indeed provide fruitful critique founded on a thorough engagement with the fundamentals of economics.

Second, while the study of money and finance may be dominated by economics, in recent years the disciplines of sociology and anthropology have broken new ground in the study of economic topics. Perhaps the most prominent example is the field of the social studies of finance, which is constituted by such publications as Michel Callon's *The Law of the Market*, Karin Knorr-Cetina and Alex Preda's *The Sociology of Financial Markets*, Donald MacKenzie's *An Engine, Not a Camera*, Caitlin Zaloom's *Out of the Pits*, and Karen Ho's *Liquidated*. Along similar lines, we should add publications from the field of the anthropology of money, such as Viviana Zelizer's *The Social Meaning of Money* and David Graeber's *Debt: The First 5,000 Years*. What we find in both of these fields are empirical studies of economic matters based on qualitative research, marking a clear distinction from economics, which tends to work either quantitatively or purely theoretically. Again, I shall be using research from both sociology and anthropology to support and inform the analyses carried out over the course of this book.

Still, the ambition of this book is to carve out a distinct field for the philosophical study of money. Philosophy is distinguished from

---

8 Davis, 'The Nature of Heterodox Economics'; Lawson, 'The Current Economic Crisis'.

economics as well as from the social sciences not so much by the capacity to provide new answers to old questions, but rather by the capacity to pose radically new questions. Good questions are the trademark of any good philosophy. And furthermore, the posing of new questions in philosophy serves as the vehicle for the creation of new concepts. The gist of philosophy is not the application of existing theories to new empirical fields and problems, but the very production of new theoretical concepts to facilitate thinking. I do not wish to imply that philosophical thinking is completely absent from studies carried out under the label of economics, sociology or anthropology, just as any good philosophical analysis is informed by findings from other fields. The point is merely that the ultimate benchmark for an analysis that calls itself philosophy is whether it pushes our conventional thinking beyond the verification or refutation of existing hypotheses.

In this introduction, I have used Heidegger to open up the question of money for philosophical inquiry. But once we get started with the actual analyses, the primary theoretical point of reference will be Slavoj Žižek. I have found his distinction between the three ontological orders – the real, the symbolic and the imaginary – to be well-suited to conceptualize the functioning of financial markets as well as the multiple dimensions involved in the constitution of money. While an engagement with contemporary capitalism is intrinsic to Žižek's oeuvre, reflections about money as such appear only as rudimentary fragments scattered throughout his writings. The ambition of *Making Money* is to redeem the potential in Žižek's philosophy for pushing the boundaries of our current thinking about money and finance.

What Žižek offers to the analysis is, first and foremost, immense conceptual firepower. The triad of real–symbolic–imaginary is the foundation of a rich system of interrelated concepts that allows us to explore the philosophical implications of several aspects of the constitution of contemporary money, including financial markets, financial speculation, price, value, risk, gold, state, credit, commercial banking, central banking, derivatives, and so on. One of the positive results of the economic crisis that started in 2007–8 was the awakening of a critical public interest in the constitution and functioning of the international finance and banking system. As ever new aspects of this system come to light, we see the contours of a highly complex global machine that serves to not only facilitate global trade and production, but also to systematically concentrate large amounts of wealth in the hands of a very small minority of people. The complexity and perversity of the contemporary money system must be countered with a theoretical framework that is even more complex and more perverse. This is what Žižek provides. He is the Goldman Sachs of contemporary philosophy.

The outline of the book is structured along the lines of the two meanings of the phrase 'making money'. Part one starts out from the first and most immediate meaning. The purpose of this part is to analyze how speculators and investors make money in financial markets. Chapter one presents the basic coordinates of Žižek's thinking, as the triad of real–symbolic–imaginary is applied to the analysis of financial markets. In this chapter I also present two schools of speculation in financial markets – technical analysis and fundamental analysis – and review their philosophical properties. Chapter two proceeds by tracing the intellectual history of modern neoclassical finance. The evolution of the notion of the efficient market is a key component in the neoclassical approach to financial speculation. I demonstrate how this theoretical notion functions as a fantasy with profound implications for the conditions of actual financial trading.

The relevance of the analysis of financial speculation rests on the assumption that today we live in the age of financial capitalism. When Marx studied money in the context of industrial capitalism, he looked at the way capital functioned to structure the production and circulation of commodities. In order to study money today, we need to look at the way capital functions to structure the buying, selling and pricing of stocks, bonds, currencies, derivatives and other forms of financial securities that are traded in global financial markets. This is the 'natural habitat' of contemporary money.

The assumption that today we live in the age of financial capitalism does not imply that industrial production or other forms of economic interaction no longer exist. In fact, the amount of industrial production today greatly exceeds the amount of industrial production at the time Marx wrote *Capital*. Still, the importance of financial markets today lies in the fact that the logic of these markets seems to pervade more and more spheres of economic life. The logic of finance is no longer confined to financial markets. As the pricing of an increasing array of assets – and even the pricing of money itself – is ultimately determined in financial markets, agents engaged in the so-called 'real economy', such as farmers, manufacturers, or even private homeowners, become subject to the logic of these markets. Finance is the defining logic of contemporary money.

Part two proceeds along the lines of the second meaning of the phrase 'making money'. The purpose of this part is to investigate how money comes into being and how certain objects come to function as money. Following Heidegger, this is the ontological question proper: How *is* money? Chapter three presents a further dimension of Žižek's philosophy, as his theory of the subject as $ is appropriated for a philosophical understanding of money. I apply this theory to an analysis of the commodity theory of money (Smith/Marx) and the fiat theory of money (Knapp/Keynes). In chapter four, I apply Žižek's theory to an analysis of the credit theory of money (Innes). This includes an analysis of the ontological properties of banking.

Part three conflates the two meanings of making money; it presents the idea that contemporary capitalism is characterized by very distinct conditions for making money by making money. In this part, I put the ontological issue of money into an historical and sociological context and pose the question: What *is* money today? Chapter five investigates the monetary paradigm shift that occurred with the collapse of the Bretton Woods system in 1971. I argue that this shift led to the current state of money, which is marked by the dominance of post-credit money. Chapter six demonstrates how the proliferation of post-credit money is driven by the concurrent exponential growth in financial derivatives trading. The combined effect of these two trends leads to a general destabilization of money, where control of the creation and pricing of money is transferred from the sphere of democratic politics to the sphere of financial markets, in which certain private agents hold privileged positions.

The conclusion attempts to point beyond the contemporary paradigm of money by imagining what revolution would look like in the age of financial capitalism.

Part One:

The Philosophy of Finance

CHAPTER ONE

Analyzing Financial Markets

A key element in the emergence of modern finance in the twentieth century is the application of models and methods from the natural sciences to the study of financial markets. Arguably, modern finance was born with Louis Bachelier's *Théorie de la Spéculation* in 1900. Bachelier discovered a homology between the movement of prices on the Parisian exchange for bond trading and the diffusion of heat through a physical substance. This discovery allowed him to apply common mathematical models developed in the field of physics – most notably the Gaussian normal distribution model – to the study of financial phenomena.

The guiding methodological idea of this book is to make a comparable interdisciplinary connection. Instead of using natural science as the paradigm for the study of finance, we want to make a connection between finance and philosophy. By re-describing the functioning of financial markets in philosophical term, we want to open up the field to an application of philosophical models and concepts. This application is primarily structured around Slavoj Žižek's distinction between real, symbolic and imaginary.

Modern finance is a discipline of great systemic complexity and methodological rigour. These qualities have come about largely through the appropriation of mathematics and the empirical natural sciences as the methodological foundations of the discipline. What philosophy has to offer in the study of financial markets is certainly neither of these qualities. Some might even argue that philosophy is characterized by the opposite qualities: speculative analysis and haphazard methodology. While I do not concur with such a view of philosophy, it is indeed the case that the purpose of this investigation is not to support the widespread self-conception among scholars in the field that finance is really a sub-discipline of the natural sciences. Perhaps the purpose of the analysis may be summed up in a very old-fashioned Marxist way: the unveiling of the ideological component in the functioning of financial markets.

The analysis starts with the question: How does money function in financial markets? This is not necessarily a philosophical question. It could just as well initiate an economic analysis. The difference between the philosophical and economic analysis turns on the way we hear the question. Both the philosophical as well as the economic analysis may start out by understanding money in terms of the distinction between value and price. The economic analysis might explain the functioning of money as the pricing of valuable assets. One of the key competencies in economics and finance is the ability to compose models for estimating the price of valuable assets. Black and Scholes's option pricing model, which we will return to, is perhaps the most prominent of such models in the history of modern finance. Thus, the economic analyst hears the question about the functioning of money in financial markets as, 'How are valuable assets priced in the market?'

In the terminology of Heidegger, economics is an ontic investigation of the question of money. It translates the question of money into 'what does money do'. The ontic is an investigation of beings (*Seiende*) in terms of their 'what-ness' (*Was-sein*). Hence, economics will provide an answer to the question of money by unveiling the pricing mechanisms inherent in the market. Our philosophical approach to money is an ontological investigation, as we are concerned with the very 'to be' (*Sein*) of money. Although we will investigate money in relation to the distinction between value and price, the main purpose of this analysis is to map out the functioning of the market in terms of the interrelation between different ontological domains, which is the very precondition for the phenomenon of money. The question of money is broken down into a series of questions: What *is* value? What *is* price? What *is* the market? The philosophical answer to these questions comes about by assigning each of the components to different ontological domains and explaining their interrelation. To help us turn money and financial markets into objects of philosophical study, we shall invoke the thinking of Slavoj Žižek, in particular his distinction between three ontological orders: the real, the symbolic and the imaginary.

THE REAL OF VALUE

At the heart of Žižek's philosophy we find the threefold distinction between real, symbolic and imaginary.[1] These concepts each refer to a distinct ontological order. In this sense, Žižek's thinking resembles

---

1 Žižek, *The Sublime Object of Ideology*.

that of Heidegger insofar as both start out by distinguishing different ontological orders. Heidegger makes a twofold distinction between 'to be' (*Sein*) and beings (*Seiende*).

Applying Žižek's thinking to finance, we can conceive of financial markets as systems of symbolization. In their simplest form, financial markets refer to different underlying assets in the productive economy. A stock refers to the assets of the company that has issued the stock, and it entitles the holder of the stock to a share of the cash flow generated by these assets. A bond refers to the debt of a nation, and it entitles the holder to the cash flow generated by the interest payments on this debt. When a stock or bond is traded at a certain price, this price functions as a symbolic representation of the value of the underlying assets and the value of the expected cash flow.

The meaning of Žižek's notion of the symbolic becomes clear only when we think of it in relation to the order of the real. Along these lines, we can think of the relation between securities in financial markets and their underlying assets in terms of the distinction between the symbolic and the real. Prices, as established in financial markets, are symbolic expressions of the real value of their underlying assets. Žižek defines the symbolic as a system of signs that emerge as the real is integrated into a social order of language, meaning, law, etc. However, as anyone who has even the slightest experience with financial markets knows, value is an extremely elusive concept. We might even suggest that it is the very elusiveness of value that generates financial trading.

According to Žižek, the operation of symbolization is not determined by qualities inherent in the symbolized objects of the real. On the contrary, certain paradigms of meaning and regularity are reproduced within the symbolic order on the basis of structures inherent in this order. In this respect, Žižek concurs with mainstream social constructivist thinking, as represented by figures such as Wittgenstein, Luhmann or Foucault. If we observe here Žižek's distinction between the social *reality* and the *real*,[2] we see how the symbolization of the real is a social construction of reality. Along these lines, prices in the financial markets are not determined by some kind of value absolutely inherent in the real assets. Prices are rather social constructions of reality. Prices are determined by market-immanent mechanisms rather than independent qualities of the real.

---

2 Žižek, *Looking Awry*, 3–20.

As the real is transformed into the reality of our social world, the real is at the same time lost. Symbolization bars our access to the real. There is here an affinity with Heidegger's idea that our preoccupation with the world as beings prevents us from experiencing the world in its immediate 'to be'. Once the real has become integrated into the symbolic order of language and meaning, it is inaccessible in its immediate and undifferentiated state. We may compare this to the way that the sound and rhythm of a voice eludes us once we become occupied with working out the meaning of the words spoken by the voice. In the world of finance, we see how the trading of stocks at the exchange is typically carried out with regard to nothing except the price and expected future developments in the price of the stock. This means that the qualities of the underlying company are effaced to such an extent that they have no bearing on the price. We thus see how the introduction of a company into a stock exchange sometimes has the effect of diverting the attention of management and owners from the social, ethical and environmental aspects of the company's activities, narrowing their focus to short-term fluctuations in the stock price. The effect of effacing the qualities of underlying economic entities is further magnified when trading moves into the sphere of derivatives. These financial products, to which we shall return, do not even refer directly to real existing economic entities, but merely to rights and obligations involved in the trading of other financial products at specified future points in time. In the virtual reality of derivatives trading, the real existing economy is often reduced to a mere abstraction and thus lost from view.

Still, it would be a gross oversimplification to reduce financial markets to mere social constructs. In the fluctuations of financial markets, there is a constant interplay between market-immanent forces and events outside the markets. Žižek's distinction between symbolic reality and the real is well-suited to theorizing this interplay. The point where Žižek breaks off from mainstream social constructivist thinking is in his insistence on the incompleteness or even the impossibility of every system of symbolization. The relation between the real and the symbolic is characterized by an ontological imbalance. On the one hand, symbolization bars our access to the real. But on the other, there is in every operation of symbolization a leftover in the form of a surplus or a deficit of the real. Thus emerges the strange paradox that the real is something we can never reach, but also something we can never get rid of.

This paradox captures the condition of the financial speculator. Sometimes prices in financial markets seem to move independently of the real conditions of the underlying assets. For instance, there may be a drastic increase in the stock price of a company on a day when there no new information is released about the operation of the company. In such cases, the market seems to have taken on a life of its own. At other times, the market is extremely responsive to external events related to the real assets being traded, and new information is immediately registered in stock prices. In philosophical terms, the market has a double epistemology. The speculator is constantly faced with the dilemma of how to mediate between these two epistemologies.

The real is a key component in all of Žižek's thinking, and he theorizes the real in different ways at different points in his work. At one point, the real is located in a positive existence beyond the sphere of symbolization. He defines the real as 'that which resists symbolization' and 'as the rock upon which every attempt at symbolization stumbles'.[3] At other points, the real is located in a negative existence, i.e. as merely a void or an aporia inherent in the symbolic order. Žižek states that 'the symbolic order itself, is . . . *barré*, crossed-out, by a fundamental impossibility, structured around an impossible/traumatic kernel, around a central lack'.[4] These two ways of theorizing the real may seem contradictory, and perhaps they are. Yet, this contradiction is in itself a symptom of the impossibility of conceptualizing (symbolizing) the real. Žižek summarizes the two accounts of the real this way:

> In a first move, the Real is the impossible hard core which we cannot confront directly, but only through the lenses of a multitude of symbolic fictions, virtual formations. In a second move, this very hard core is purely virtual, actually, non-existent, an X which can be reconstructed only retroactively, from the multitude of symbolic formations which are 'all there actually is'.[5]

3 Žižek, *The Sublime Object of Ideology*, 69, 169.

4 Ibid., 122.

5 Žižek, *The Parallax View*, 26.

This is a dense philosophical passage, but it captures very well the status and dilemma of the relation between value and price in financial markets. Had Žižek been a scholar of finance, he might have said: 'In a first move, value is the impossible hard core which we cannot confront directly, but only through the lenses of a multitude of price formations'. Even though we have a sense that assets are endowed with a certain intrinsic value, it is difficult to talk about value without immediately invoking the notion of price. And when trading assets, it becomes downright impossible to avoid talking about value in terms of price. Indeed, one of the key functions of markets is to assess the value of assets in terms of price.

At the same time, there is discrepancy between value and price inherent in the constitution of a market. Ideally, the seller of an asset believes that the price he receives exceeds the value of that asset. Conversely, the buyer should believe that the value of the asset exceeds the price. Hence, trading is only possible insofar as prices are *not* able to represent the value of an asset in any definite sense, i.e. insofar as it is impossible to confront value directly.

In consumer markets, the elusiveness of value is obvious, since the seller and the buyer are heterogeneous entities with different wants and desires. The seller typically wants to make a profit by trading a commodity he has either produced himself or bought from a third party. The buyer, however, has completely different reasons for engaging in the trade. He may be hungry, cold, or just in the mood for buying a new pair of jeans to look good for a prospective partner. The heterogeneity of seller and buyer means that very different standards of evaluation are at play in determining the value of the commodity. In the words of Žižek, value is confronted through the lenses of a multitude of price formations. The seller will confront the value of the commodity in terms of a calculation of the cost of production, the cost of marketing and selling the commodity, the price of similar commodities in the market, etc. Of course the buyer may also consider the price of similar commodities in the market, but he will also confront the value of the commodity in terms of its ability to satisfy his particular wants and desires. The trade will come about at a given price as the two parties invoke different measures of value that render the trade attractive for both of them.

In financial markets, the problem of the discrepancy between price and value is much less straightforward. The textbook account of stock markets is that they are a place where companies in need of capital for investment and expansion meet with investors with an excess of capital. The excess capital is traded for shares of the companies. Along similar lines, foreign exchange markets are viewed as places where companies may convert between currencies to facilitate international trading.

However, if we look at the actual functioning of contemporary financial markets, this begins to look like a romantic image, one that explains very little about the explosion in the volume of financial trading over the last three to four decades. In currency markets, for instance, trading volumes are several hundred times higher than the volume of global commodity imports and exports.[6] This indicates that the vast majority of transactions in foreign exchanges do not reflect heterogeneous needs in companies for buying and selling commodities in other countries, but are simply motivated by the desire to make a speculative profit as exchange rates fluctuate.

Under these circumstances, we cannot take heterogeneity between seller and buyer in financial markets for granted. What then drives trading in financial markets? Even though there is no qualitative difference between seller and buyer in most trades in financial markets, they still have different beliefs regarding the values of the assets they are trading. In contrast to a consumer market, in a financial market the difference between the seller's and the buyer's perception of the value of an asset is quantitative rather than qualitative. They differ not in the nature of their desires but only in their opinion of how to best satisfy these desires. For instance, imagine that one party sells a stock at a given price because he thinks the price is going to decrease in the foreseeable future, i.e. the current price exceeds the value. Another party agrees to buy the stock in the belief that the price is going to increase, i.e. the current value exceeds the price. Both parties want to make money and both believe they are going to make money from the transaction.

In fact, it is the fundamental discrepancy between price and value which allows a 'multitude of price formations' to co-exist and hence to enable trading to take place. Neither seller nor buyer can 'confront value directly'. Each is relegated to indirect estimations of the true value of the asset in question. As we can see, Žižek's definition of the

6 Knorr-Cetina and Preda, *The Sociology of Financial Markets.*

real applies to value, since value 'resist symbolization' and functions as 'the rock upon which every attempt at pricing stumbles'. Paradoxically, the impossibility of pricing is the condition of possibility for the market. Only insofar as the value of assets cannot be unambiguously determined does trading take place. If we imagine God coming down from heaven to put a definite price tag on all the companies registered on the stock exchange, most of the trading in these stocks would cease.

According to Žižek, the efficiency of any form of social interaction presupposes an element of ignorance on the part of the participants:

> The social effectivity of the exchange process is a kind of reality which is possible only on condition that the individuals partaking in it are *not* aware of its proper logic; that is, a kind of reality *whose very ontological consistency implies a certain non-knowledge of its participants* – if we come to 'know too much' . . . this reality would dissolve itself.[7]

In financial markets, this implies that there must be a certain non-knowledge about the value of the assets traded in the market in order for this trade to take place. It is crucial to stress that the discrepancy between price and value is not merely epistemological. It is ontological. Prices do not correspond with value because there is insufficient knowledge in the market. In turn, prices do not correspond with value because value is essentially elusive, because value belongs to the order of the real. The discrepancy between price and value propels an ongoing negotiation of their relation. This negotiation is what constitutes the market. We can observe the ongoing negotiation as prices in financial markets fluctuate.

The constant volatility of prices in markets takes us to the second part of Žižek's account of the real, as this volitility produces the conditions for value to appear in another form. If Žižek were a finance scholar, he might have said: 'In a second move, the very hard core of value is purely virtual, actually, non-existent, an X which can be reconstructed only retroactively, from the multitude of price formations'. Imagine a trader taking a position in British Petroleum stock

7 Žižek, *The Sublime Object of Ideology*, 20–21.

for £1,000,000. He may even be doing this with borrowed money. A month later, the stock has risen 3 percent and he liquidates the position. This obviously turned out to be a very 'valuable' investment. In fact, we can retroactively determine the value of the investment exactly: £30,000 minus whatever transaction costs and interest payments he might have incurred on the initial loan. But where does this value come from?

Maybe we can point to an event in the operation of BP – say, the discovery of a promising oil field – which justifies the increase in the stock price. Maybe nothing unusual has happened with BP and the price increase is judged to be the result of sheer speculative trading in the market. Maybe there have been rumours in the market about a possible discovery of an oil field which have caused the stock price to go up, but then months later these rumours turn out to be unfounded. Even with very detailed information about BP, we can never know for sure what actually caused the price of the stock to go up. Even if we know with certainty that BP did find oil, why should this cause an increase of 3 percent rather than 1 percent, 5 percent or 10 percent?

The point is that we have no direct access to the value of BP. All we have is a 'multitude of price formations'. Even the initial price of £1,000,000 is nothing but a compromise between the price formations of the buyer and the seller. We cannot be sure that this price is the expression of the true value of BP. Both buyer and the seller probably have an idea of what 'the right price' would be, and at the time of the trade both probably think that they got a bargain. Hence, the value of the investment can also only be approached through a retroactive reconstruction from the multitude of price formations. The value of the investment emerges as nothing but the difference between the price formation at the time the stock is bought, and the price formation at the time when it is sold again.

We have seen how Žižek's twofold account of the real captures the two primary ways value functions in financial markets. Both forms of value are invariably present in the market. We might be tempted to invoke the classic distinction between investment and speculation to distinguish between the two forms. Investment would correspond to trading based on asset pricing in terms of value that is inherent in the material properties of the asset. Speculation would correspond to trading based on pricing that takes into account only the temporal fluctuations in the market. However, the point in Žižek's concept of the real is precisely that such distinctions are impossible to uphold, as the nature of the real is essentially elusive. The two movements of the real are intertwined. We should think of them as two sides of the same Möbius band rather than two distinct categories.

DESIRE IN THE MARKET

Žižek's philosophy is also a psychoanalytical theory of the subject. The way he thinks about the relation between the subject and desire may serve to further elaborate the way value functions in the market. Contrary to most other theories of the subject, Žižek states that *mis*identification rather than identification is what constitutes the subject. Every individual becomes a social subject by being integrated and positioned in the symbolic order through a series of symbolic designations (electrician, Polish, woman, amateur soccer player, etc.). The subject may recognize and perceive itself through these categories, but at the same time it has a fundamental sense that these social designations do not fully capture 'who I really am'. Even if it were possible to list all relevant symbolic designations of a particular individual, this would still leave as a remainder, unaccounted for, the subject's sense of 'I'ness'.

Žižek's point is not that every individual has in him or her an authentic kernel of selfhood. It is rather that every individual believes he or she has this kernel which transcends every symbolic designation, and which therefore never fully identifies with its social mandate. Subjectivity emerges not as we identify with our social roles. Nor is subjectivity something which we may eventually discover beyond our social roles. Subjectivity is nothing but the constant insistence on being 'more than that', and it emerges in the very process of shuffling through the social order in search of 'who I really am'.

This insistence is what propels the desire of the subject. Desire is the perpetual projection of an ontological 'lack of Being' onto different objects in the world that might resolve the lack (money, a car, a man, a bigger house, another child, etc.). The subject's desire is structured by the need to discover and obtain those objects that are believed to confirm and demonstrate 'who I really am'. Žižek describes the intricate interplay between the subject and the objects projected by desire:

> The subject . . . and the object-cause of its desire . . . are strictly correlative. There is a subject only insofar as there is some material stain/leftover that *resists* subjectivation, a surplus in which, precisely, the subject *cannot* recognize itself. In other words, the paradox of the subject is that it exists only through its own radical impossibility, through a 'bone in the throat' that forever prevents it (the subject) from achieving its full ontological identity.[8]

Obviously, there is desire in financial markets. Whether it takes place in an open-outcry trading pit or in the digitized environment of an online exchange, financial trading evokes great passions, emotions and other affects. Academic as well as literary accounts of desire in the market abound.[9] One way of understanding desire in financial markets is by locating it in the individual traders' desire for money, competition and action. However, Žižek's account of the subject and desire seems to fit neatly with the functioning of the market as such. In this sense, we can speak of a form of desire in the market as such.

It is important to stress the empty nature of the object of desire. Žižek invokes Lacan's concept of '*objet petit a*' to make this point: '*objet petit a* is a pure void which functions as the object-cause of desire'.[10] Value is the *objet petit a* of the financial market. The market is driven by the desire to attain this object, i.e. for the prices in the market to coincide with the true value of the assets traded in the market. In the market, we find the same paradox that Žižek describes in relation to the subject: The paradox of the market is that it exists only through its own radical impossibility, through a 'bone in the throat' that forever prevents it (the market) from achieving its full ontological identity. The market exists only insofar as prices never coincide fully with the value of their corresponding assets, otherwise there would be no reason for trading; desire in the market would wane.

The paradoxical nature of desire means that the subject achieves enjoyment not through the appropriation of the objects of desire, but rather through the very search for these objects and the struggle to

8 Žižek, *The Fragile Absolute*, 28.

9 Wolfe, *The Bonfire of the Vanities*; Leeson, *Rogue Trader*; Hassoun, 'Emotions on the trading floor'; Zaloom, *Out of the Pits*.

10 Žižek, *The Sublime Object of Ideology*, 163.

attain them. In fact, the complete satisfaction of desire can be fatal for the subject. I have elsewhere demonstrated how this works in the case of drugs consumption.[11] The market functions in a similar fashion. Financial traders make money not necessarily by being accurate or right in their estimations of the value of various assets. Rather, their frantic activity of constantly pricing and re-pricing assets through trading them creates fluctuations in the market, and these fluctuations themselves allow the traders to make (or lose) money. By searching for the real *objet petit a* of value, the traders generate the very mechanisms that allow them to profit from being in the market. Value now emerges as a virtual creation. If a trader earns $100,000 in five minutes by making a smart move, value must have been created somewhere in the process. But this value is probably best described as a pure void, one that is nevertheless exchangeable for money the trader can use to buy very real things.

THE FANTASY OF THE MARKET

So far we have touched only briefly on the third order of Žižek's threefold ontological distinction, the order of the imaginary. The imaginary order is where the irreconcilable gap between the symbolic and the real is managed. Since there is no logically consistent solution to the problem of the relation between the real and the symbolic, the imaginary order has the form of fantasy. The symbolic order presents itself as the order of logic, calculation, the rule of law, predictability, coherence, completeness etc. The order of the imaginary, on the contrary, has the form of paradox, tautology and incoherence. In the order of the imaginary, we find a vague and often not fully articulated fantasy about a completed state of the symbolic order where contradictions and antagonisms have been overcome:

> The function of fantasy is to fill the opening in the Other, to conceal its inconsistency . . . Fantasy conceals the fact that the Other, the symbolic order, is structured around some traumatic impossibility, around something which cannot be symbolized.[12]

---

11 Bjerg, 'Drug Addiction and Capitalism'.
12 Žižek, *The Sublime Object of Ideology*, 123.

Fantasy projects an image of the ontological gap between the symbolic and the real as merely a technical, practical, and temporary problem, which may be overcome if the proper measures are taken and incidental obstacles are cleared out of the way. If price and value belong to the orders of the symbolic and the real respectively, the imaginary is constituted by different fantasies about the reconciliation of the two. There is no one definite fantasy of financial markets. Different people have different approaches to the market, and they will differ in their projected images of the market. Furthermore, there are different fantasies which are more or less prominent at different times in history. In this chapter and the next, we will explore different fantasies about the market and their implications for the configuration of the relation between price and value. Even though the substance of the different fantasies that serve to structure trading in financial market may differ, we can already say something general about fantasy and the market.

We can start by making a simple observation about the way people commonly speak about 'the Market'. This applies not only to professionals working in finance, but also to ordinary citizens. There seems to be a popular perception of the market as an autonomous entity, one that operates according to its own immanent mechanisms and temperaments. The fact that many news programmes have adopted financial news as a regular segment indicates the ontological status of the market. Financial news occupies a place in news programmes similar to that of the weather forecast. This is no coincidence. In contemporary financial capitalism, we have come to accept 'the Market' as in independent force in our lives. As with the weather, we can prognosticate the development of the market with some mixture of accuracy and uncertainty. The individual may act on forecasts by taking precautions and exploiting opportunities. With regard to the weather, this may imply buying shorts and planning a picnic. With regard to finance, it may imply selling bonds and buying stocks. But the idea of the individual changing the course of the weather or 'the Market' is absurd.

It could be argued that the market as such does not exist. All that exists are individual people making individual trades. If I wanted to see the market, where would I go? Even if I went to a physical trading room, all I would see are individuals engaging in trades with other individuals. Where would 'the Market' be? However, such an argument makes little sense, as it does not take into account the way that people relate to the market. When the news anchor announces that 'the Dow is up 3 percent from yesterday', or when we watch prices scrolling across a Bloomberg screen, the idea that this is the result of individual trades is very abstract. Instead, we think of this as 'the Market'. Even if we know that the market is ultimately made up of individual trades, this knowledge is suppressed in order for us to conceive of the price fluctuations as expressions of the market.

We can think of this image of 'the Market' in terms of a fantasy. In the above passage, Žižek describes how 'the symbolic order is structured around some traumatic impossibility, around something which cannot be symbolized'. In the previous sections, we have seen how the market is, in these terms, structured around value and how value is impossible to price decisively. The fantasy of 'the Market' functions to 'conceal' the impossibility of reconciling price and value. It functions to 'fill the opening in the Other' by transforming prices from contingent results of arbitrary encounters between fallible individuals into expressions of trans-individual rationality.

Žižek often uses the terms 'imaginary', 'fantasy' and 'ideology' interchangeably. The function of the imaginary should not, however, be confused with the popular notion of ideology as a veil covering up the true state of reality. On the contrary, if we keep in mind the distinction between the real and reality, ideology is part of the very fabric of reality. In a key formulation, Žižek puts it this way:

> Ideology is not a dreamlike illusion that we build to escape insupportable reality; in its basic dimension it is a fantasy-construction which serves as a support for our 'reality' itself: an 'illusion' which structures our effective, real social relations and thereby masks some insupportable, real, impossible kernel . . . The function of ideology is not to offer us some point of escape from our reality but to offer us the social reality itself as an escape from some traumatic, real kernel.[13]

The imaginary may indeed serve to cover up an underlying traumatic split, but the cover-up is an inherent part of the very functioning of reality. The imaginary is not a derivative form of ontological

13 Ibid., 45.

order, the neutralization of which would result in a state of truth. The truth does not reside somewhere behind or beyond the order of the imaginary, but in the very imaginary interweaving of the real and the symbolic. As we shall see, there are numerous configurations of the fantasy of the market. Each of these configurations implies a particular interrelation between price and value, and each configuration functions to structure and motivate a particular form of trading. Fantasies do not have the form of a logical and consistent argument. This is very much the case with speculative fantasies of the market. They manage to uphold the belief that prices represent value, while at the same time admitting several exceptions to this rule that allow the speculator to make a profit.

Žižek is sometimes said to imply a negative ontology. One axiom of his thinking about the relation between the symbolic (language, signification, law, etc.) and the real is that there is a reciprocity between the possibility and impossibility of symbolization. Any symbolic order is constituted by a 'lack' of symbolization, a point where symbolization is impossible. This lack is not just a mark of the insufficiency of the symbolization. It functions as the very structuring principle of the symbolic order. Žižek states that 'the symbolic field is in itself always already barred, crippled, porous, structured around some extimate kernel, some impossibility'.[14] He even goes on to state that this impossibility is the very condition of possibility for symbolization and for the constitution of social reality: 'Reality itself is nothing but an embodiment of a certain blockage in the process of symbolization. For reality to exist, something must be left unspoken'. 'There is 'reality' only insofar as there is an ontological gap, a crack, at its very heart – that is, a traumatic excess, a foreign body that cannot be integrated into it'.[15]

Financial markets are conglomerates of activities of buying and selling. On the one hand, this activity constantly generates symbolizations in the form of prices. The endless quotations generated by different exchanges demonstrate that the symbolization of value is certainly possible. On the other hand, trading in different financial markets is conditioned by the very impossibility of the symbolization of value. If it were possible to put a definite price on the value of a stock, most of

---

14 Žižek, *Looking Awry*, 33.

15 Ibid., 45; Žižek, *The Ticklish Subject*, 60.

the reasons for trading it would disappear. If all future dividends as well as future price movements were already incorporated into the current price for all stocks and securities available for trade, investors might as well just hold on to their stocks. Most trading activity would cease.

The indeterminacy of the value of stocks, the impossibility of definite symbolization, is what drives trading in financial markets. In this sense, we can paraphrase Žižek to describe the functioning of these markets: 'There is a market only insofar as there is an ontological gap, a crack, at its very heart – that is, a traumatic excess, a foreign body that cannot be integrated into it'. The traumatic excess at the heart of the market is the real of value. Fantasies of the market serve to manage this excess.

MAKING MONEY IN FINANCIAL MARKETS

How is it possible to make money in financial markets? On the one hand, this is a very practical question asked by most people who engage in the trading of stocks and other financial assets. On the other hand, it may also serve as the vantage point for an analytical inquiry into the functioning of financial markets.

In the above sections, we have seen how it is possible to think philosophically about financial markets through the use of Žižek's distinction between the real, the symbolic and the imaginary. This gives us a theoretical frame for the analysis of financial markets. In the following, we shall use this frame to analyze different strategies for investment and speculation in terms of their configurations of the real, the symbolic and the imaginary. Each of these strategies is based on a particular form of market analysis. Žižek thus provides us with the theoretical coordinates for understanding the different forms of analysis that already exist in the field of finance. We shall distinguish between three different approaches to financial trading: value investing, momentum investing and arbitrage.[16] Value investing is based on fundamental analysis, momentum investing is based on technical analysis and arbitrage trading is based on the so-called Efficient Market Hypothesis (EMH) of modern neoclassical finance.

---

16 Beunza and Stark, 'How to recognize opportunities', 87.

The purpose of the analysis is not to investigate whether these trading strategies are viable paths to profit. Instead, we shall seek to grasp these strategies in terms of their implied assumptions about the relation between price and value. As we have already seen, this relation is an expression of the relation between the symbolic and the real. The philosophical exposition of the relation between price and value thus provides an exposition of the ontology inherent in different investment and speculation strategies. Each of the trading strategies constitutes an ideal typical configuration of the relation between price and value, symbolic and real. And each of the approaches implies a fantasmatic image of the market, which serves to manage the relation between price and value.

The remaining part of the current chapter focuses exclusively on fundamental analysis and technical analysis. Even though all three trading strategies are applied in financial markets, I would argue that arbitrage trading and the modern theory of market efficiency enjoy a special status in contemporary financial capitalism. As we shall see, this theory emerged over a period of two decades from the 1950s to the 1970s and has served to propel the so-called 'financialization' of the world economy, which characterizes our current predicament. Hence, the purpose of the current chapter is not only to philosophically explicate fundamental and technical analysis, but also to provide background for the more elaborate analysis of modern finance theory in chapter two.

TECHNICAL ANALYSIS AND FUNDAMENTAL ANALYSIS

When looking at a live chart of price fluctuations in a financial market, e.g. the quotes that track trading in a particular stock or the development of the EUR/USD exchange rate, it is tempting to view the movements of the chart as not only as recordings of past events, but also as containing a hidden meaning that may be deciphered in order to predict the course of future events. This is precisely the strategy of the momentum trader. On the basis of previous trends in the movement of prices and the volume of trading, he aims to predict future movements in the price of a stock or other security. He then uses these predictions to decide when to buy and sell different positions so as to maximize profits and minimize losses. His goal is to be in tune with the momentum of the market. The momentum trader's approach to the market relies on so-called 'technical analysis' of the market. This form of analysis is sometimes also referred to as 'chartism', since the primary component of technical analysis is the study of charts that show previous price changes.

Charles Dow, who was co-founder of the Dow Jones Indexes, was one of the pioneers of technical analysis. Dow also founded *The Wall Street Journal*, where he wrote many editorials sketching out his ideas about speculation and the stock market. Only subsequently were Dow's writings compiled to produce a coherent theory, which is referred to as Dow's Theory.[17] At the core of Dow's Theory is the identification of cycles in the price movements of the stock market:

> Nothing is more certain than that the market has three well defined movements which fit into each other. The first is the daily variation due to local causes and the balance of buying and selling at that particular time. The secondary movement covers a period ranging from ten days to sixty days, averaging probably between thirty to forty days. The third move is the great swing covering anything from four to six years.[18]

In an illuminating metaphor, the three movements are also referred to as 'ripple', 'wave' and 'tide'. The interplay between these cycles is governed by certain laws, which allow the attentive speculator to predict the movements of the market. One of these is the 'law of action and reaction':

> It seems to be a fact that a primary movement in the market will generally have a secondary movement in the opposite direction of at least three-eighths of the primary movement. If a stock advances ten points, it is very likely to have a relapse of four points or more. The law seems to hold good no matter how far the advance goes. A rise of twenty points will not infrequently bring a decline of eight points or more.[19]

---

17 Hamilton, *The Stock Market Barometer*; Rhea, *The Dow Theory*.
18 Dow, 1902 quoted in Hamilton, *The Stock Market Barometer*, 23.
19 Dow, 1902 quoted in ibid., 37.

Other patterns idenfitied by the chartist in order to predict price movements include 'head and shoulders', 'flags', 'pennants', 'triangles', etc.

There is a kind of double ontology at play in the 'technicians' approach to the market. On the one hand, he believes that there is some form of correspondence between the stock market and the condition of business. Stock prices reflect the accumulated knowledge and expectations in the market about the current and future value of underlying companies.[20] On the other hand, technical analysis, in its pure form, ignores data about the actual state of companies and focuses entirely on market data. Technical analysis is uninterested in the question: what is it *really* worth? It makes little sense to pose this question within the framework of technical analysis, as the notions of value and price are entirely conflated. In the words of Dow:

> In reading the market . . . the main point is to discover what a stock can be expected to be worth three months hence and then to see whether manipulators or investors are advancing the price of that stock toward those figures.[21]

With Žižek we have seen how symbolization bars our access to the real. When the undifferentiated matter of being is incorporated into the symbolic system of signs, law and meaning, the immediate perception of being is lost. Technical analysis seems to parallel this move from the real to the symbolic, since it does not aim to excavate the real value of the companies underlying their symbolic representation in the form of stock prices. The object of analysis is not the relation between the real of value and the symbolic price. Instead, the focus is exclusively on the symbolic order and the laws inherent in this order. Hamilton sums up the ontological assumption of Dow's Theory this way: 'We have said that the laws we are studying are fundamental, axiomatic, self-evident'.[22]

An alternative approach to trading in financial markets is so-called 'fundamental analysis'. In fundamental analysis, decisions about buying, selling or holding stocks or other securities are based

---

20 Ibid., 41–42.
21 Dow, 1902 quoted in ibid., 38.
22 Ibid., 20.

on a careful analysis of the current state and future prospects of the underlying companies or assets. A classic formulation of the basics of fundamental analysis is found in John Burr Williams' *The Theory of Investment Value*. Williams begins the book with a key distinction between value and price:

> Separate and distinct things not to be confused, as every thoughtful investor knows, are real worth and market price. No buyer considers all securities equally attractive at their present market prices whatever these prices happen to be; on the contrary, he seeks 'the best at the price'. He picks and chooses among all the stocks and bonds in the market until he finds the cheapest issues . . . Of investment value in this sense some men will make one estimate, others another, and of all the estimates only one will coincide with the actual price, and only one with the true worth.[23]

We find here the notion of 'true worth'. The aim of Williams's text is to demonstrate how the value of a stock or other security is ultimately the present value of all future dividends, coupons and principal. In the case of a stock, the intrinsic value is thus constituted by the future profitability of the underlying company insofar as this results in dividends paid out to the holder of the stock. Williams provides a formula for the calculation of this so-called 'investment value'.[24] Of course, the calculation of future dividends is based on a number of assumptions and projections which are subject to uncertainty. Williams is well aware of this, and the bulk of his book consists of tools that can be used to improve the accuracy of such estimates. The quality and profitability of an investment strategy basically comes down to the estimation of investment value.

Similar to his distinction between value and price, Williams makes a distinction between investor and speculator: 'We shall define an investor as a buyer interested in dividends, or coupons and principal, and a speculator as a buyer interested in the resale price'.[25] We see here how the definition of the speculator fits nicely with the approach of the technical analyst. While Williams does little to conceal his

---

23 Williams, *The Theory of Investment Value*, 3.
24 Ibid., 56.
25 Ibid., 4.

professional and even moral contempt for the speculative approach to trading, he still allows the speculator a role in the formation of prices in the market:

> Both wise men and foolish will trade in the market, but no one group by itself will set the price. Nor will it matter what the majority, however overwhelming, may think; for the last owner, and he alone, will set the price. Thus *marginal* opinion will determine the market price.[26]

This means that even though the value of stocks and other securities is ultimately determined by their intrinsic investment value, the prices at which these are traded in the market do not necessarily correspond with this value. 'The market can only be an expression of opinion, not a statement of fact'.[27] Since some opinions in the market are based on unqualified speculation or even intentional ignorance of actual business conditions, discrepancies between intrinsic value and market price inevitably arise. These provide profitable trading opportunities for the attentive investor.

Fundamental analysis revolves around the very question that is bracketed in technical analysis: 'What is the *investment value* of a given security?'[28] Once the investor has acquired a stock at a price below the actual investment value, he need not worry about the future speculative whims of the market. Even if the market price of the stock should fall, he can still hold the stock for value and, as the company pays out dividends, gradually cash in at a rate above the average return on his investment.

THE FANTASY OF BEATING THE MARKET

There is an obvious contrast between the implied ontologies of the technician and the fundamentalist. While the technician accepts the real as inaccessible – i.e. he predicts the future price of a stock without making any assumptions about its real value – the fundamentalist aims to get as close as possible to this real value by observing the

26 Ibid., 12.
27 Ibid.
28 Ibid., 5.

actual business conditions of the underlying company. We see here the contours of a classic philosophical controversy.

The technician's approach to the relation between price and value is a form of idealism. We might also talk of a form of transcendentalism or structuralism, depending on our conceptual framing of the position. The technician reduces the question of value to a question of price in the same way that idealist philosophy reduces the question of being to a question of perception or knowledge. From an idealist perspective, it is impossible to speak of the being of objects as independent from our perception of these objects. The task of philosophy is therefore to analyze patterns in the conditions of possibility for perception and knowledge. Depending on the branch of idealism, these patterns may take the form of transcendental structures of subjectivity (Kant, Husserl), or general structures of language (Saussure, Lévi-Strauss). The idealist analysis of the conditions of possibility for perception and knowledge is comparable to the technical analysis of the 'fundamental, axiomatic, self-evident'[29] laws of the formation and movement of prices in the stock market.

In contrast, the distinction between value and price that underlies fundamental analysis implies a realist approach to knowledge. In philosophy, the realist position may come in the form of empiricism, materialism and positivism. Through careful analysis of the factual circumstance of a business, the fundamentalist believes it is possible to determine the 'ultimate worth of investments' independent of their price in the stock market. We see here the separation of the question of being from the question of perception and knowledge, which is characteristic of realist philosophy. The aim of much realist philosophy is to clear the way for objective, scientific investigation of factual reality and to provide a basis for knowledge that is informed by empirical observation rather than metaphysical speculation. A scepticism towards speculative knowledge unites the various schools of realist philosophy, from the empiricism of Locke and Hume, through the materialist analysis of the true value of a commodity in Marx, to the positivist thinking of the early Wittgenstein and Popper. As we have already seen, a similar scepticism towards speculation, bordering on downright condemnation, characterizes the fundamental analysis outlined by Williams.

29 Hamilton, *The Stock Market Barometer*, 20.

The obvious philosophical contraction between the idealism of technical analysis and the realism of fundamental analysis should not, however, prevent us from seeing that the two approaches to financial markets concur on a very crucial point. Although they might disagree on the appropriate method, both believe that it is possible to make an above-average return on investments in financial markets. In order to uncover the philosophical constitution of this concurrence, we shall return to Žižek's two definitions of the real.

His first definition of the real describes it as a positive existence beyond the sphere of symbolization. The real is 'that which resists symbolization' and 'the rock upon which every attempt at symbolization stumbles'.[30] A similar notion of the real lurks in the background of Williams's fundamental analysis. Insofar as the investment value of a stock is constituted by future dividends, there is an inherent chronological displacement in the relation between the symbolic and the real. While the price is always quoted in the present, intrinsic value only reveals itself in the future. Williams himself imagines that the gap between the symbolic price and the real value of an investment gradually closes:

> Concerning a stock's true worth, every man will cherish his own opinion; as to what price really is right, time only will tell. Time will not give its answer all at once, though, but only slowly, word by word, as the years go by; nor will the last word be spoken till the corporation shall have closed its books forever and ever.[31]

Williams seems to commit a chronological fallacy here. It is true that when dividends are paid out as 'the years go by', we get an answer to the question of the 'right' price. But this answer regards only the historic price, i.e. what *was* the right price at the time of the investment. This information is about as useful as knowing the outcome of the spin of a roulette wheel after having placed the bet. Not only has the market moved and produced a new current price, but the intrinsic value of the investment is also based on a new series of future dividends. Even though an investment in a stock has turned out to be profitable, yielding dividends above what was expected at the time of

30 Žižek, *The Sublime Object of Ideology*, 69, 169.
31 Williams, *The Theory of Investment Value*, 11.

the purchase, time may have generated a new situation with a seemingly inflated current price and a seemingly dire prospect for the future profitability of the company, thus forcing the investor to make a new decision to sell rather than hold. In philosophical terms, there is an inherent gap between the symbolic and the real. The real value 'resists symbolization' in the same way that the future resists subordination to the present.

Žižek's second definition of the real describes it as a negative existence, a lack, a void, an impossibility or an aporia inherent in the symbolic order. It its pure form, technical analysis abstains from making any estimates about the intrinsic value of a stock or other investment. In this sense, value as a positive real existence is absent from technical analysis. Williams characterizes speculators this way: 'Some old traders think it a handicap, a real handicap, to let themselves reach any conclusion whatsoever as to the true worth of the stocks they speculate in'.[32] Instead, the value of a stock or other investment is constituted by the difference between the current price and the price at some point in the future when the stock is realized. We see here how value in technical analysis figures as a relation between two points within the symbolic order of the market. Value is, in other words, the difference between two prices.

In seeming concordance with Žižek, technical analysis assumes that movements in the symbolic order of the market are governed by certain laws. The technician claims to be able to profit from his knowledge of these laws by predicting market movement. However, the scientific validity of technical analysis – and thus also its claim of profitability – is highly disputed.[33] It has been argued that technical analysis is nothing but guesswork; it has even been referred to as 'financial astrology'.[34] But even if we assume the laws of technical analysis to be accurate, the functioning of these market laws depends on a curious paradox. The market moves according to the law only insofar as this law is not fully recognized and believed by the market.

This paradox of technical analysis was already identified by Sidney S. Alexander, who believed he had proven the profitability of the so-called 'filter technique' by using statistical analysis. He

32 Ibid., 33–34.

33 Cowles, 'Can Stock Market Forecasters Forecast?'

34 Mandelbrot and Hudson, *The (Mis)Behaviour of Markets*, 9.

concludes his paper reporting this discovery by saying: 'I leave to the speculation of others the question of what would happen to the effectiveness of the filter technique if everybody believed in it and operated accordingly'.[35]

Imagine that Dow's Theory predicts that the price of a particular stock in a bear market will continue to fall until it reaches a certain threshold, after which it will start rising. If everyone in the market knew about this prediction and acted accordingly, no one would be willing to buy the stock before the threshold was reached, and no one would be willing to sell the stock after the threshold had been passed. Instead of a gradual fall and rise, which would allow speculators to profit from the prediction by selling the stock on its way down and buying it on its way up, the market price would jump instantaneously to the predicted end price as soon as the prediction was known to the market. If everyone in the market knew that within a certain amount of time the price of a given stock would rise by 5 percent, every potential seller of the stock would instantaneously ask this price, effectively eliminating the possibility for speculative buyers to make a profit.

In philosophical terms, this paradox is a case of the real emerging out of an aporia in the symbolic order. In order for the market to move according to the prediction of a given technical analysis, the market must not know about the prediction itself. The prediction implicitly excludes itself from the market and from the analysis. In this sense, the prediction itself becomes 'that which resists symbolization'. It is possible to have knowledge about the laws of the stock market only insofar as the market itself is driven by beliefs rather than knowledge. Technical analysis thus seems to fit Žižek's definition of the unconscious as 'knowledge that doesn't know itself'.[36]

We have seen how Žižek's general theory of symbolization is based on the axiom that there is an inherent discrepancy between the symbolic and the real in any form of symbolization. The application of this negative ontology to financial markets was summed up as follows: 'There is a market only insofar as there is an ontological gap, a crack, at its very heart – that is, a traumatic excess, a foreign body that cannot be integrated into it'. At first glance, fundamental analysis

---

35 Alexander, 'Price Movements in Speculative Markets: Trends or Random Walks', 26.

36 Žižek, *How to Read Lacan*, 52.

and technical analysis seem to conform to this idea of a discrepancy between the symbolic and the real. Even though the two forms of analysis differ in their approaches to investment and speculation, they share the fundamental assumption of a discrepancy between price and value. Fundamental analysis takes as its starting point the fact that prices in the stock market do not necessarily represent the real intrinsic investment value of the underlying businesses. And technical analysis takes as its starting point the fact that current prices in the stock market do not necessarily reflect the foreseeable development of future prices.

However, it is important to note that in Žižek, the discrepancy between the symbolic and the real is *ontological*. In fundamental and technical analysis, by contrast, the discrepancy between price and value is treated as *epistemological*. Both approaches believe that through knowledge, the gap may be closed. While fundamental and technical analysis differ in the kinds of knowledge they think can do this, both contain a fantasy of closing the gap. This closing is not performed by the market in general but by the individual investor/speculator.

'Of investment value', Williams writes, 'some men will make one estimate, others another, and of all these estimates only one will coincide with the actual price, and only one with the true worth'. He then goes on to state that the purpose of his theory is 'to explain the price as it is, and to show what price would be right'.[37] At play here is a fantasy of the 'intelligent investor' who is able to determine the 'right price' and to locate the point where price and value 'coincide'.

Along similar lines, Hamilton writes:

> If it is true, as we have seen, that nobody can know all the facts which at any one time influence the stock-market movement, it is true, as any of us can record from personal experience, that some have far more knowledge than others . . . There has usually been and I hope there always will be, the right man to take the right objective view at the right moment.[38]

Both of these approaches hold out the promise that it is possible for the individual trader to identify profitable trading opportunities

---

37 Williams, *The Theory of Investment Value*, 3.

38 Hamilton, *The Stock Market Barometer*, 17, 19.

in the market. We can understand this promise as a fantasy of beating the market. This fantasy functions to structure the desire of the trader in a particular fashion. The market is structured around an ontological gap that is manifested by the impossibility of determining the 'right price'. In this gap, we find the real of value as an excess constantly eluding definite symbolization. The desire of the trader is aimed at appropriating, taming this excess, this elusive piece of the real.

CHAPTER TWO

Modern Finance and the Fantasy of the Efficient Market

> Before Harry Markowitz's 1952 essay on portfolio selection, there was no genuine *theory* of portfolio construction – there were just rules of thumb and folklore. It was Markowitz who first made risk the centerpiece of portfolio management by focusing on what investing is all about: *investing is a bet on an unknown future.* Before Bill Sharpe's articulation of the Capital Asset Pricing Model in 1964, there was no genuine *theory* of asset pricing in which risk plays a pivotal role – there were just rules of thumb and folklore. Before Franco Modigliani and Merton Miller's work in 1958, there was no genuine *theory* of corporate finance and no understanding of what 'equilibrium' means in financial markets – there were just rules of thumb and folklore. Before Eugene Fama set forth the principles of the Efficient Market Hypothesis in 1965, there was no *theory* to explain why the market is so hard to beat. There was not even a recognition that such a possibility might exist. Before Fischer Black, Myron Scholes, and Robert Merton confronted both the valuation and the essential nature of derivative securities in the early 1970s, there was no *theory* of option pricing – there were just rules of thumb and folklore.[1]

Modern neoclassical finance is a paradigm of thinking about financial markets that may be crudely traced back to a number of canonical theories published between 1952 and 1973.[2] While these theories were initially worked out in academic environments with the purpose of explaining and understanding the functioning of finance, they would gradually be adopted by practitioners trading in financial markets, thus coming to shape the functioning of these very same markets. Bernstein provides an historical account of this interplay between theory and practice, which he refers to as a move 'from gown

1 Bernstein, *Capital Ideas Evolving*, xii–xiii.

2 Bernstein, *Capital Ideas: The Improbable Origins of Modern Wall Street.*

to town'.[3] Along similar lines, MacKenzie invokes the concept of 'performativity' to explain, from a sociological perspective, how financial theories function not only to shape but perhaps even to produce markets that conform to the predictions of those theories.[4]

While both Bernstein and MacKenzie describe the evolution of modern finance with a degree of richness and empirical detail that this book shall not attempt, their respective historical and sociological accounts leave open a number of philosophical questions. This chapter is an analysis of the philosophical properties of modern neoclassical finance theory, i.e. an analysis of the ontology of markets implied by these theories. The analysis is structured around three key ideas that are held to constitute the paradigm of modern finance. These ideas are the Efficient Market Hypothesis (EMH), the impossibility of speculation, and the separation of finance and economics.

THE EFFICIENT MARKET HYPOTHESIS

If modern finance, as Bernstein suggested, was born with the publication of Harry Markowitz's paper on *Portfolio Selection*, then the discipline was arguably conceived with the publication of Louis Bachelier's doctoral thesis on the *Theory of Speculation* in 1900. In its own time, the thesis was an original yet odd work in the field of stochastic analysis. It was only when the work was discovered in the 1950s by American finance scholars that its truly pioneering qualities were fully recognized. The novelty and importance of Bachelier's work resides in the formulation of two interrelated ideas that define the paradigm of modern finance: the treatment of price fluctuations in financial markets as random, and the application of stochastic analysis to the study of these price fluctuations.

Bachelier makes a fundamental distinction between two forms of probability. The first is 'the probability that one could call *mathematical*, that is, that which one can determine a priori. This is what one studies in games of chance'. The second is 'probability depending on future events, which is, consequently, impossible to predict in a mathematical fashion'.[5] Bachelier is interested only in the first form of

3 Bernstein, *Capital Ideas Evolving*.
4 MacKenzie, *An Engine, Not a Camera*.
5 Bachelier, *Theory of Speculation*, 26.

probability. An ingenious theoretical assumption allows him to disregard the latter form:

> It is this last probability that the speculator tries to predict; he analyses the causes that can influence the rise or the fall of the market and the amplitude of the movements. His inferences are entirely personal, since his counterpart necessarily has the opposite opinion. It seems that the market, that is to say, the set of speculators, must not believe *at a given instant* in either a rise or a fall, since for each quoted price there are as many buyers as sellers . . . *At a given instant the market believes neither in a rise nor in a fall of the true price.*[6]

What we find here is a crude formulation of the Efficient Market Hypothesis. Price fluctuations in financial markets indeed depend on actual events in the real economic circumstances of the assets represented in these markets. Yet the accumulated knowledge of buyers and sellers in the market means that the anticipation of relevant future events is already incorporated into the current price of stocks and securities. A key figure in the 'rediscovery' and reception of Bachelier's work in the English-speaking world of finance theory is Paul Samuelson. Samuelson's main contribution to modern finance lies in refining the idea of market efficiency. He provides a succinct formulation of the Efficient Market Hypothesis: 'In competitive markets there is a buyer for every seller. If one could be sure that a price will rise, it would have already risen'.[7]

There is an obvious strain of Kantian thinking in Bachelier's distinctions between the two forms of probability. A key component in Kant's critical investigation of the limits of pure speculative reason is the distinction between a priori and a posteriori cognition.[8] The latter is knowledge derived from fallible sensory experience, while the former is knowledge about the very conditions of possibility structuring the experience of the world. These conditions of possibility can be arrived at through purely deductive reasoning independent of fallible empirical experience. Bachelier himself designates the first of his two forms of probability, i.e. mathematical probability, as a

6 Ibid.

7 Samuelson, 'Proof that Properly Anticipated Prices Fluctuate Randomly', 41.

8 Kant, *Critique of Pure Reason*, 127.

priori, which suggests that we should designate the second form, i.e. probability depending of future events, as a posteriori probability.

The idea of market efficiency, propagated by Bachelier, Samuelson and many others, rests on the assumption that a posteriori probability is unpredictable. This does not mean that the future is wholly unpredictable. If we were interested in investing money in a farming business, we might reasonably predict that crops planted in the spring can be harvested and sold in autumn. But all other potential buyers or sellers of stocks in the farming industry also possess this basic knowledge, and it is always already calculated into the current prices at which stocks are bid or sold for in the market. Hence, stock prices in the farming industry obviously do not fluctuate in sync with the predictable change of the seasons; they do not decrease in the winter when the fields are empty and boom in the summer as the crops are growing and harvest is approaching.

What may cause prices to change are *unforeseen* events. If one year there is a severe drought, thus reducing crop yields, this will probably cause a drop in farming stock prices. However, this drop does not occur when the drought sets in, but rather at the moment when the forecast of the drought becomes known. In order to profit from price changes due to future events, the individual investor has to know about the coming of this event before the rest of the market. If one investor had a superior weather forecasting technique, he might be able to profit by trading on his more accurate knowledge about future crop yields.

Cootner sums up this point:

> If any substantial group of buyers thought prices were too low, their buying would force up the prices. The reverse would be true for sellers. Except for appreciation due to earnings retention, the conditional expectation of tomorrow's price, given today's price, is today's price. In such a world, the only price changes that would occur are those that result from new information. Since there is no reason to expect that information to be non-random in appearance, the period-to-period price changes of a stock should be random movements, statistically independent of one another.[9]

The Efficient Market Hypothesis says that in an ideal state, the

9 Cootner, *The Random Character of Stock Market Prices*, 232.

market adjusts itself instantaneously to new information. In the efficient market, it is impossible to trade profitably on new information, since all potential buyers and sellers of a stock or security react simultaneously as this information becomes known. This feature spells out the Efficient Market Hypothesis as formulated by Eugene Fama. Since this is often regarded as the authoritative formulation, we shall quote Fama at length:

> The primary role of the capital market is allocation of ownership of the economy's capital stock. In general terms, the ideal is a market in which prices provide accurate signals for resource allocation: that is, a market in which firms can make production-investment decisions, and investors can choose among the securities that represent ownership of firms' activities under the assumption that security prices at any time 'fully reflect' all available information. A market in which prices always 'fully reflect' available information is called 'efficient'.[10]

The most obvious question posed by the Efficient Market Hypothesis is, of course, whether actual markets are indeed efficient. However, before we look into this question, it is worth considering the epistemological status of the Efficient Market Hypothesis. What does it actually say? And what does it say this *about*? Samuelson raises this issue when he considers different interpretations of the notion of market efficiency:

> 1) Is this a correct *fact* about well-organized wheat or commodity markets? About stock exchange prices for equity shares? About futures markets for wheat or other commodities as contrasted to the movement of actual 'spot prices' for the concrete commodity?
> 2) Or is it merely an interesting (refutable) *hypothesis* about actual markets that can somehow be put to empirical testing?
> 3) Or is it a valid *deduction* (like the Pythagorean Theorem applicable to Euclidean triangles) whose truth is as immutable as 2 + 2 = 4?[11]

10 Fama, 'Efficient Capital Markets', 383.

11 Samuelson, 'Proof that Properly Anticipated Prices Fluctuate Randomly', 41, numbering and italics added.

Again, there seems to be a key Kantian distinction at play, namely, the distinction between analytic and synthetic judgments.[12] Crudely speaking, an analytic judgment is a clarification of the meaning of a concept. When I say, 'gold is yellow', the predicate 'yellow' is already contained in the defining characteristics of the subject 'gold'. The judgment merely states this implication. Synthetic judgments, by contrast, move beyond the defining characteristics of a concept. When I say, 'gold is sometimes used as money', this predicate is not already implied in the notion of gold. If the proposition is true, it contains new knowledge.

In interpretations 1) and 2) listed by Samuelson, the EMH has the status of a factual or hypothetical statement about actually existing markets. The truth value of such a statement is determined through empirical testing. In these interpretations, the EMH is a synthetic judgment. In interpretation 3), the EMH does not presume to say anything about any real markets. It is merely a clarification of the concept of 'market efficiency'. In this interpretation, the EMH is an analytic judgment, the truth value of which may be proved through logical deduction. It is precisely such proof that Samuelson proceeds to deliver. The article in which all of this appears is pointedly titled 'Proof That Properly Anticipated Prices Fluctuate Randomly'.[13]

If we review Fama's formulation of the EMH, it is obvious that he is not talking about actually existing markets either. In the above quote he refers to the 'ideal' market and concludes with an exemplary analytic judgment: 'A market in which prices always 'fully reflect' available information is called 'efficient.'' As an analytic judgment, the EMH states that in an ideally efficient market it is impossible to make profitable predictions about future price movements.

Yet, the purpose of Fama's paper is not only to explicate the theoretical implications of the EMH, but also to test the empirical validity of the statement. Fama distinguishes between three forms of efficiency: weak, semi-strong and strong efficiency. In weak-form efficiency, it is assumed that traded prices reflect all past public information. In semi-strong-form efficiency, it is further assumed that prices adjust instantly to new information. And in strong-form

---

12 Kant, *Critique of Pure Reason*, 130–134.

13 Samuelson, 'Proof that Properly Anticipated Prices Fluctuate Randomly'.

efficiency, it is further assumed that prices even reflect non-public or 'insider' information. Through a comprehensive review of the existing literature, Fama concludes that markets conform to the first two forms of efficiency, and even though some evidence seems to cast doubt on the latter form of efficiency, the existence of traders with monopolistic access to information does not seem to interfere with the overall efficiency of the market. Hence, Fama concludes that 'the evidence in support of the efficient markets model is extensive, and (somewhat uniquely in economics) contradictory evidence is sparse'.[14]

We see here how Fama treats the EMH not only as an analytic but also a synthetic proposition. He is even able to validate this proposition. Fama's paper constitutes a culmination in the evolution of modern neoclassical finance. The EMH is no longer merely a theoretical idea in the mind of abstract economic thinkers, it is also an accurate model of actually existing financial markets.

THE IMPOSSIBILITY OF SPECULATION

The mathematical expectation of the speculator is zero.[15]

Perhaps the most important implication of market efficiency is the impossibility of profitable speculation. When Bachelier states that 'at a given instant the market believes neither in a rise nor in a fall of the true price', he assumes the market to be in a state of equilibrium where a future upward movement in prices is just as probable as a future downward movement. This is also known as the 'Random Walk Hypothesis' because it assumes that price fluctuations in financial markets are comparable to the path taken by a zigzagging drunkard as he walks down the street.[16] His lack of control over his own legs makes any zig as probable as any zag. This means that any attempt to predict future price movements is essentially a gamble. Traders in financial markets should expect returns equivalent to nothing more than the average growth rate of the market. Profits in

14 Fama, 'Efficient Capital Markets', 416.
15 Bachelier, *Theory of Speculation*, 28.
16 Malkiel, *A Random Walk Down Wall Street*.

the excess of this average are attributable to sheer luck rather than skill.

The impossibility of speculation implied in the EMH also shows how modern neoclassical finance constitutes a radical break with fundamental and technical analysis. Both of these approaches rely on the assumption that it is possible for the individual trader to outperform the market through careful financial analysis. From the perspective of neoclassical finance, the fundamental analyst as well as the chartist are principally gamblers. The fundamental analyst is comparable to a roulette player who examines the roulette wheel for physical irregularities that make certain numbers more likely to come up than others. The chartist is comparable to a player who looks for patterns in the previous outcomes of roulette games in order to predict the next round.

The impossibility of profitable speculation provides the benchmark for testing the efficiency of a market. In the studies he reviewed, Fama tested the EMH against various hypotheses for the existence of continuously profitably trading rules. Since no such rules seem to stand up to proper scientific scrutiny, the EMH is confirmed. While technical analysis is typically written off by neoclassical finance as financial 'alchemy' or 'astrology', i.e. pre-scientific guesswork, the neoclassical view of fundamental analysis is ambiguous. On the one hand, fundamental analysis is viewed as a futile investment strategy in efficient markets, since all available information about the underlying assets is already reflected in the current prices. On the other hand, fundamental analysis is recognized as a necessary precondition for the development and maintenance of efficient markets. It is the presence of a multitude of diligent and ever-attentive fundamental analysts which allows the neoclassical financier to make his assumptions about market efficiency. In the view of neoclassical finance, fundamental analysts are what Stalin once referred to as 'useful idiots'.

In terms of Žižek's real–symbolic–imaginary distinction, the notion that in efficient markets 'prices always 'fully reflect' available information' suggests that the financial market, as symbolic order, is able to completely symbolize the real of value. In the neoclassical account of efficient financial markets, there is no gap between the symbolic and the real, between price and value. The market price is always already an accurate reflection of the value of the underlying asset.

Since there is no gap between the symbolic and the real, there is also no need for the order of the imaginary to manage this gap. Neoclassical finance is, seemingly, a theory without fantasy, a statement of pure facts. It is noteworthy how the EMH is validated through the refutation of the fantasy of beating the market that is found in technical and fundamental analysis. The validity of the EMH hinges on the impossibility of speculation. Modern neoclassical finance is what is left when we have eliminated all speculative illusions. No wonder that neoclassical finance is the hegemonic theory of markets in contemporary post-ideological capitalism.

THE COPERNICAN REVOLUTION OF FINANCE

As we touched upon above, already in Bachelier we find modern finance's aspiration to transcend the fuzzy domain of a posteriori probabilities based on guessing the future, and to enter the world of mathematically proven a priori probabilities. The ingenuity of the EMH lies in the way it enables this leap by setting up a correlation between the capacity of the market to 'fully reflect' available information about underlying assets and the unpredictability of future price movements.

At first glance, this correlation between market efficiency and random price fluctuations seems to do the opposite of providing scientific footing for finance theory, since it traps the discipline into a choice between two evils. If the EMH is true as an empirical description of actually existing markets, neoclassical financial theory can provide nothing in the way of predicting prices other than a form of Socratic scepticism: 'all I know is that I know nothing . . . of future price movements'. If the EMH is false as an empirical description of actually existing markets, the whole paradigm of neoclassical finance rests on an erroneous assumption and thus does not even qualify as science.

This dilemma is comparable to the one faced by Kant in his ambition to found a theory of pure reason: 'The real problem of pure reason is now contained in the question: How are synthetic judgments a priori possible?'[17] This famous passage appears in Kant's

17 Kant, *Critique of Pure Reason*, 146.

Critique of Pure Reason. Kant was aware of the fallible character of empirical knowledge, i.e. knowledge derived from sensory experience of the world. His ambition was to establish a theory of knowledge and reason that was not contingent on this kind of experience. The notion of 'pure reason' comes from Kant's belief that absolute knowledge is indeed possible, even if empirical knowledge is inherently uncertain. Kant's critique is an effort to investigate the limits of human reason. How much can we know with certainty if our knowledge about the empirical world is tainted by uncertainty?

Kant's is a theory of pure speculative reason. The same goes for Bachelier and his progeny in modern neoclassical finance. We have already seen how Bachelier makes a distinction between mathematical a priori probability and probability that depends on future events. And just as Kant would discard sensory experience as a source of absolute knowledge, Bachelier discards the predictions made by individual traders in the market as purely subjective. He then proceeds to investigate in a deductive fashion the domain of a priori probabilities.

Bachelier's notion of a priori probabilities is comparable to Kant's notion of synthetic judgments a priori. Kant's investigation of the question, 'How are synthetic judgment a priori possible?', is at the same time an investigation of the very possibility of philosophical knowledge as such. In answering this question he claims that, on the one hand, philosophy is concerned with a priori cognition and not with the investigation of empirical objects. On the other hand, this cognition is not merely a clarification of things, as we already know. Philosophy is in fact able to produce new and absolute knowledge.

Bachelier's adoption (whether he was aware of the philosophical roots or not) of the Kantian distinction between a priori and a posteriori is also a distinction between finance and economics. A central feature, perhaps even the defining feature, of modern finance is the idea that it is in principle possible to study the mechanisms of financial markets with no knowledge of the functioning of the underlying economy. In other words, you can analyze the markets without getting your hands dirty examining the books of companies or the demand for and supply of commodities. The evolution of modern finance as a distinct discipline is at the same time the history of the differentiation of finance from economics.

The result of Kant's investigation of reason was the mapping out of the very conditions of possibility for experience, i.e. the structures of transcendental subjectivity. Knowledge of these structures does not tell us what is and what is not the case. It does not imply factual statements about the empirical world. Rather, the transcendental structures of subjectivity are the categories of experience that must be in place for us to even conceive of the world in whatever contingent empirical state. An empirical table may be round or square, but for the individual to experience the table in whatever form, we must presuppose that he or she has certain cognitive prerequisites for experiencing objects in time and space. The structures of transcendental subjectivity are the conditions of possibility for any experience of the empirical world.

Kant's move from the domain of the empirical to the domain of the transcendental is comparable to Bachelier's move from exact predictions – such as the ones found in technical and fundamental analysis – to probabilistic estimates of future price movements. Bachelier's scepticism regarding the possibility of knowledge about financial markets concerns only immediate up/down movements in prices. In Kantian terms, these are predictions based on a posteriori probabilities. When it comes to a priori probabilities, it is in fact possible to make predictions, albeit in probabilistic rather than absolute terms. The whole point of Bachelier's thesis is precisely to show that such predictions are possible. Bachelier's introduction of stochastic analysis into the study of financial markets enables the calculation of different probabilities. It thus provides a mapping of the conditions of possibility of different price trajectories.

It is precisely the EMH – encapsulated by Bachelier's statement that the mathematical expectation of the speculator is zero – which paves the way for the treatment of future price fluctuations as random events conforming to Brownian motion. The implicit Kantian question underlying Bachelier's work is: How are predictive judgments a priori possible? By answering this question, Bachelier does for modern finance what Kant did for modern philosophy. He provides the foundation for finance as an independent discipline studying the a priori laws of the market without recourse to fallible assumptions about the underlying economy. Along these lines, he concludes his thesis with these words:

'The market, unwittingly, obeys a law that rules it: the law of probability'.[18]

THE REAL AS RISK

With Žižek, we can understand this paradigmatic leap from predictions in exact terms to probabilistic mapping of a range outcomes as a way of treating the real as risk. In Williams, the real is the intrinsic value of a stock. The gap between the symbolic and the real is constituted by the 'error' of the fundamental analyst's estimate of the true investment value of a stock or other security. The aim of fundamental analysis is to minimize if not close this gap through the accurate pricing of value, thus approaching a full symbolization of the real. Williams treats the payment of future dividends as a predetermined trajectory. If only the analyst were in possession of full knowledge, he would be able to predict the future cash flow.

Williams's reasoning is the type of reasoning that Bachelier writes off as 'entirely personal'. Neoclassical finance moves beyond such reasoning and into the domain of 'a priori' probability by embracing uncertainty instead of trying to eliminate it through forecasting. In neoclassical finance, uncertainty is not a product of the limitations of human knowledge and judgment. Uncertainty is an intrinsic element of business life in general, and of the life of financial markets in particular.

Treating uncertainty as risk enables modern finance to approach it with statistical analysis. Probability theory is a system for the symbolization of the real. If we look at a situation determined by randomness, the outcome of the situation may be regarded as a manifestation of the real which 'resists symbolization'. At the roulette table, there is no way to predict whether the outcome is going to be red or black, and once the outcome is determined, there is no sufficient reason why it was one and not the other. However, once we abstract from the single instance and start looking at the game on an aggregate level, i.e. once we move from the 'short run' to the 'long run', the outcome of roulette is no longer a meaningless enigma. From the perspective of probability theory, the series of outcomes of a roulette wheel constitutes a very predictable pattern, which is fully

18 Bachelier, *Theory of Speculation*, 77.

comprehensible through the theory. For the true gambler who bets all his fortune on the outcome of a single game, the whimsical nature of the roulette wheel may be a great mystery. But for the disengaged statistician, the mystery is solved and the game is nothing but a series of outcomes normally distributed around a mean value.[19] Roulette is just another instance of Brownian motion.

The groundbreaking idea of treating financial uncertainty as risk should probably be attributed to Harry Markowitz, on account of his work on portfolio selection.[20] While Markowitz takes fundamental analysis, as formulated by Williams, as his point of departure,[21] he also makes a paradigmatic break with this approach to financial markets.

We have already seen how Bachelier's theory is introduced through a fundamental distinction between the two forms of probability. In comparable fashion, Markowitz starts with an analytic distinction:

> The process of selecting a portfolio may be divided into two stages. The first stage starts with observation and experience and ends with beliefs about the future performances of available securities. The second stage starts with the relevant beliefs about future performances and ends with the choice of portfolio.[22]

He then very explicitly notes: 'This paper is concerned with the second stage'. We can easily recognize the first stage as precisely the operation of fundamental analysis. But Markowitz adds a very crucial dimension to the estimation of expected future returns. Prices in financial markets not only reflect the expectation of future returns, but also the variance of these future returns. Markowitz refers to this as the 'expected returns – variance of returns rule', or simply the 'E-V rule'. In efficient markets there is a tradeoff between high expected returns and low variance of returns. If securities A and B trade at the same price but A has a higher expected return than B, this is due to B

---

19 Bjerg, *Poker – The Parody of Capitalism*, 17–22.

20 Markowitz, 'Portfolio Selection'.

21 Bernstein, *Capital Ideas: The Improbable Origins of Modern Wall Street*, 46–47.

22 Markowitz, 'Portfolio Selection', 77.

having a lower variance of returns. When deciding whether to buy, hold or sell a security, an investor considers not only his estimate of the future dividends that might flow from this security, but also the chances that these future dividends will deviate from what's expected.

As noted above, deviations from the expected, in Williams, can only be attributed to shortcomings in the judgment of the individual fundamental analyst. While Markowitz certainly does not deny the possibility of such misjudgements, he also introduces another possible source of deviation from the expected. This is the notion of risk as variance of return.

In Markowitz, risk is included as an inherent component of investing. Instead of striving for absolute certainty, which is anyhow impossible, we should adjust our theories of financial markets to accommodate the presence of risk. What Markowitz offers is a 'probabilistic reformulation of security analysis'.[23] We see here how Markowitz's distinction between the two phases of portfolio selection corresponds to the aforementioned distinction between a posteriori and a priori probabilities. While misjudgements in the fundamental analysis of securities occur in the domain of a posteriori probabilities, risk is an a priori source of uncertainty.

In fundamental analysis, securities are treated as separate entities. The analysis provides recommendations on whether to buy, hold or sell each security individually. From this perspective, the introduction of risk as variance of return is relevant only to align a particular investment with an investor's particular level of risk aversion. Individual investors may prefer different sides of the tradeoff between expected return and risk. By introducing the second phase of portfolio selection, Markowitz transforms financial trading from being a matter of individual 'stock picking' to being a matter of the composition of complete portfolios of several securities.

Of course, the variance of returns of securities ultimately derives from the uncertainty inherent in the economic circumstances of the underlying assets. Yet, by looking at securities collectively rather than individually, Markowitz directs our attention to the way some securities tend to fluctuate synchronically, whereas other securities fluctuate in uncorrelated fashion. In other words, the collective approach to securities analysis reveals different levels of 'co-variance' between

23 Ibid., 91.

different sets of stocks. Taking co-variance into consideration in portfolio selection allows the investor to offset the risks of different stocks against each other. This means that an otherwise risk-averse investor may tap into the 'risk premium' on highly volatile securities without compromising his preference, as long as he composes a portfolio that consists of a number of *uncorrelated* high-risk securities. Here we see the rationale behind the age-old strategy of diversification. What Markowitz initially provides is thus not a distinctively new investment strategy, but rather a mathematical justification for an existing 'rule of thumb'.

Markowitz's theory of portfolio selection and the notion of risk were further elaborated by William Sharpe in his Capital Asset Price Model (CAPM).[24] Markowitz's model requires as input estimates of co-variance between each pair of securities to be considered for inclusion in the portfolio. As the number of such co-variance estimates increases exponentially with the number of securities under consideration, the model quickly becomes very complex, even for a limited amount of securities. Sharpe's contribution to the theory consists first and foremost in replacing these numerous co-variance measures between pairs of securities with just one estimate for every stock, namely the stock's co-variance with the market as a whole expressed in some form of market index. Sharpe refers to this estimate of co-variance with the market as β (beta).

Sharpe's contribution to portfolio theory is not just a simplification of the model, making it more operable in actual trading. His model also allows for a stringent distinction between two forms of risk which pertain to the holding of a financial asset. The first is the volatility of the asset deriving from its fluctuation in relation to overall economic activity. The second is the remainder, i.e. a kind of idiosyncratic risk that pertains to the individual asset independent of the general condition of the market. Sharpe calls the former 'systematic risk', or beta, and the latter the 'unsystematic component' of risk.[25] As with Markowitz, the practical usefulness of Sharpe's model lies in the way it helps to devise a strategy of diversification:

---

24 Sharpe, 'Capital Asset Prices'.

25 Ibid., 439.

> Diversification enables the investor to escape all but the risk resulting from swings in economic activity – this type of risk remains even in efficient combinations. And, since all other types can be avoided by diversification, only the responsiveness of an asset's rate of return to the level of economic activity is relevant in assessing its risk.[26]

In the 1980s there was a popular R&B hit that included the line: 'There's not a problem that I can't fix / Cause I can do it in the mix'. At least as far as unsystematic risk is concerned, this is the promise of a strategy of diversification devised on the basis of Sharpe's CAPM. The distinction between unsystematic and systematic risk is, in effect, a distinction between risk that can be diversified away and risk that cannot be diversified away.

PROBABILITY AS SYMBOLIZATION

> The epistemological value of probability theory is based on the fact that chance phenomena, considered collectively and on a grand scale, create a non-random regularity.[27]

In philosophical terms, Kolmogorov describes here the transformation of an otherwise chaotic and unpredictable real into an ordered and predictable symbolic order by means of probability theory. This is what happens in the 'probabalistic turn' of modern finance initiated by Bachelier and completed by Markowitz and Sharpe. To explicate how probability theory works in terms of Žižek's triad of real-symbolic-imaginary, it is useful to invoke a particular illustration of the conversion of the real into the symbolic provided by Lacan.

The game of tossing a coin is often used in finance theory to illustrate the way chance and probability works in financial markets. Here is how Lacan uses the game to illustrate the interplay between the real and the symbolic.[28] Imagine the following: By tossing a coin 10 times, a random sequence of heads and tails is produced. We may get the following result:

---

26 Ibid., 441–442.

27 Gnedenko and Kolmogorov, *Limit Distributions for Sums of Independent Random Variables.*

28 Lacan, 'The Function and Field of Speech and Language in Psychoanalysis'.

1	2	3	4	5	6	7	8	9	10	Toss No.
H	H	H	T	H	H	T	T	H	T	Heads/Tails

Figure 1: Sequence of Tosses

In the first instance, this sequence is a purely chaotic, irregular and meaningless manifestation of the real. Now we organize the individual tosses into overlapping units of three, that is No. (1,2,3), (2,3,4), (3,4,5) etc. These aggregate units are then symbolized according to the following rule: (HHH, TTT) = (α); (HTT, THH, TTH, HHT) = (β); (HTH, THT) = (γ). A new sequence is thereby generated:

1	2	3	4	5	6	7	8	9	10	Toss No.
H	H	H	T	H	H	T	T	H	T	Heads/Tails
		α	β	γ	β	β	β	β	γ	Symbolic Chain

Figure 2: Sequence of Symbolizations

While the outcome in the sequence of individual tosses is of course still completely random, the symbolization has introduced an element of regularity and order into the symbolic chain. Certain successions have been made impossible and others necessary. For instance, γ cannot follow immediately after α since this would imply a shift in the row of tosses from heads to tails or vice versa. Such a shift would generate the unit β between the two other units. Another example is the fact that between two α-units, there must necessarily be an even number of β-units. β symbolizes a shift in the series from heads to tails, or vice versa. If there have been three heads in succession, there will have to be 0, 2, 4, 6, etc. such shifts before we can come back to three heads in succession again.

Lacan's point with the model is to show how order and regularity emerge *ex nihilo* from the symbolization of the pure randomness of the real, even though the symbolization might initially appear to be an 'innocent' recording of real events. This is comparable to the introduction of order into chaos through the symbolization and aggregation procedures of probability theory. Lacan sums up the point of the coin game in a remark that is strikingly similar to Kolmogorov's above: 'We see separate out from the real a symbolic determination which, as faithful as it may be in recording any partiality of the real, merely produces all the more clearly the disparities that it brings with it'.[29]

In Markowitz, we find two such procedures for aggregation. First, the treatment of the uncertainty of the future price trajectory of a security as risk redirects the focus from the immediate up/down movement of the price to the perspective of the long run. This allows the financial decision-maker to disregard short-term fluctuations and base his trading strategy on the mapping of probabilities. Second, the transition from individual stock picking to portfolio composition is also a way of viewing securities on an aggregate level. Again, the trading strategy is not based on predictions of the performance of the individual security, but rather on a probabilistic mapping of the performance of the collective of securities in the portfolio. In other words, the calculation of probabilities constitutes a symbolization of the real by which it becomes possible to make rational decisions in the face of otherwise unpredictable events. In this kind of risk management, we see what Hacking refers to as 'the taming of chance'.[30]

THE FANTASY OF JOINING THE MARKET

It is important to note that in the case of probability theory, Žižek's assertion that any symbolization is incomplete also holds true. The Law of Great Numbers is precisely that: a law of *great*, not *small*, numbers. Only at the aggregate level does the sequence of events represent a principle of order. Only at the aggregate level is chance tamed. The singular event remains disorderly, untamed and 'lawless'. Historian Thomas M. Kavanagh summarizes the limitations of probability theory:

> The theory of probability does offer a response to chance, does generate a distinct scientific enterprise. It is able to do so, however, only by first relinquishing any claim it might make to speak of what, from the viewpoint of the player, the gambler, the person awaiting the outcome of the chance event, is most crucial: the present moment, what will actually happen next, the specific event. As a science of

29 Ibid., 51.
30 Hacking, *The Taming of Chance.*

> chance, probability theory may speak of the real; but is does so only by first stepping outside the real, by adopting as its vantage point a distant, removed position excluding all real involvement with any one outcome as opposed to another. The reality about which probability theory speaks is always an abstracted real without compelling pertinence to any specific moment or situation.[31]

The singular event thus constitutes a surplus of the real that is not contained by symbolization. The singular event marks the limitation of probability theory. The point here is none other than the one already made by Bachelier. Modern finance theory cannot say much about the up/down movement of the price of a single stock or other security in the immediate future. The immediate up/down price movement thus constitute a surplus of the real that 'resists symbolization'.

According to Žižek, systems of symbolization are supported by fantasies in the order of the imaginary that function to make the process of symbolization work, despite its inherent limitations. In the case of probability theory, this function is performed by what we might call the 'Fantasy of the Long Run'. In a series of random events a certain pattern will, according to the Law of Great Numbers, eventually become apparent after a 'great number' of events. This pattern is what Kolmogorov refers to as a 'non-random regularity', and it takes the form of a normal distribution around a certain mean value. To take the perspective of the long run is to redirect attention from the immediate outcomes of singular events to the pattern that will eventually emerge out of the collective of events.

We may recall that Žižek's concept of fantasy does not imply that an idea is 'wrong', 'false' or 'illusionary'. Nor does it imply that 'behind' the fantasy there is a true reality. By characterizing probability theory as a fantasy, the point is not to say that probability theory is false or illusionary. The imaginary idea of the long run allows us to perceive a certain probabilistic reality in which the real of the singular event is abstracted away.

We have seen how both technical and fundamental analysis point toward a trading strategy that aims to identify discrepancies in the market between price and value – between the symbolic and the real

31 Kavanagh, *Enlightenment and the Shadows of Chance*, 14–15.

– in order to take advantage of such discrepancies. As we have also seen, trading strategies based on Markowitz and Sharpe are not aimed at picking individual bargain stocks or shuffling in and out of the market at the right moment. Assuming that markets are efficient and that prices in the market are governed by the E-V rule, such strategies must be regarded as futile.

If there is a discrepancy between the symbolic and the real in Markowitz and Sharpe, it is not a discrepancy between the price and value of individual securities. Rather, the discrepancy lies between the market as a whole and the underlying productive economy as a whole. While Williams's fundamental analysis points out individual bargains among the stocks and securities in the market, the bargain in Markowitz and Sharpe is the market itself. Fundamental analysis is a theory of investing in one stock rather than another. Markowitz and Sharpe advance a theory of investing in financial markets as opposed to putting money in the bank or under the mattress. The E-V rule may apply to the determination of prices in financial markets relative to each other – hence the adage of no return without risk. But the promise that diversification enables the investor 'to escape all but the risk resulting from swings in economic activity' minimizes the risk of being in the market relative to not being in the market. Depending of course on the assessment of systemic risk, this almost translates into a promise that we may violate the E-V rule on the aggregate level. In 'the long run', a well-diversified portfolio is predicted to generate a return equivalent to the market average, while only incurring the 'systemic risk' of overall economic activity. Hence, the market in general provides the most optimal combination of expected return relative to risk.

In fundamental and technical analysis, we found a *fantasy of beating the market*. Since this is impossible under conditions of market efficiency, portfolio theory is based instead on a *fantasy of joining the market*. This fantasy relies on a particular image of the market, one that is based on two key assumptions. First, the financial market as a generalized entity moves in synch with the level of productivity in the underlying economic. This means that if the prices of financial assets in the market as a whole increase over a substantial period of time – for instance, as expressed in an increase in the Dow Jones Index – this signifies real economic growth. It also means that it takes a decline in the productivity of the real economy to produce a decrease in overall price levels in the financial market. Second, the relative fluctuations between the prices of individual stocks or other securities in the market will, in the long run, conform to a pattern of normal distribution.

This fantasy conveys an image of the financial market as a place where the collective profits of society are distributed 'equally' among investors who have put their capital into the market. 'Equally' here does not mean that everyone gets the same share, but rather that everyone gets the same share relative to the amount they have invested. This image frames the market as basically fair. In the vision of Markowitz and Sharpe, the market is not a place where smart people make money at the expense of people who are less smart. If investors adhere to a set of almost mechanical rules, they may rest easy in the knowledge that the market will provide them with a fair return on their investments.

There is an illuminating affinity between modern portfolio theory and game theory as conceived by John von Neumann and Oskar Morgenstern. On the basis of a two-player game of simplified poker, Neumann and Morgenstern devised the notion of the so-called 'mini-max strategy'.[32] This is an optimal strategy based on the assumption that each player is perfectly rational and fully knowledgeable about the other player's strategy. Under these conditions, each player should aim to minimize his opponent's maximum gain. Similar to modern portfolio theory, the mini-max strategy is expressed in probabilistic terms. The optimal mini-max strategy does not prescribe specific individual moves for specific situations in the game. Instead, the strategy consists of a set of different probabilities that dictate which moves should be executed. If, for instance, a poker player holds a medium hand in a certain situation, the mini-max strategy tells him to bet with a frequency of X percent, call with a frequency of Y percent, and fold with a frequency of Z percent. Similar to the way Markowitz changes the perspective from the individual security to the portfolio, game theory looks not at the individual move but rather at the way a series of moves plays out in the long run. The two theories also share the assumption that it is impossible to beat one's opponent. Neumann and Morgenstern's assumption of each player's perfect

---

32 Neumann and Morgenstern, *Theory of Games and Economic Behavior*, 143–168.

rationality is comparable to the assumption of market efficiency found in Markowitz and Sharpe. Neumann and Morgenstern note that while mini-max strategies 'are perfect from the defensive point of view, they will (in general) not get the maximum out of the opponent's (possible) mistakes – i.e. they are not calculated for the offensive'.[33] If we compare modern portfolio theory to trading strategies based on fundamental and technical analysis, we see how the latter two are offensive strategies aimed at beating the market, whereas the former is a defensive strategy aimed at merely minimizing the maximum potential loss on investments.

When a player applies the optimal mini-max strategy, he transforms the game from a playful and unpredictable activity to a mechanical execution of strategic rules which enforces a certain probabilistic distribution of outcomes. Imagine that one player in a game of rock-paper-scissor applies a strategy of deciding his throws at random. In this scenario, each of the three possible moves – rock, paper or scissors – has a 33.3 percent probability of being chosen. Regardless of the opponent's strategy, this would force the outcome of the game into a pattern of normal distribution, with each player having a 50 percent chance of winning. Arguably, this way of playing would take the ludic element out of the game.

Modern portfolio theory does the same with trading in financial markets. According to Markowitz and Sharpe, the market is not a game where 'players' compete at trying to predict the movements of the market. Modern portfolio theory transforms financial trading into the mechanical execution of strategic rules, which distributes the profits of the underlying economy among investors in proportion to their investment in the financial market. In this way, modern portfolio theory takes the play element out of trading in financial markets.

PRICING FANTASIES

It is crucial to remember that the model for portfolio selection created by Markowitz and refined by Sharpe still relies on input data to determine what should be included in the portfolio; this data consists of the estimated returns and the variance of the different securities being considered for the portfolio. This input requires some form of

33 Ibid., 164.

fundamental analysis. Markowitz notes: 'To use the E-V rule in the selection of securities we must have procedures for finding reasonable μi the expected return and σij the covariance. These procedures, I believe, should combine statistical techniques and the judgment of practical men'.[34] Such 'practical men' are fundamental analysts.

What Markowitz provides is basically a quantitative method for solving the problem of diversification. In the terminology of Bachelier, Markowitz's portfolio theory explores the *mathematical* domain of a priori probabilities. Yet Markowitz's theory still relies on data generated in the domain of a posteriori probabilities, i.e. the domain of fundamental analysis. In Bachelier, we find the aspiration for a science of finance wholly independent from this latter domain. There is in Bachelier an obvious disregard for the inferences made in this domain, as they appear to be 'personal' rather than mathematically grounded.

After the advances made by Markowitz and Sharpe in the area of portfolio theory, the next step in the evolution of modern finance was arguably the development of the theory of options pricing by Black, Scholes and Merton. This theory represents a climax in the history of the discipline, as it seems to realize Bachelier's aspiration for a purely quantitative theory of finance uncontaminated by the register of qualitative judgment.

The theories of Black, Scholes and Merton concern the market for derivatives. Derivatives are financial products that do not refer to underlying assets in the productive economy. They may take a variety of forms, such as options, futures, swaps, etc. Derivatives refer only to the prices of securities, which may then refer to some externality outside the market. In this sense, the markets for derivatives constitute a meta-market inside the financial markets. A stock option, for instance, grants the holder the right but not necessarily the obligation to buy a specified amount of company stocks at a specified price at some specified time in the future. Derivatives are curious as they do not represent ownership of the underlying asset in the same way that a stock represents ownership of a share of a company. This makes the pricing of derivatives a very intricate matter.

In fact, Bachelier already provided a formula for the pricing of a derivative in the form of a government bond option. Even though

34 Markowitz, 'Portfolio Selection', 91.

Black, Scholes and Merton did provide a number of corrections and refinements to the original Bachelier model, their primary achievement perhaps lies more in the way that they conceptualize and justify their model than in the content of the model itself, which was published by Black and Scholes in 1973. The novelty in Black, Scholes and Merton is that they use the efficient market itself as a benchmark for the estimation of the correct price of an option. This idea is spelled out in the very first sentence of the seminal Black and Scholes article: 'If options are correctly priced in the market, it should not be possible to make sure profits by creating portfolios of long and short positions in options and their underlying stocks'.[35]

Here, Black and Scholes build directly upon Bachelier's statement that the mathematical expectation of the speculator is zero. When this axiom is applied to the markets for derivatives, it means that, in an efficient market, it is impossible to make profits through arbitrage between the derivatives markets and the markets of the underlying assets. The idea of the impossibility of arbitrage is also developed by Merton.[36]

Options provide the holder with the possibility of profiting on an increase in the price of the underlying stock (or other asset), while only incurring the risk of losing the price paid for the option if the stock price stays constant or decreases. Thus, we might imagine a strategy where a trader buys a stock option and at the same time short-sells a certain quantity of the underlying stock. If the price of the stock increases, he makes money on the option but loses money on the short position. If the price of the stock decreases, he loses the price paid for the option but makes money on the short position. In an efficient market – so the axiom of Black, Scholes and Merton's theory says – the profit of such a trading strategy is zero regardless of the development in the stock price, as the option will be priced in a way as to make the two sides of the trade cancel each other out. Arbitrage is impossible.

A formula for the 'rational' or 'fair' pricing of options can be derived by working backwards from this axiom of the impossibility of arbitrage. The price of an option should reflect the likelihood of making money on a portfolio of underlying assets, which replicates

35 Black and Scholes, 'The Pricing of Options and Corporate Liabilities', 637.
36 Merton, 'Theory of Rational Option Pricing', 164–165.

the option. If the likelihood of making money on the portfolio of underlying assets is high, the price of the corresponding option should be high. If the likelihood of making money on the portfolio is low, the price of the corresponding option should be low.

The Black and Scholes formula for the calculation of a European call option is the following (the difference between European and American call options will be explained later):

$$C_t = S_t N(d_1) - Xe^{-r\tau} N(d_2)$$

where

$$d_1 = \frac{\ln\left(\frac{S_t}{X}\right) + \left(r + \frac{\sigma_s^2}{2}\right)\tau}{\sigma_s \sqrt{\tau}}$$

and

$$d_2 = d_1 - \sigma_s \sqrt{\tau}$$

$N(\cdot)$ is merely the cumulative density function of normal distribution, so the price of the option (C) is ultimately a function of five variables: (1) The strike price, i.e. the price at which the stock can be bought at the expiry of the option (X). (2) Time to expiry of the option (τ). (3) The current price of the underlying stock (S). (4) The risk-free interest rate (r). (5) The variance of the stock price (σ).

The first two variables, strike price and time, are directly specified in the contract of the option. The third and fourth variables, current price and interest rate, can ideally be observed directly in the current market. It is assumed that the interest rate is constant. The key variable is the fifth, the variance of the stock price. This variable is a measure of the volatility of the stock. Basically, the option price is a reflection of the volatility of the underlying stock. Even if the intricacies of the formula are complex, this is in fact a very simple point.

Since the call option gives the holder the right but not the obligation to buy the stock at a certain price at a certain time in the future, an option on a volatile stock is more valuable than an option on a stable stock. Consider two different companies. Company A is a ferry boat company operating twenty routes in Scandinavia and surrounding countries. Company B is a small biotech company that develops and patents components for medical products. Successful patents are sold to larger medical companies for further development and marketing. The current stock price of each of the companies is €100. Now consider two identical options in each of the companies, which give the holder the option to buy 10,000 stocks in the company in one year at a strike price of €130. Even though the stock prices of the companies are identical, it is reasonable to assume that they have different levels of volatility. Company A is a traditional company in a relatively predictable line of business. This is typically a low volatility stock, and the likelihood of the option expiring 'in the money' is very low. Company B is in an unpredictable line of business. The development of new ideas is a risky affair and there is a significant chance of failure. However, if the company is successful with one of its products, profits may suddenly soar. An option in company A is almost worthless, as the probability of the stock price increasing by 30 percent within one year is negligible. Even though there is a considerable risk that company B might go bankrupt in one year, the option in this company is much more valuable, since there is also a significant probability that the price of the stock has risen more than 30 percent already.

While this simple example is easily grasped though economic common sense, the achievement of Black and Scholes is that their formula allows us to abstract from common sense and to understand this and even more complex situations in purely mathematical and financial terms. Reviewing the five input variables of the formula, we see that four are immediately given in the contract or in the current state of the market. With a few seemingly innocent assumptions, even the fifth variable, variance of the stock, can be derived directly from price data in the market.

The first assumption is that price fluctuations in financial markets are stochastic and normally distributed. This is a direct consequence of the Random Walk Hypothesis. The second assumption is that the variance of these fluctuations is constant over significant periods of time. These assumptions allow us to calculate the volatility of a stock on the basis of historic price data. In other words, all we need to calculate the right price of a stock option is a chart showing the fluctuations in the stock price for the past, say, one or two years. Here is how Merton reviews the Black and Scholes formula in terms of the minimal requirements of input data:

> An exact formula for an asset price, based on observable variables only, is a rare finding ... The manifest characteristics of the Black and Scholes formula is the number of variables that is does *not* depend on. The option price does not depend on the expected return on the common stock, risk preferences of investors, or on the aggregate supplies of assets. It does depend on the rate of interest (an 'observable') and the *total* variance of return on the common stock which is often a stable number and hence, accurate estimates are possible from time series data.[37]

We have seen how Markowitz and even the CAPM ultimately rely on 'fundamental' input, i.e. input based on fundamental analysis, in the form of estimates of expected future return and co-variance between different stocks. With the Black and Scholes formula, finance seems to have finally cut its umbilical cord to economics. The formula works without any 'economic' input, i.e. qualitative estimates regarding the underlying economy. The theory allows us to calculate the right price of certain securities in the market with no recourse to market-external data. All we need to do in order to analyze the market is observe the market itself. In this sense, the theory of option pricing is a form of neo-chartism.

VERTICAL ARBITRAGE

A recurring theme in Žižek is the intricate relation between desire and law. We should note here that Žižek's notion of law does not only refer to legal but also religious, moral, and even scientific laws. On the one hand, law restricts the subject's access to various objects of desire. 'You shall not commit adultery' is an obvious example. On the other hand – and this is the psychoanalytic point – the very prohibition instituted by law is what makes the prohibited object desirable in the first place.[38] Besides being a symbolic expression of a prohibition, the law also implies a fantasmatic underside, which structures the

37 Ibid.
38 Žižek, *The Plague of Fantasies*, 10–13.

subject's desire towards the prohibited object. The law carries an injunction for transgression.

If we regard the aforementioned Black and Scholes axiom of the impossibility of making a 'sure profit' (arbitrage) as the expression of a law of the efficient market, we can detect the fantasmatic underside of the law by simply moving the 'not' in the very first sentence of the paper. The formulation thus reads: 'If options are *not* correctly priced in the market, it should not be possible to make sure profits by creating portfolios of long and short positions in options and their underlying stocks'. We see here that the logical meaning of the sentence is not changed by the alteration of the formulation. The original formulation states that sure profits are impossible in a perfect market. This formulation seems merely to draw out the logical implication that in an imperfect market it is possible to make sure profits. At the symbolic level, the two formulations are merely two ways of making the same point. However, at the level of the imaginary, two very different fantasmatic images are created.

The first is the image of the efficient market, which adheres to immanent market laws, thus serving its functions of generating correct prices and governing the distribution of capital for the productive economy. The second is the image of the inefficient market, which is a kind of financial Sodom and Gomorrah where the sublime object of the market, the sure profit through arbitrage, may be immediately appropriated. Even though these images may seem to be diametric opposites, they are not, given their fantasmatic character, mutually exclusive. Both images are present in the shaping of contemporary financial markets. Perhaps the most eminent illustration of the functioning of both of these images is the fact that in 1997, Myron S. Scholes and Robert C. Merton were awarded the Nobel Prize. (Fischer S. Black died in 1995 and could therefore not be included in the award). At the same time, Scholes and Merton were both part of the hedge fund Long Term Capital Management (LTCM), which made billions identifying arbitrage opportunities in the market using trading strategies built on the options pricing model. We shall return to LTCM. This seeming paradox between receiving the Nobel Prize for having discovered an immanent law in the market, while at the same time profiting from deviations from this law in the actual market, is emblematic of the functioning of contemporary financial markets. We shall return to this paradox in the next chapter.

Black, Scholes and Merton's theory of option pricing was an historic breakthrough for a number of reasons. Not only did it constitute the climax of the differentiation of finance from economics, but the theory and the formula also sparked the proliferation of a new paradigm of speculation. This paradigm is characterized by the appropriation of speculative profits through arbitrage.

Arbitrage works by taking advantage of a difference in the price of the same asset in two or more different market. A simple example would be buying gold at a certain (low) price in the London bullion market (LBMA) and selling it at another (high) price in the New York Mercantile Exchange (NYMEX), provided that the delivery conditions are similar in both markets. Arbitrage is by no means a new phenomenon, and in its general form it does not originate with Black, Scholes and Merton. What the theory of option pricing achieves, however, is a new form of linking between different markets, thus opening hitherto unseen opportunities for arbitrage.

In the simple example of trading gold, arbitrage emerges between two epistemologically homogeneous markets, the LBMA and the NYMEX. These two markets trade in the same assets, but in two different locations. Derivatives markets are meta-markets, since the value of options, futures, swaps and other securities traded in these markets are derived from the price behaviour of the underlying assets. The Black and Scholes formula enables the linking of these two epistemologically heterogeneous markets: on the one hand, the immediate markets for trading in stocks (or other securities), and on the other, the meta-markets for the corresponding derivatives. The formula can be used first to identify derivatives that are not correctly priced, and second to calculate how to compose and adjust a portfolio of the underlying assets in order to carry out arbitrage.

We may conceptualize the difference between the two forms of arbitrage as horizontal and vertical arbitrage. In this terminology, horizontal arbitrage refers to arbitrage between homogenous markets, e.g. the trading gold of in LBMA and NYMEX. Vertical arbitrage would then designate a form of arbitrage that operates between epistemologically heterogeneous markets, e.g. between a stock market and the corresponding meta-market for derivatives of these stocks.

In the previous chapter, we saw how fundamental analysis aims at identifying discrepancies between the current price of a stock and the 'true worth' of the underlying company. Fundamental analysis takes advantage of this through so-called value trading. In philosophical terms, this is a discrepancy between the symbolic and the real. Technical analysis, by contrast, works by predicting future price fluctuations purely on the basis of previous fluctuations, and it profits from such predictions through momentum trading. The technical analyst does not try to transcend the symbolic order of the market. Instead, he deciphers signs in the symbolic order of the market. Knowing the inherent laws of the market, these signs purportedly allow her to foresee future price movements.

Modern neoclassical finance typically presents itself as being the diametric opposite of technical analysis. Neoclassical finance regards itself as being founded on rigorous scientific methods, and it views technical analysis as nothing but speculative guesswork, a kind of financial quackery. A key element in the empirical proof of the Efficient Market Hypothesis is the statistical refutation of the possibility of profiting from momentum trading. As we have already seen, in 1961 Sidney S. Alexander thought he had statistically proven the profitability of the filter technique. Yet, three years later he published a second paper in which he revised his conclusions and raised serious doubts about the profitability of this technique.[39] Alexander's retreat from his own initial hypothesis is sometimes regarded as proof of the demise of technical analysis and confirmation of the validity of the EMH.[40]The relationship between neoclassical finance and fundamental analysis is more ambivalent. On the one hand, the EMH states that in an efficient market it is impossible to profit from value trading based on fundamental analysis, since all relevant information about assets is always already incorporated into the current prices in the market. In this view, fundamental analysis is a waste of time. On the other hand, neoclassical finance recognizes that somebody has to do the 'dirty job' of empirically scrutinizing the economic circumstances of companies and other assets in order for financial markets to function efficiently. In 1980, Grossman and Stieglitz proposed a solution to this ambivalence by arguing that a minimal amount of inefficiency is necessary to the functioning of an efficient market, as this inefficiency allows fundamental analysts to be rewarded for doing the work

---

39 Alexander, 'Price movement in speculative markets'.

40 Fama, 'Efficient Capital Markets', 395; Bernstein, *Capital Ideas: The Improbable Origins of Modern Wall Street*, 109.

required to obtain information about assets in the market.[41] If the market were perfectly efficient, there would be no incentive to gather market-relevant information. But without this information the market would not be able to function efficiently. So even if fundamental analysis is not part of the paradigm of modern finance, and even if fundamental analysis lacks the stringent mathematical foundation that plays such a crucial part in the self-perception of neoclassical finance, empirical investigation of the underlying economy is still regarded as a necessary precondition for market efficiency. In this view, fundamental analysts are the foot soldiers of financial markets.

Even though neoclassical finance is indeed a new paradigm for thinking about financial markets, it also shares important continuities with fundamental and even technical analysis. If we look at vertical arbitrage speculation from a philosophical perspective, we see that it is a hybrid of the forms of speculative profits found in fundamental and technical analysis. Fundamental analysis operates between two different ontological levels. The first is the symbolic order of the financial market, where prices of stocks are quoted. The second is the real order of business, where the intrinsic value of companies may be found. In the neoclassical idea of informationally efficient markets, this ontological difference is initially levelled out, since it is assumed that all relevant information about the value of underlying assets is always already incorporated into current market prices. However, with option pricing theory and vertical arbitrage, the distinction between the different levels is reintroduced in a new form. It is no longer a distinction between real business (value) and symbolic market (price). It is rather a distinction between, on the one hand, the meta-markets for derivatives, and on the other, the underlying markets for stocks, bonds, and currencies.

In contrast to the distinction between value and price in fundamental analysis, option pricing theory and vertical arbitrage do not transcend the domain of the symbolic. Instead, there is a doubling of the market within the order of the symbolic, which creates a difference between two distinct levels of prices. This is where vertical arbitrage becomes a form of neo-chartism. Similar to old-fashioned chartism, neoclassical option pricing theory does not have to rely on

41 Grossman and Stiglitz, 'On the Impossibility of Informationally Efficient Markets'.

market-external data. It does not have to move beyond the order of the symbolic. The underlying assets are just another price series. Vertical arbitrage is a hybrid that combines the metaphysics of fundamental analysis with the decoupling of finance from the underlying economy found in technical analysis.

Part Two:

The Philosophy of Money

CHAPTER THREE

Analyzing Money

We shall now set aside the examination of financial markets in order to look at the phenomenon of money itself. The analyses of financial markets in the preceding chapters looked at how financial assets are traded at fluctuating prices, and how the trajectories of these prices may or may not be predicted. An obvious precondition for the functioning of financial markets is, of course, money. As we touched upon at the beginning of this book, the philosophical properties of money are usually overlooked or taken for granted. This is not only true of our daily use of money for buying groceries or paying our mortgage. This is also true of theories of modern finance. The role of philosophy at this stage is to linger over the taken-for-grantedness of money and subject the phenomenon to careful analysis.

The most curious thing about the contemporary philosophy of money is that it does not exist. This is perhaps a crude and arrogant postulate, since there are indeed a number of contemporary philosophers who write about money. Nevertheless, the philosophy of money is not an established field of research, and it is certainly not regarded as an obligatory part of a philosopher's education in the way that the philosophy of science, the philosophy of ethics, the philosophy of language, or the philosophy of art are. At best, the philosophy of money resides at the margins of the discipline.

When it comes to the question of money, the twentieth century seems to have been marked by a particular division of labour between philosophy and economics. When Smith wrote *The Wealth of Nations* in the eighteenth century, or even when Marx wrote *Capital* in the nineteenth century, there was no clear distinction between philosophy and economics. Both of these works are regarded as classics within both fields. But in the twentieth century, the discipline of economics was separated from philosophy and developed into an autonomous field of research based on a distinct set of concepts and methods. Ironically, the publication of Simmel's *Philosophy of Money* in 1900 marked the end rather than the beginning of the philosophical study of money.

From the point of view of philosophy, economics came to be regarded as the natural place for the study of money. At best, philosophers, sociologists and other scholars of the humanities would study the effects of capitalism and other forms of economic organization on the social and psychological life of people. The nature of the phenomenon of money itself was regarded as beyond the scope of their disciplines.

Over the course of the twentieth century, economics developed in the direction of the natural sciences such as physics and chemistry.[1] This trend was signified by the movement of neoclassical economics into the mainstream of the discipline and by the growing importance of mathematics. Mainstream economics takes as its point of departure a number of meta-theoretical assumptions about economic agents as rational, utility maximizing and fully informed about their options.[2] These assumptions allow for the posing of questions and testable hypotheses that are typically formulated in terms of causal relations between economic variables. How is inflation correlated with unemployment? How do changes in the interest rate effect GNP? Does economic inequality stimulate economic growth? And so on. In the study of such problems, the question of the nature of money is an obstruction rather than a precondition. Mainstream economics tends to study the *effects* of money and monetary dispositions rather than the object itself. Reflection on the nature of money seems invariably to lead to metaphysical philosophizing, which is far beyond the scope of mathematical testing. At best, the question 'What is money?' is brushed aside with reference to the fourfold definition of money as a medium of exchange, a measure of value, a standard of account and a store of value, which leaves the economist free to proceed to more important matters. At worst, the question is simply ignored.

This leaves the question of money falling between two stools. While philosophy has the proper methods for studying the object of money, this is not regarded as a proper object of philosophic inquiry. Economics, on the other hand, is indeed the scientific discipline concerned with the study of money, but the discipline lacks the proper methods for approaching the object in any direct fashion. The purpose of the following chapters is to bridge the gap between philosophy and

---

1 Mirowski, *More Heat than Light*.

2 Weintraub, 'Neoclassical Economics'.

economics by developing a philosophical theory of money. The method for the development of the theory is similar to the one applied to the analysis of financial markets. We shall again use Žižek's threefold distinction between real, symbolic and imaginary to map out the functioning of money.

As noted in the introduction, it is of course a simplification to claim that the question of money has been completely neglected for the past one hundred years. Several scholars within the fields of heterodox economics, economic sociology and the anthropology of money have indeed explored this topic. Still, the distinct potential of a philosophy of money lies in the development of new concepts that will constitute an actual theory of money, one that goes beyond empirical studies of what money does. This is the purpose of the following exposition.

'MONEY DOES NOT EXIST'

When framing an analysis of money with the question 'What is money?', it is invariably assumed that money is a definite thing and that it is possible to define this thing through one coherent theory. In the following analysis, I am going to disavow this assumption.

The title of this section is of course a paraphrase of Lacan's infamous slogan 'Woman does not exist'.[3] The point of the slogan is not that there are no women in the world, but rather that the essence of what it means to be a woman does not lend itself to a general definition. Lacan's statement has been the cause of much controversy, especially among feminists. It is beyond the scope of this book to enter into this debate. Regardless of the validity of Lacan's theory about women, his point seems immediately applicable to money. Hence, the assumption of the following analysis is precisely that 'Money does not exist'. This renders the ambition to develop a philosophical theory of money into a paradoxical endeavour, as the theory will have to incorporate the fact that money cannot be captured by one coherent theory.

Money comes in a variety of forms. Today, most people immediately associate the concept of money with the notes and coins they carry in their wallet. However, cash money makes up only a fraction

---

3 Lacan, *Television*, 38.

of the total amount of money in circulation. Most money consists of the various liabilities of banks and financial institutions. Furthermore, the boundaries of what counts as money and what does not are not clearly defined. They are themselves a matter of scientific dispute. For instance, some people have asked whether derivatives should be regarded as a distinct form of money.[4] I will return to this particular question in chapter six. The point here is merely that instead of looking for a theory or a definition of money that can account for the nature of money across its various empirical manifestations, I will concede the fact that money eludes a comprehensive theory. In the language of Žižek, money is the real that resists symbolization. At the same time – and this is a point I will elaborate in the next chapter – the very functioning of money relies on the illusion among the users of money that different forms of money are in the last instance one and the same thing.

Instead of framing the analysis with the question 'What is money?', I am going to use the kind of question I posed in my analysis of financial market. This was the question: How is it possible to make money in financial markets? Since we are no longer concerned with money merely in the context of financial markets, I will rephrase the question in a more general form: How is it possible to make money? It is important to note the ambivalent meaning of the phrase 'make money'. Most often when we use this phrase – for instance, when we say 'let's make some money' – we actually mean 'acquire some money'. In this sense, 'making money' does not imply adding to the pool of existing money in the world, but merely appropriating some of the money already in existence. In the context of my analysis of financial markets, 'making money' was implicitly interpreted in this fashion. But in the current analysis of money I am going to turn to the more literal interpretation of the phrase. The question is thus, how is it possible for money to come into being?

In the field of economics, there is no consensus about the nature and evolution of money. In the following, I will distinguish among three theories of money: commodity theory, chartalist theory and credit theory. Besides presenting the main ideas of each of these theories, I will analyze the theories in terms of their philosophical

---

4 Bryan and Rafferty, 'Money in Capitalism or Capitalist Money?'; Bryan and Rafferty, 'Financial Derivatives and the Theory of Money'.

properties and assumptions. The ambition of my analysis is not to settle the controversy between the different accounts of money in favour of one or the other theory. Rather, the purpose is to demonstrate how the theoretical controversy about money is a symptom of the very nature of the thing itself. Since money does not exist, it's no wonder there is controversy about what it is! As we will see, it is an intrinsic part of the functioning of money in different historical and social contexts that money implies different answers to the question 'What is money?' These answers function as the ideological fantasies that sustain the functioning of money.

THE TRAUMATIC CONSTITUTION OF MONEY: FROM $ TO $

The analysis of money proceeds along the same lines as the preceding analysis of financial markets. The starting point of the analysis of financial markets was the distinction between price and value. Price is the symbolic expression of the real value of an asset. The symbolic order of the financial market generates a price that is an answer to the question: *What* is it worth? The functioning of money is even more fundamental than the functioning of the market insofar as money is the very precondition that allows us to speak of something in terms of price. Money is the precondition for the distinction between value and price.

In order for money to enable the distinction between value and price with regard to commodities that we buy and sell, the money system also has to be able to account for the distinction between value and price when applied to money itself. This is where the analysis of money becomes tricky. When we start asking about the price of money, we invariably get caught in a tautology, insofar as the price of money can only be expressed in terms of money itself. The price of $100 is $100. When we start asking about the value of money, some form of ontological ambiguity instantly emerges. On the one hand, the value of money is expressed by the amount of commodities that we can buy with this money. On the other hand, the precondition for the purchasing power of money is that it has some kind of other value in the first place. Crudely speaking, the difference between the three theories of money presented in this chapter boils down to their respective conceptions of what grounds the value of money.

In *Being and Time*, Heidegger deliberately circumvents the question 'what is a subject?' by proposing the following definition of 'Dasein', the term he uses to designate human beings:

> Dasein is an entity which does not just occur among other entities. Rather it is ontically distinguished by the fact that, in its very Being, that Being is an issue for it. But in that case, this is a constitutive state of Dasein's Being, and this implies that Dasein, in its Being, has a relationship towards that Being – a relationship which itself is one of Being. And this means further that there is some way in which Dasein understands itself in its Being, and that to some degree it does so explicitly. It is peculiar to this entity that with and through its Being, this Being is disclosed to it. Understanding of Being is itself a definite characteristic of Dasein's Being. Dasein is ontically distinctive in that it is ontological.[5]

The point is that we cannot define Dasein in terms of 'what it is'. Dasein is ontically distinguished from other beings (rocks, chairs, lizards) by the fact that Dasein is concerned about itself with regard to 'what it is'. From this concern (*Sorge*) originates the very distinction between beings and Being, between what-ness and mere thatness. This distinction applies not only to Dasein itself but also to entities in the world of Dasein. It is the very Being of Dasein that introduces this distinction into the world. In a later work, Heidegger makes the point that in a world populated by lizards only, there would be no disclosure of the world in terms of separate entities, there would be no distinction between the what-ness and the mere that-ness of the world.[6]

Heidegger's analysis of Being and Dasein is methodologically relevant to the study of money. The point here is not that we can simply equate the concept of Dasein with money. This would be a grave mistake. Nevertheless, I would argue that Heidegger performs a methodological move that is applicable to the analysis of money. In Heidegger, the concept of Dasein comes to have two meanings. On the one hand, it is the designation for that particular form of Being which pertains to the individual human being. On the other hand,

---

5 Heidegger, *Being and Time*, §. 4.

6 Heidegger, *The Fundamental Concepts of Metaphysics*, 197–8.

Dasein also invariably comes to stand for the human being as an entity. Even though Heidegger may want to eschew this latter meaning of the word, it is impossible to avoid this interpretation when reading Heidegger. Dasein is both a form of Being and the name for a particular entity.

In the case of money, we find a comparable ambiguity. The most straightforward understanding of money is to view it as the name for the coins and notes we carry in our pockets. At the same time, we can also understand money as a particular form of Being that pertains to particular entities. When a group of people play a game of poker, the plastic chips in the game take on the Being of money. When the game ends and wins and losses are settled in ordinary cash, the chips cease to be money. In this sense, we could speak of 'being-money' rather than money.

The particular Being of money is characterised by a particular configuration of the distinction between value and price. In Heidegger's analysis of the ontological difference, we have seen how the distinction between Being and being blurs when it is applied to Dasein itself. A similar ontological feature applies to money. Money is simultaneously the source of the distinction between value and price and the point where this distinction breaks down.

We find the same kind of thinking in Žižek, more specifically in his theory of the subject. As we have seen, Žižek describes the subject as constituted by a fundamental lack. The perpetual attempt to fill this lack is what propels the desire of the subject. Žižek also refers to the subject as a 'split subject'. In Lacan's intricate system of notations, the subject is thus given the symbol $. It is hard to believe that this symbol's similarity to the dollar sign is merely a coincidence. In the following, we shall appropriate this theory for the analysis of money.

The concept of the split subject refers to the subject's position as an intermediary between the order of the real and the order of the symbolic. Žižek explains:

> The subject is not directly included in the symbolic order: it is included as the very point at which signification breaks down. Sam Goldwyn's famous retort when he was confronted with an unacceptable business proposition, 'Include me out!', perfectly expresses this

intermediate status of the subject's relationship to the symbolic order between direct inclusion and direct exclusion.[7]

The notion of the split subject can be illustrated by the way we ordinarily think of ourselves as individuals. Individuality implies that something is a unity, it is *in*-dividable. We refer to ourselves as such a unity all the time: 'I don't like cheese', 'I live in an apartment', 'I owe you $500', etc. We assume the existence of a self that is the origin of our feelings, preferences, opinions, etc. The famous liar's paradox is precisely a paradox because it contradicts this sense of the self as a unity. The paradox consists of the simple statement 'I am lying', and it thrives on the double position of the self in the proposition. The self figures both as the object of the proposition, i.e. as the thing the proposition refers to, and as the subject of the proposition, i.e. as the origin of the utterance. The paradox arises because the selves of the two positions are not identical. If the proposition is true, the self is a liar, thus refuting the proposition, and vice versa. The liar's paradox is self-contradictory in both meanings of the term: the proposition contradicts itself, but the paradox also contradicts the very idea of the self as a unity.

Žižek starts from the completely opposite view of the subject. Subjectivity is not a unity but rather the product of an irreconcilable gap. A person is incorporated into the symbolic order when he or she attains a certain position in the social structure of society. The ritual of giving a person a name signifies this incorporation. As the person is incorporated into the structure of the symbolic order, this structure also provides the conditions of possibility for that person's reflective self-conception. This is Foucault's point about the social constitution of subjectivity, which has become a central component of mainstream social constructivist theories of the self.

Žižek breaks from these theories when he insists that the incorporation of a person into the symbolic order is always incomplete. The subject will indeed identify with the symbolic designations attributed to him in the symbolic order; I will identify myself as a male, Danish, a father, a taxpayer, etc. But at the same time, my identification with these designations is marked by a sense of misrecognition. As noted in chapter one, even if it were possible to make a complete

7 Žižek, *The Ticklish Subject*, 109–110.

list of all my symbolic designations, I would still have the feeling that I am 'more than this'. This feeling is constitutive of Žižek's understanding of subjectivity.

The point here is not that beyond the sphere of our symbolic identity there is some external kernel of true subjectivity. This is the mistake made by neurobiological conceptions of subjectivity that locate subjectivity in the materiality of the brain. Just as the person confronted with the complete listing of his or her symbolic designations will insist on being 'more than this', so a person confronted with a real-time scanner image of his or her brain will insist the same. Subjectivity can be reduced neither to the order of the symbolic nor to the order of the real. Subjectivity is rather the gap separating the two.

Žižek also refers to this constitution of subjectivity as 'de-alienation'. Subjectivity is experienced when the individual is minimally misrecognized, when conformity to social ideals and norms as expressed through the symbolic order is slightly off. This produces a sense of 'something' manifesting itself in the individual's actions that cannot be deduced from the symbolic premises of a the given situation. Žižek refers to the following Marx Brothers joke to illustrate this point:

> 'You remind me of Emanuel Ravelli.'
> 'But I am Emanuel Ravelli.'
> 'Then no wonder you look like him!'[8]

In this joke there is an insistence on the non-identity between the symbolic mandate of the subject – the signification of the subject by the name Emanuel Ravelli – and the real presence of the person designated as Emanuel Ravelli. It is in this minimal gap between the incomplete signification and the real presence of the subject that subjectivity manifests itself. The insufficiency of the symbolic order opens a space for the subject's imaginary projections of his or her own subjectivity.

In the spirit of Heidegger, I suggested above that instead of posing the typical question 'What is money?', we should structure our investigation around the question 'How *is* money?' A tentative answer to

8 Žižek, *The Sublime Object of Ideology*, 3.

this question can be modelled on Žižek's theory of the split subject: The Being of money consists in the opening of the gap between the value and the price of commodities, even as this gap is sustained by various fantasmatic projections that render money itself as a valuable object. In order to see what that means, we shall start by looking into the relation between money and gold.

MAKING MONEY OUT OF GOLD

A conventional way of thinking about money is to understand it through some version of the commodity theory of money. This theory claims that modern money has evolved from a particular kind of commodity – typically gold or some other precious metals – which at some point was singled out to perform the function of money. In the wake of the 2007–8 financial crisis, some commentators who were sceptical about the functioning of our current money system recommended a return to the gold standard. The financial crisis was seen as a symptom of the decoupling of money from a material base, and gold was seen as a way to re-establish the link. This suggestion invokes a commodity theory of money and illustrates how gold comes to stand for concreteness in the world of money. But closer inspection reveals gold to be anything but concrete.

A fundamental mystery in the functioning of money is that people believe in it. How is it that people are crazy enough to accept the exchange of a loaf of bread, a sheep or even a brand new BMW for a number of paper bills that have no immediate use? When we look at historical money systems based on coins made of gold or other precious metal, this mystery seems not to arise, since these monetary objects seem to have intrinsic value. The exchange of a gold coin for twelve sheep seems to be nothing but an advanced form of barter. As indicated by the incessant use of the word 'seem' in the preceding formulations, there is something wrong with this kind of reasoning.

We can explain the role of gold in relation to money by way of analogy: gold is to money what Jesus is to God. We might ask: Why do people believe in God? And we might answer: Because His son Jesus descended to earth to deliver the good message of God. However, in order to believe in Jesus, even if you were to meet him face to face, you would have to believe in God first. If you did not believe in God, how could you believe someone claiming to be His son? The same problem occurs when gold is invoked to guarantee or explain the value of money. This is not really a guarantee or an explanation. It is rather the displacement of a mystery by an even greater mystery.

A classic account of the commodity theory of money is found in Adam Smith:

> When the division of labor first began to take place, this power of exchanging must frequently have been very much clogged and embarrassed in its operations. One man, we shall suppose, has more of a certain commodity than he himself has occasion for, while another has less. The former consequently would be glad to dispose of, and the latter to purchase, a part of this superfluity. But if this latter should chance to have nothing that the former stands in need of, no exchange can be made between them. The butcher has more meat in his shop than he himself can consume, and the brewer and the baker would each of them be willing to purchase a part of it. But they have nothing to offer in exchange, except the different productions of their respective trades, and the butcher is already provided with all the bread and beer which he has immediate occasion for. No change can in this case be made between them. He cannot offer to be their merchant nor they his customers; and they are all of them thus mutually less serviceable to one another. In order to avoid the inconvenience of such situations, every prudent man in every period of society, after the first establishment of the division of labor, must naturally have endeavored to manage his affairs in such a manner, as to have at all times by him, besides the peculiar produce of his own industry, a certain quantity of some one commodity or other, such as he imagined that few people would be likely to refuse in exchange for the produce of their industry . . . Many different commodities, it is probable, were successively both thought of and employed for this purpose. In all countries, however, men seem at last to have been determined by irresistible reasons to give the preference, for this employment, to metals above every other commodity.[9]

In this account of the evolution of money we recognize the starting point as the imaginary pre-monetary barter economy. Money is essentially the solution to the problem of barter. This is still the

---

9 Smith, *The Wealth of Nations*, 24–25.

standard account of the evolution of money in most economics textbooks.

Along similar lines, Marx also relies on a commodity theory of money. In his analysis of the genesis of the value form and the evolution of capital, a crucial step is the emergence of the 'general equivalent', which serves as a standard measure of commodities. In concordance with the historical circumstances of his time, Marx points to gold (or silver) as the particular commodity which is singled out among all other commodities to play the role of universal equivalent. This means that gold becomes the standard against which the value of all other commodities is measured. Even the evolution of paper money is merely the continuation of this process, as paper money is the symbol of the value of gold:

> Just as the exchange value of commodities is crystallized by their process of exchange into gold money, so is gold money sublimated in its currency into its own symbol first in the form of worn coin, then in the form of subsidiary metal currency, and finally in the form of a worthless token, paper, mere sign of value.[10]

There is something seductively simple about the commodity theory of money. Gold (or other precious metals) has an intrinsic value which makes it generally accepted in the exchange for other commodities, the use-value of which is contingent upon the contextual circumstances of the exchange. The use-value of meat, for instance, may depend on the potential buyer's immediate level of hunger. The use-value of a bicycle may depend on whether the potential buyer already has a bicycle or some other means of transportation. And so on. Gold may thus serve as the basis for money. In the form of coins, gold may itself circulate, making it simultaneously a commodity with intrinsic value and a form of money symbolizing value. In other words, gold coins are simultaneously real value and symbolic representations. We see here, in a very simple form, the difference between value and price. In the form of paper money or account money, the real and the symbolic are separated and gold functions merely as a real 'anchor' guaranteeing the credibility of symbolic representations of value. At this stage, the difference between

10 Marx, *A Contribution to the Critique of Political Economy*, 149.

value and price has evolved into a more advanced form.

However, if we start inquiring into the value of gold itself, things become rather more complicated, and the elusive nature of the real soon becomes apparent. Gold is not merely the origin of the difference between value and price; it is also the point where this difference breaks down. Smith talks about the 'irresistible reasons' why men finally settle on gold and other precious metals as the specific commodities that will perform the function of money. And Marx writes about the aesthetic properties of gold and silver that 'make them the natural material of luxury, ornamentation, splendor, festive occasions, in short, the positive form of abundance and wealth. They appear, in a way, as spontaneous light brought out from the underground world'.[11] It seems to be the almost magical properties of gold that make it stand out as 'the Lord of commodities'.[12]

Indeed, Marx is ambiguous in his account of the value of gold. Besides pointing to these material properties as the basis of gold's inherent use-value, Marx sometimes applies his labour theory of value to gold as well. According to this theory, the true value of a commodity is expressed by the amount of abstract labour time embodied in the production of the commodity. In the case of gold, the true value of the commodity is expressed by the amount of labour required to mine and process the material. In turn, the value of labour is expressed by the amount of commodities required for the reproduction of the labour power. What Marx aims to do in his labour theory of value is to institute abstract labour time as the 'gold standard' of value:

> Now suppose that the average amount of the daily necessaries of a labouring man require six hours of average labour for their production. Suppose, moreover, six hours of average labour to be also realized in a quantity of gold equal to 3s [shillings]. Then 3s. would be the price, or the monetary expression of the daily value of that man's labouring power. If he worked daily six hours he would daily produce a value sufficient to buy the average amount of his daily necessaries, or to maintain himself as a labouring man.[13]

---

11 Ibid., 211.

12 Ibid., 166.

13 Marx and Engels, *Selected Works*, 211.

The measurement of the value of gold in terms of abstract labour is a complication rather than a solution to the paradoxical relationship between money and gold. Marx's reasoning in this quote provokes a number of questions. First, a simple question: Why would anyone struggle to dig gold out of the ground in the first place? If the purpose of commodities is ultimately to serve in the reproduction of labour, what is it about gold that warrants any interest in it as a commodity? It is true that gold may be used to buy the commodities required for the reproduction of labour, but this is only the case once gold has been established as money. Furthermore, the use of labour time as an abstract measure of value requires a distinction between labour activities and non-labour activities (leisure, consumption, reproduction). This raises a second question: How can we know that the production of the average labourer's 'daily necessities' or the production of 3s. worth of gold require six rather than eight or ten hours of labour? How do we know when to start and stop the clock when measuring the amount of labour going into the production of a commodity? The answer is again provided by money itself. We start the clock when the worker starts getting paid, and we stop it when he is no longer getting paid. Money itself serves as the criterion for the distinction between labour time and non-labour time. In addition, the 'monetary expression' of the value of labour is provided only through the unquestioned assumption that the monetary value of gold is immediately expressed in shillings. This brings us to a third question: Is not the symbolization of gold in shillings only possible once a monetary system that designates gold as money in already in place? Again, we see that the labour theory of value cannot explain the emergence of money in the form of gold.

Finally, it is tempting to ask what happens to Marx's theory of money and gold if reality does not conform to this imaginary situation where the labour time embodied in the production of the daily necessities of the average labourer equals the labour time required to produce 3s. worth of gold, which in turn equals the price of the daily necessities. What if 300s. worth of gold could be produced in six hours of labour, while the price of the daily necessities was still 3s.? Would the true value of gold still be those six hours of abstract labour embodied in its production? Or would it be the six hundred hours of labour that could be reproduced through the exchange of gold for daily necessities?

The fundamental problem here is that it is impossible to speak of value without simultaneously invoking some kind of symbolic system that sets the standard for the determination of value. Even though gold may indeed possess the qualities listed by Marx, it is possible to speak of gold as valuable only insofar as there is already a symbolic system in place that enables us to compare the value of gold to the value of other commodities. And even though it takes a certain amount of labour time to produce a certain quantity of gold, this does not explain the value of gold as money. As we have already discussed in the case of financial markets, the notion of 'real value' or 'intrinsic value' is highly elusive. The determination of real value presupposes a system that can perform the symbolic operation of pricing. In the case of money and gold, this leads to the paradox that in order for gold to be singled out as valuable and thus to perform the function of money, there needs to already be a system of money in place that is able to perform this valuation. Another way of stating this paradox is to say that gold may indeed function as the general equivalent setting the standard for the valuation of all other commodities, but it cannot function as a standard for the valuation of gold itself.

Marx also writes about how the function of a general equivalent can only be fulfilled by 'that part of the products which are not immediately required as use-values'.[14] In this formulation, it is not superior use-value but rather the lack of immediate use-value that is particular to gold. The lack of use-value allows gold to be excluded from the ordinary exchange of commodities meant for consumption. This exclusion does not follow necessarily from the immanent properties of gold. It is rather an operation performed within the system of exchange itself, much in the same way that the sovereign king is not a sovereign because of his inherent qualities but because his subjects *think* he is king. 'A commodity', Marx writes,

> can only function as general equivalent because, and insofar as, all other commodities *set it apart* from themselves as equivalent. Not until this setting apart is definitively concentrated upon one particular kind of commodity does the uniform relative value form of

14 Marx, *A Contribution to the Critique of Political Economy*, 168.

commodities at large acquire objective fixity and general social validity.[15]

We see here how gold functions as money by being simultaneously included and excluded from the exchange of commodities, in the same way that the split subject is included and excluded from the symbolic order. Gold is a 'split commodity'. It incarnates simultaneously the symbolic function of money and the real value of the commodity.

THE VALUE OF GOLD IS PRICELESS

In the case of the subject, the system of symbolization breaks down because it is unable to signify who the subject 'really is'. Every symbolic account of the Being of the subject falls short, as the subject insists 'I am more than this'. However, the impossibility of symbolization is at the same time the condition of possibility for symbolization. It is the very breakdown of symbolization that allows the subject to imagine himself or herself as an individual subject. We may think of the way that people typically explain who they are, not by listing a number of characteristics that define them, but rather by pointing to inconsistencies in these symbolic definitions: 'I am religious but I do not believe in the Christian God'. 'I am a manager but I do not like to tell other people what to do'. 'I like toast but only with the crust cut off', etc. Along these lines, Žižek proposes the following definition of the subject:

> The subject has no substantial actuality, it comes second, it emerges only through the process of separation, of overcoming its presuppositions, and these presuppositions are also only a retroactive effect of the same process of their overcoming. The result is thus that there is . . . a failure or a negativity inscribed into the very heart of the entity we are dealing with. If the status of the subject is thoroughly 'processual', it means that it emerges through the very failure to fully actualize itself. This brings us again to one possible formal definition of the subject: a subject tries to articulate ('express') itself in a signifying chain, this articulation fails, and by means of and through this

15 Marx, *Capital – Volume 1*, 42.

failure, the subject emerges: the subject is the failure of its signifying representation – this is why Lacan writes the subject of the signifier as $, as 'barred'.[16]

A similar impossibility occurs when we attempt to symbolically value gold in terms of its use-value. Even though gold may indeed have some kind of use-value as 'the natural material of luxury, ornamentation, splendor, festive occasions', this does not seem to warrant the special value attached to gold. It is as if gold insists, 'I am more than this', 'My value cannot be expressed in terms of the kind of value inherent in ordinary commodities'. In chapter one, we saw how Žižek defines the real as 'that which resists symbolization' and 'as the rock upon which every attempt at symbolization stumbles'.[17] These definitions perfectly fit the role of gold in relation to money and the exchange of commodities.

A defining characteristic of money is the capacity to price all kinds of assets. In the analysis of financial markets, we have seen how price functions as the symbolic expression of value. In the case of gold, this function breaks down. In a money system based on gold, the pricing of a quantity of gold merely states the identity of the gold with itself. The pricing function of money turns into a tautology, which merely states that a kilogram of gold is worth a kilogram of gold. This means that unlike all other assets, the value of gold cannot be expressed in terms of the price of gold. The value of gold is priceless.

However, this tautology does not mean that the system breaks down. The point in Žižek's definition of the subject is precisely that the failure of symbolization is the precondition for the existence of the subject. The impossibility of adequately symbolizing the real Being of the subject gives rise to the subject's imaginary self-understanding as an individual subject that is the origin of its own actions, emotions, and thoughts. Hence, the impossibility of symbolization is the condition of possibility of subjectivity. A similar dialectic is at play in the case of gold as money. The impossibility of adequately accounting for the value of gold gives rise to an imaginary fantasy of gold as being endowed with some form of value beyond the ordinary sphere

16 Žižek, *Living in the End Times*, 232.
17 Žižek, *The Sublime Object of Ideology*, 69, 169.

of use-values. We have already seen how this fantasy is at play even in Marx, who is otherwise a true master of cynicism.

This argument may be pushed one step further by suggesting that even the special aesthetic qualities of gold – which, according to Marx, 'make them the natural material of luxury, ornamentation, splendor, festive occasions', and which appear 'as spontaneous light brought out from the underground world' – are nothing but the reflections of our own fantasmatic projections, which in turn spring from the knowledge of the privileged position of gold in the money system. In this fashion, gold provides what Žižek refers to as an 'answer of the real'. Žižek defines this concept in relation to communication:

> Some accidentally produced 'little piece of the real' . . . attests to the success of the communication . . . For things to have meaning, this meaning must be confirmed by some contingent piece of the real that can be read as a 'sign'. The very word *sign*, in opposition to the arbitrary mark, pertains to the 'answer of the real': the 'sign' is given by the thing itself, it indicates that at least at a certain point, the abyss separating the real from the symbolic network has been crossed.[18]

In the context of money, gold provides this indication that the gap between the real of value and the symbolic sphere of exchange has been bridged. It is important to note that the gap between the real and the symbolic is not bridged through a relation of representation. The answer of the real emerges in a space of indistinction between the real and the symbolic, thus establishing so-called 'quilting points' (*points de capiton*) where the real is weaved into the fabric of reality. These quilting points are in turn the precondition for all other relations of representation between the symbolic and the real.

Even though the position of gold as general equivalent in the system of money is perhaps arbitrary, it can only function as an answer of the real as long as this arbitrariness is concealed. This is what happens when we imagine that gold has a privileged position in the system of money *because* of its inherent, real qualities, and not the other way around. Žižek explains how this logic works:

---

18 Žižek, *Looking Awry*, 31–32.

> If an object is to take its place in a libidinal space, its arbitrary character must remain concealed. The subject cannot say to herself, 'Since the object is arbitrary, I can choose whatever I want as the object of my drive'. The object must appear to be *found*, to offer itself as support and point of reference for the drive's circular movement . . . While it is true that any object can occupy the empty place of the Thing, it can do so only by means of the illusion that it was always already there, i.e., that it was not placed there by us but *found there as an 'answer of the real'*. Although any object can function as the object-cause of desire – insofar as the power of fascination it exerts is not its immediate property but results from the place it occupies in the structure – we must, by structural necessity, fall prey to the illusion that the power of fascination belongs to the object as such.[19]

The illusion, which has to be maintained in order for gold to function as a *point de capiton* in the money system, is the illusion of the intrinsic value of gold. The value of gold must seem to be 'found' rather than 'placed there by us' in the very designation of gold as money. In the commodity theory of money, gold functions as the incarnation of real value. We have seen how Marx points out that the functioning of gold as general equivalent comes about only when 'all other commodities *set it apart* from themselves as equivalent'. Paradoxically, gold can only function as the sublime incarnation of value insofar as it is excluded from the ordinary circulation of commodities. We like to think that the reason why gold is stowed away in the vaults of banks is to provide security against the outstanding debt of the bank. Perhaps the actual reason is the complete opposite. Gold is kept out of the ordinary exchange and consumption of commodities in order to conceal the fact that it is in fact an ordinary commodity with very little actual use-value beyond serving as the surface for our fantasmatic projections about its magical capacities.

In summary, the commodity theory is based on the idea that the value of money is grounded in the order of the real. Gold is elevated to the status of money due to the intrinsic real qualities of the material. These qualities make gold an object of a very general desire

19 Ibid., 32–33.

among participants in the marketplace. Not everyone desires potatoes all the time, but everyone desires gold all the time.

MAKING MONEY BY LAW

> Today all civilized money is, beyond the possibility of dispute, chartalist.[20]

There are several problems with the commodity theory of money. One very important problem is that the theory is historically wrong. The account of money as evolving from primitive barter systems, which is not only found in Adam Smith's age-old account but is still recycled in contemporary textbooks on economics, is anthropologically unfounded. After extensive studies on barter, anthropologist Caroline Humphrey writes: 'No example of a barter economy, pure and simple, has ever been described, let alone the emergence from it of money; all available ethnography suggests that there never has been such a thing'.[21] As pointed out by David Graeber, the simple barter society from which money is supposed to have emerged is a fantasy world in the imagination of a certain strand of economists.[22]

The problem with this story of the origins of money (critics refer to is as 'the barter myth') is not merely one of historical inaccuracy. The way we narrate the origins of money has profound implications for the way we think about the functioning of money, even in contemporary society. One of the implications of the idea of money as a practical solution to the so-called 'problem of the double coincidence of wants' is that it conceives of money as a spontaneous creation of the market. Money is merely a mediator between honest manufacturers and merchants, who make their living by producing and trading commodities with intrinsic value. In this account, the value of money is backed by the kind of values we find in the market. The commodity theory thus tends to veil the role of force and government in the creation of money.[23]

---

20 Keynes, *A Treatise on Money*, 4–5.
21 Humphrey, 'Barter and Economic Disintegration', 48.
22 Graeber, *Debt*, 23.
23 Hudson, 'The Archaeology of Money'.

This objection is at the heart of the chartalist theory of money, which proposes that money is essentially fiat money. The classic formulation of this approach to money is found in Georg Friedrich Knapp's *The State Theory of Money.*[24] As we will see, Keynes makes explicit reference to Knapp. Indeed, much of Keynesianist economics is based on the idea of fiat money. More recent formulations of chartalism are found in Mosler, Bell and Wray.[25]

The basic idea of the chartalist theory is this: 'Money is a creature of law'. And hence: 'The soul of currency is not in the material of the pieces, but in the legal ordinances which regulate their use'.[26] Obviously, this approach is diametrically opposed to the one found in the commodity theory. The 'moneyness' of an object comes not from the intrinsic qualities of the object, but rather from the symbolic designation of the thing as money. Declaring something as money can in principle be done by any authority that has sufficient power to write and enforce the law. Chartalists typically make reference to coinage in Lydia (now Turkey) around 600 BC as the first instance of fiat money.[27] In contemporary society, this money-issuing authority is of course the nation-state.

> Money in the modern sense first comes into being when the morphic means of payment have their validity settled by proclamation and become Chartal . . . The nominality of the unit of value is . . . created by the State in its capacity as the guardian and maintainer of law.[28]

Chartalism also differs from the commodity theory insofar as it is first and foremost a theory of modern money. The purest form of fiat money is found within the context of the modern nation-state. However, Knapp still maintains that any kind of money necessarily includes an element of chartality. He makes the distinction between hylogenic and autogenic money. If a means of payment is accepted because of its 'possibility of 'real' use', it is hylogenic, and if a means of payment is accepted merely because it can pass on in further

---

24 Knapp, *The State Theory of Money.*

25 Mosler, 'Full Employment and Price Stability'; Bell, 'Do Taxes and Bonds Finance Government Spending?'; Wray, *Understanding Modern Money.*

26 Knapp, *The State Theory of Money*, 1–2.

27 Keynes, *A Treatise on Money*, 10; Graeber, *Debt*, 224.

28 Knapp, *The State Theory of Money*, 38–39.

circulation, it is autogenic. For instance, gold coins are hylogenic, whereas paper money is purely autogenic. But even hylogenic means of payment require an element of chartality in order to become money. 'The use in exchange is a legal phenomenon.'[29] Only when certain objects are proclaimed to be valid means of payment in exchange and the settlement of debt are they money. Gold does not become money merely on account of the intrinsic qualities of the material, but because it is proclaimed to be money within the legal sphere of a sovereign authority. In this sense, the chartalist theory does not deny that commodity money exists. However, this form of money is merely a subcategory of chartal money. It is hylogenic chartal money. This is opposed to autogenic chartal money, which we may regard as the pure form of fiat money insofar as its value is *only* sustained by its legal status.

When the state, or another sovereign authority, proclaims certain objects to be money, it performs a double movement. It is not enough to just declare that 'from now on gold is money'. The proclamation only comes to have economic effects when it is supported by the recognition of the object as payment in economic transactions with the state:

> The modern state can make anything it chooses generally acceptable as money and thus establish its value quite apart from any connection, even of the most formal kind, with gold or backing of any kind. It is true that a simple declaration that such and such is money will not do, even if backed by the most convincing constitutional evidence of the state's absolute sovereignty. But if the state is willing to accept the proposed money in the payment of taxes and other obligations to itself, the trick is done. Everyone who has obligations to the state will be willing to accept the pieces of paper with which he can settle the obligations, and all other people will be willing to accept those pieces of paper because they know that taxpayers, etc., will accept them in turn.[30]

Chartal money, therefore, does not have to rely on a general desire for the real qualities of the money object. Even in a state where gold

---

29 Ibid., 7.

30 Lerner, 'Money as a Creature of the State', 313.

coins are proclaimed to be legal tender, the value of these coins does not necessarily depend on whether people are generally interested in gold as such. It is enough that they are generally interested in not being thrown in prison for failing to pay their taxes. Hence, it is easy for chartalist theory to explain the progression from metallic money to paper money backed by metal, and even to unconvertible paper money. Since the true value of the money does not depend on the intrinsic value of the metal in the first place, but rather on the state's proclamation that the thing is money, it is no mystery how the trick can be done just as well with useless paper.

When the state proclaims certain objects to be money and to be acceptable for various payments to the state, such as fines, customs, rent, and most importantly taxes, this generates enough demand for these objects such that they can function as general means of payment, not only in relation to the state but also among private individuals. In contrast to the assertions of the commodity theory, we see here how chartalist theory views the emergence of the market as concomitant with the emergence of sovereign authority.[31] Money is not a spontaneous creation of the market. Instead, money and markets depend on sovereign government for their emergence in the first place.

In economies where currency is in fact made out of gold, silver or other precious metals, these coins tend to circulate at a price above the market price of these metals. This phenomenon has been referred to as 'fiduciarity'.[32] The mechanism behind this phenomenon is not unlike the mechanism described in Marx's theory of surplus value. According to Marx, capitalist exploitation comes about through the discrepancy between the use-value and the exchange-value of labour. In the labour market, labour is exchanged for money at a price, which is below the actual use-value of labour. The use-value of labour consists in its productive capacity for creating new value. Surplus-value is this difference between the use-value and the exchange-value of labour. Exploitation is the appropriation of surplus-value, which happens when the capitalist sell the fruits of labour in the consumer market.

In comparable fashion, we can also understand fiduciarity as the result of a discrepancy in the pricing of money. Instead of talking

31 Graeber, *Debt*, 49–50.

32 Seaford, *Money and the Early Greek Mind*, 136–146.

about this discrepancy in terms of use-value and exchange-value, we might better conceive of it in terms of two different prices. Fiduciarity comes about because of the coexistence of two different pricing systems for the valuable coins. On the one hand, the coins may be priced as commodities simply on account of their material properties. On the other hand, the coins may be priced as money on account of their 'fiducial' properties, that is, their capacity to function as money. Fiduciarity is the difference between the first and the second price. We can think of this difference as a kind of monetary surplus-value. If we continue along the lines of Marx, we should ask the simple question: Where does this monetary surplus-value come from?

YOU MUST (NOT) MAKE MONEY!

We have already seen that the value of fiat-money is generated when the government legally proclaims something to be money and to be acceptable for payments to the state. Still, this does not properly explain the constitution of the value behind this money. In order to understand this constitution, we shall resort to Žižek's ideas about the relation between law, desire and enjoyment. At first glance, law seems to take the form of a prohibition banning our access to certain objects and acts. We may think of the law as an institution that is necessary for disciplining our wild and otherwise uncontrolled desires for different forbidden things, such as other people's property ('Thou shalt not steal') or transgressive sexual acts ('Thou shalt not commit adultery'). In this line of thinking, a society without law would be an anarchical, all-against-all society, with everybody satisfying their every desire at the expense of everybody else.

However, Žižek argues that law also has the latent function of structuring our very being as subjects, since the law is what institutes our desires in the first place. When the law tells us not to do this or that, it carries an underlying fantasmatic message promising that beyond the prohibition of the law lies the objects that can satisfy the desire of the subject. Inherent in the law is the fantasy of what might happen if the law were not there to prevent me from pursuing my immediate desires.

As was the case with his concept of law, it is important to note how Žižek's concept of fantasy differs from the usual meaning of the term. Here is how Žižek explains it:

> Fantasy is usually conceived as a scenario that realizes the subject's desire. This elementary definition is quite adequate, on condition that we take it *literally*: what the fantasy stages is not a scene in which our desire is fulfilled, fully satisfied, but on the contrary, a scene that realizes, stages, the desire as such. The fundamental point of psychoanalysis is that desire is not something given in advance, but something that has to be constructed – and it is precisely the role of fantasy to give the coordinates of the subject's desire, to specify its object, to locate the position the subject assumes in it. It is only through fantasy that the subject is constituted as desiring: *through fantasy, we learn how to desire.*[33]

The creation of chartal money is a prime example of the creation of both an object of desire and the desire itself through the interaction between law and fantasy. The proclamation of a particular thing as money necessarily entails the prohibition against the private creation of money. If someone were to imitate the government's creation of money – for instance, by printing money that looks like government money – he would be judged as a counterfeiter and severely punished. The institution of fiat money is also the prohibition against unlimited access to money.

The creation of chartal money simultaneously creates the very desire for money. This is where the monetary surplus-value of fiduciarity comes from. The institution of fiat money creates a desire for money that goes beyond the mere material of money. This is most obvious in the case of paper money insofar as its material value is almost nothing. We desire this money even though it is materially worthless. As we have already touched upon, the law implies a fantasmatic underside that serves to structure the subject's desire for the prohibited object. In the case of the institution of chartal money, the two sides of the law hinge on the double meaning of 'making money'. At face value the law says: 'You must not make money'. But at the same time it implicitly says: 'You must make some money'.

Since the acceptance of chartal money in the payment of taxes and other obligations to the state is a key component of the institution of fiat money, it seems reasonable to assume that chartal money is a kind of debt relation. This is indeed the case, but it takes a rather

33 Žižek, *Looking Awry*, 6.

curious form. At first glance, chartal money may seem to represent a credit with the state. For instance, British pound notes bear the inscription: 'I promise to pay to the bearer on demand the sum of . . .', followed by the denomination of the particular note. Still, we cannot understand money as a credit the way we ordinarily understand credit.

First of all, it is not entirely clear who is actually liable for redeeming the credit implied in fiat money. It is true that we may use fiat money to pay off debts to the state, but most of the time we use fiat money to purchase goods or services in the market. And even though some of this money does eventually come back to the state when merchants and manufacturers pay taxes, a large amount of money remains in circulation in the market without being redeemed. In this sense, the market rather than the state seems to redeem the value of fiat money.

Second, the state can only function as debtor to the bearers of fiat money if the users of money are at the same time interpellated as debtors. This is what happens in the double movement of the state. The state proclaims something (gold, silver, bank notes, etc.) to be money and at the same time proclaims the citizens as liable to pay some of this money back to the state. Even if we think of fiat money as a credit with the state, this credit merely represents the right to be absolved from a debt that was initially imposed on the bearer of the money by the state in the first place. When money is sent into circulation by the state's purchase of goods and services from citizens, this seems to be an ordinary equal exchange of commodities and money. But this exchange presupposes another action whereby the state imposes a debt on its citizens by law and force. And third, even if we ignore the above and regard fiat money as a credit against the state, this is a credit which can only be redeemed in fiat money itself. As long as fiat money is subject to convertibility under some form of gold standard, the holder of the money has the option of redeeming his credit through conversion into gold. But once convertibility is abandoned and fiat money appears in its pure form, the credit against the state becomes *ontologically irredeemable*. The following experiment by N. Stephan Kinsella illustrates what this means:

> There's some funny language on the money in England. The five-pound note contains the statement, 'Bank of England: I promise to

pay the bearer on demand the sum of five pounds'. Five pounds of *what*? If you ask anybody on the street, the note is five pounds, and they obviously aren't talking about units of weight – so what could that statement possibly mean? I decided to visit the Bank of England in downtown London to make them make good their promise. What would they do – hand me back another five-pound note in exchange for the one I offered? I was stopped at the door by a security guard. I explained that my note said that the Bank would give me five pounds upon demand for it, and that I was hereby demanding they fulfill their obligation. He explained I couldn't get past the front desk without wearing a three-piece suit and having 'official business'. The man behind the front desk had little patience, telling me that perhaps I'd find some information if I went to the Bank of England Museum around the comer. So I left and went to the museum, which is quite nice, actually. I explained to a curator what had happened, and that I was interested in finding out what exactly the language could mean. It obviously didn't function as a promise to pay me five pounds – the bank wouldn't even let me through the door! She disappeared into a back room and, finally, dug up an old photocopy from God-alone-knows-where, which attempts to explain the meaning and evolution of the 'I promise to pay the bearer' language. I took the pages home and tried to understand them. Apparently, the Bank is now contending that the language only means, and only ever meant, that it has an obligation to replace old, out-of-circulation pound notes with new, in-circulation ones. Right. That's what 'I promise to pay the bearer on demand the sum of five pounds' means.[34]

The experiment serves to unveil how the state is only capable of paying back its 'debt' to the bearer of money in the form of state money. In other words, the debt can only be paid back by an equivalent debt. The strange logic at play here seems to resemble Lacan's definition of love: 'Love is giving something one doesn't have . . . to someone who doesn't want it'.[35] When the state issues money, it issues a promise to eventually give something in return for this money, something which it does not have. Luckily the receiver does not want

---

34 Kinsella, 'Funny Money', 12.
35 Lacan in Žižek, *Violence*, 48.

this thing which is allegedly represented by the money. Most users of money (excluding Kinsella) are happy to get the money without making good on the state's promise. The state issues the money as a form of credit, even though there is nothing but more money to back up this credit.

By the way, the strategy applied by Kinsella is a perfect example of Žižek's notion of 'traversing the fantasy'. According to Žižek:

> Fantasy designates precisely this unwritten framework which tells us how we are to understand the letter of the Law . . . Sometimes, at least, the truly subversive thing is not to disregard the explicit letter of Law on behalf of the underlying fantasies, but to *stick to this letter against the fantasy which sustains it*.[36]

Kinsella exposes the impossibility of the law precisely by sticking to the letter of the law imposed by the Bank of England: 'I promise to pay the bearer on demand the sum of five pounds'. Knapp was already aware of this paradox inherent in fiat money:

> On their face they may admit that they are debts, but in point of fact they are not so if the debts are not meant to be paid. In the case of paper money proper the State offers no other means of payment; therefore it is not an acknowledgment of the State's indebtedness, even if this is expressly stated.[37]

Curiously, even though fiat money is not a debt in the ordinary sense, it obviously still functions as a means of exchange. The reason is that the institution of chartal money, as we have seen, is not merely a relation between the individual citizen and the state insofar as state-proclaimed money also comes to function as the general medium of exchange in the market. The institution of chartal money thus also implies the institution of a particular nominal unit of value, a particular sign that functions as the universal signifier of all other values in the community. This nominal unit is currency, which is in some cases even designated by a particular symbol such as $, £, ¥, or €. What do these symbols stand for?

---

36 Žižek, *The Plague of Fantasies*, 29.

37 Knapp, *The State Theory of Money*, 50.

We have already touched upon the similarity between the sign for the subject in Lacanian psychoanalysis and the US dollar sign. In Lacanian psychoanalysis, $ stands for the failure of signification. The only way to truly represent the subject in the symbolic order is through the breakdown of symbolization itself. Žižek gives the example of a love letter to illustrate this paradox:

> A subject tries to articulate ('express') itself in a signifying chain, this articulation fails, and by means of and through this failure, the subject emerges: the subject is the failure of its signifying representation – this is why Lacan writes the subject of the signifier as $, as 'barred'. In a love letter, the very failure of the writer to formulate his declaration in a clear and effective manner – his vacillations, the letter's fragmentary nature, and so on – can in themselves be proof (perhaps are the necessary and only reliable proof) that the professed love is authentic: here the very failure to deliver the message properly is the sign of its authenticity.[38]

'I cannot tell you how much I love you' is the only way to tell my partner how much I love her. A similar paradox applies to the institution of $ or another nominal unit of monetary value. To paraphrase Žižek, 'money is the failure of its signifying representation'. $ (the dollar sign or any other currency) is the signifier of a failure in the signification of value. $ does not stand for any particular incarnation of value. Not even in a money system operating under a gold standard does $ stand for the value of gold. This is clearly illustrated by the phenomenon of fiduciarity. The symbolization of the metallic coin creates a surplus-value which can be accounted for only through recourse to the symbolization itself.

Returning to the signification of the subject, here is Žižek again:

> The surplus of signification masks a fundamental lack. The subject of the signifier is precisely this lack, this impossibility of finding a signifier which would be 'its own': *the failure of its representation is its positive condition*. The subject tries to articulate itself in a signifying representation; the representation fails; instead of a richness we have a lack, and this void opened by the failure *is* the subject of

38 Žižek, *Living in the End Times*, 232.

> the signifier. To put it paradoxically, the subject of the signifier is a retroactive effect of the failure of its own representation; that is why the failure of representation is the only way to represent it adequately.[39]

In the case of paper chartal money, it is obvious that the value of this kind of money is nothing but symbolic. But even further, the value symbolized by chartal money is the surplus-value created through the symbolization itself. The introduction of a monetary system into the world is not the introduction of a symbolic system for the recording of preexisting valuable assets. Again paraphrasing Žižek: 'the value of the signifier $ is a retroactive effect of the failure of its own representation'.

The emergence of this kind of value entails an element of fantasmatic projection. We cannot properly account for the surplus-value of monetary symbolization. This failure of signification opens the space for the fantasy that says money incarnates a special kind of value which is beyond the sphere of 'ordinary' value found in 'ordinary' commodities. The value of money is sublime. The fact that money functions as a general equivalent in the exchange for useful commodities, *despite* the fact that money itself is utterly useless, merely adds to the enigmatic attractions of money.

We can understand the state's claim for fiat money in the payment of taxes, fines, etc. as the initial driver for the generalized desire for money. At first, nobody has to desire money for its own sake. It is enough that the state announces its 'desire' for money in the form of taxes and that it enforces on its citizens the obligation to satisfy this obligation. However, once this monetary arrangement is put in place, it quickly becomes a self-propelling system. Even though individual users of money may not believe that money as such represents any kind of value, they are still constantly confronted with a market where money is constantly treated *as if* it represents value. The individual user of money does not have to believe in money as long as he believes that there are others who do believe and who will accept money in the exchange of commodities or the settlement of debt. The individual user of money does not have to believe in money as long as he nonetheless acts *as if* he believes in money. In other words, money does not

39 Žižek, *The Sublime Object of Ideology*, 175.

care if people believe in it. Perhaps it is money that believes in people rather than the other way around.

Even though the fiat theory obviously contradicts the commodity theory of money, the commodity theory seems to reemerge here as a necessary fantasmatic component of fiat money. While the constitution of money may be logically and anthropologically explained as a creation of the state or another government authority, the system seems to have the intrinsic function of creating a situation where people use money *as if* it is indeed a valuable asset in itself. The chartalist dismissal of commodity theory may be too simple if we want to know not merely *how* but also *why* fiat money works. We find in Keynes the following metaphorical remark:

> Money is the measure of value, but to regard it as having value itself is a relic of the view that the value of money is regulated by the value of the substance of which it is made, and is like confusing a theater ticket with the performance.[40]

Perhaps this metaphor is deceptively inaccurate. Fiat money does not function as a theatre ticket insofar as the state does not offer any performance to which the ticket would grant access. Sticking with the world of theatre, the proper metaphor is rather that regarding money as having value in itself (the obvious target of Keynes's ridicule here is the commodity theory) is like confusing a theatre performance with a real-life event. However, such confusion is an intrinsic part of theatre itself. Without this confusion, theatre would not be theatre. Even though the audience *knows very well* that the events on stage are merely an act, *nonetheless* they still become emotionally involved in the events *as if* they were indeed real events. The same applies to the functioning of money. Even though we may *know very well* that money does not have value in itself, *nonetheless* we still treat it *as if* it had value in itself. Parguez and Seccareccia rightly point out: 'The very notion of a commodity money is an illusion which confuses the material support of money with money itself'.[41] They forgot to add, however, that this illusion is itself a necessary ideological support of money.

---

40 Keynes, 'Review', 418.

41 Parguez and Seccareccia, 'The Credit Theory of Money', 106.

Ingham captures this ideological function of commodity theory when he elaborates on Schumpeter's original distinction between 'practical metallism' and 'theoretical metallism':[42]

> As a theory of money . . . 'practical metallism' has been one of the means by which states have attempted to get their money accepted . . . Commodity theories of money have played a persuasive and ideological role by naturalising the social relations of credit that constitute money. But 'theoretical metallism' – that is the belief that money's origins and value is to be found in the 'intrinsic' exchange value of precious metal of which it is made or represents – has been unable to provide a satisfactory explanation of money.[43]

It is crucial once again to reiterate that for Žižek, ideology is not a distortion of the way 'things actually are'. On the contrary, ideology is a necessary precondition for things to appear the way 'they actually are'. This means that metallism may serve as a component in the ideology that functions to make state-proclaimed money work as money. As long as people believe that the money issued by the state is somehow backed by 'real value', this money will indeed circulate as if it were actually backed by 'real value', thus producing the effect that it is indeed backed by 'real value'. The ultimate real value of the money is not the gold residing in the treasury of the state or the basement of the central bank, but rather actual goods willingly exchanged for money by the very same people who use the money.

It is also worth noticing that the refutation of theoretical metallism is not necessarily a conclusive normative argument against the implementation of the gold standard or another commodity standard in actual monetary systems. Contemporary proponents of monetary reforms who advocate the reintroduction of the gold standard are often referred to as 'gold nuts' by mainstream economists, who have been brought up in a system that did away with gold four decades ago. If one reads the argument for gold as an expression of theoretical metallism, the term 'nut' seems justified according to the argument in this chapter. Yet this does not exclude the possibility that proposals for reintroducing a gold standard make sense as practical metallism.

---

42 Schumpeter, *History of Economic Analysis*, 274–276.

43 Ingham, 'The Emergence of Capitalist Credit Money', 188.

Practical metallism may be advanced on the premise, not that gold is the only true incarnation of monetary value, but rather that the institution of the convertibility of money into gold serves the purpose of curtailing the capacity of the state to issue money beyond the amount justified by the economic activity within the state. On the one hand, practical metallism and the fantasy of money as gold may be a way for the state to institute its capacity to create money, thus strengthening its power over money-users. On the other hand, even though the gold standard may be 'just' an ideological fantasy, once the money system is already in place and working, this fantasy can be invoked by money-users to hold the creators of money accountable and to shift the balance of power from creators back to the users.

Before we review the third way of thinking about money – the credit theory – we shall pause to summarize the difference between the commodity theory and the chartalist theory in terms of the ontological triad of real, symbolic and imaginary. In commodity theory, money emerges when a particular commodity, e.g. gold, is elevated to the status of money. The elevation of this particular commodity happens on account of intrinsic real qualities. For instance, gold stands out among other commodities because of its real aesthetic and material properties. The symbolization of a commodity as money is thus merely a recording of the real nature of the commodity. Commodity money is simultaneously a real commodity and a symbol of value, but the value of the money is in the last instance dependent on the real value of the commodity. Commodity theory is based on a realist ontology insofar as the 'moneyness' of an object is a reflection of the real qualities of the object.

In opposition to this, chartalist theory is a social constructivist theory of money. The determination of a particular object as money does not follow from the real properties of the object. The object may be intrinsically valuable (e.g. gold) or it may be intrinsically without value (e.g. paper). The origin of money lies in the order of the symbolic. Whatever the social norms of the law treat as money can count as money. Money is a social construct. The Žižekian analysis of both accounts of money has demonstrated how the relation between the symbolic and the real is ultimately impossible. Money does not add up in either of the two accounts. Both commodity money and fiat money necessarily rely on certain fantasies that go beyond the immediate epistemology of the theories in order to function.

Despite ontological differences, commodity theory and chartalist theory agree on one point. Money is essentially a thing. The difference lies in whether the moneyness and the value of the thing are determined in the order of the real or the order of the symbolic. This is precisely the point where credit theory departs from both commodity theory and chartalist theory.

CHAPTER FOUR

Credit Money and the Ideology of Banking

> The process by which banks create money is so simple that the mind is repelled.[1]

A crucial component in the conception of money in contemporary capitalism is a certain understanding of the way that banks create money. We have already seen how conventional economics resorts to imaginary scenarios in order to account for the origins and functioning of money. Let's create an imaginary scenario that aims to explain how banks make money:

> John, a financial entrepreneur, builds a printing press capable of producing counterfeit $100 bills that are indistinguishable from the real bills issued by the US Federal Reserve. John prints 100,000 bills at the nominal value of $10,000,000. Instead of just spending this money, John lends it out to people in the town where he lives. The money is lent on the condition that it is paid back in one year at an interest of 10 percent. The scheme works out perfectly and after one year John has been paid back a total of $11,000,000. Some of this money is his own counterfeit money that has come back to him, and some of it is genuine US Federal Reserve notes.
>
> The money John lent to his fellow townspeople has come to good use. Many borrowers used it to set up small businesses or improve existing businesses. Even the money used for immediate consumption has helped the community, as the spending has invigorating the local economy. John has become a respected and popular member of the community.
>
> However, John is riddled with guilt when he thinks about the way he cheated the good folks of his town. One day he discovers an error on his counterfeit notes. He mistakenly printed the name 'Morgan' instead of 'Franklin' under the portrait on one side. Apparently, the notes have circulated without anyone noticing this deviation from the original. This gives John an idea. In order to clear

---

1 Galbraith, *Money, Whence It Came, Where It Went*, 18.

his conscience, he puts an ad in the local newspaper revealing his scheme. He offers to exchange any counterfeit note, recognizable by the name 'Morgan' on one side, for real Federal Reserve notes. Even though many notes have already circulated beyond the local community, when word of John's scheme spreads all counterfeit notes are eventually recovered and redeemed for real notes.

John is brought before the local judge on charges of counterfeiting. Seeing that John has freely admitted his guilt and that he has already redeemed the counterfeit money, the judge lets John off with only a warning. In his decision, the judge is influenced by the positive impact John's generous lending practices had on the local economy.

As John returns home, his guilt has dissipated. This allows him to comfortably sit back and contemplate what to do with the one million dollars in real Federal Reserve notes he now has in his possession.

This scenario revolves around the double meaning of the phrase 'making money'. The initial production of the 100,000 counterfeit bills is a simple case of making money in the sense of *creating* new money that did not exist before. The subsequent collection of interest on this money is a case of making money in the sense of *appropriating* a portion of the existing pool of money in the world. The point of the scenario is that even when the newly created counterfeit money is retracted and destroyed, the other portion of real money remains in John's hands. He has managed to make money by making money. In order to unravel the logic at play here we shall take a step back from the scenario and look at the third theoretical approach to money: credit theory. Once the theory has been presented, we will return to John.

MONEY AS DEBT

Credit and credit alone is money.[2]

While commodity money emerges from the order of the real and fiat money from the order of the symbolic, the starting point for credit theory is the assumption that money is first and foremost purely

2 Innes, 'What Is Money?', 393.

imaginary. Money is not necessarily a 'thing', and exchange mediated by money does not require the physical presence of money objects. Perhaps the purest formulation of this theory is found in the work of Alfred Mitchell Innes. Innes presented his theory of money in two articles published in 1913 and 1914.

As we have seen, commodity theory tends to account for the origins of money by telling the story of traders in a barter economy who come up with the idea to use a single commodity as a common measure of value instead of exchanging bread against meat, fish against wool, etc. Innes rejects this story as a myth. Instead, he presents an alternative account of the origins of money:

> For many centuries, how many we do not know, the principal instrument of commerce was neither the coin nor the private token, but the tally . . . a stick of squared hazel-wood, notched in a certain manner to indicate the amount of the purchase or debt. The name of the debtor and the date of the transaction were written on two opposite sides of the stick, which was then split down the middle in such a way that the notches were cut in half, and the name and date appeared on both pieces of the tally. The split was stopped by a cross-cut about an inch from the base of the stick, so that one of the pieces was shorter than the other. One piece, called the 'stock' . . . was issued to the seller or creditor, while the other, called the 'stub' or 'counter-stock', was kept by the buyer or debtor. Both halves were thus a complete record of the credit and debt and the debtor was protected by his stub from the fraudulent imitation of or tampering with his tally.[3]

Even though Innes does not provide accurate reference to historical sources to support his argument, his critique of the implicit anthropology inherent in the commodity theory of money has subsequently been confirmed by more recent investigations.[4] In Innes's exposition, the argument for or against the credit theory of money does not hinge on whether the first form of money to appear in history was tallies or gold. Innes argues that even in historical societies, such

---

3 Ibid., 395.

4 Humphrey, 'Barter and Economic Disintegration', 48; Hudson, 'The Archaeology of Money'; Graeber, *Debt*.

as ancient Greece, where coins of precious metal circulated as means of payment, the weight and purity of these coins were so uneven that their intrinsic value could not have served as a stable measure of value.[5] This means that even in economies where coins of gold, silver and bronze circulated, these coins essentially functioned as tokens of value rather than commodities. The value of these coins was dependent on their nominal denomination as legally determined by the issuer, such as a sovereign or a government, rather than on their intrinsic use-value.

If we compare Innes's account to the commodity theory of money, the first thing to note is that the wooden tally does not have any use-value. It does not even purport to have use-value. The tally is merely a record of the relation of debt and credit between buyer and seller. The physical presence of a tally or similar device is not essential for the functioning of credit money. The debt relation might as well be registered by a bookkeeping system, with no physical tallies circulating.

The tally comes to function as money when its validity is not limited to the relation between the original buyer and seller. A creditor would not necessarily seek redemption of the debt from the initial debtor. He might simply pass on the debt in exchange for commodities from a third party. This third party might again pass on the debt to someone else, and so on. Insofar as tallies were generally accepted as payment in the exchange of commodities, they attained the status of a generalized medium of exchange. Innes summarizes the credit theory of money thus:

> Shortly, The Credit Theory is this: that a sale and purchase is the exchange of a commodity for credit. From this main theory springs the sub-theory that the value of credit or money does not depend on the value of any metal or metals, but on the right which the creditor acquires to 'payment', that is to say, to satisfaction for the credit, and on the obligation of the debtor to 'pay' his debt and conversely on the right of the debtor to release himself from his debt by the tender of an equivalent debt owed by the creditor, and the obligation of the creditor to accept this tender in satisfaction of his credit.[6]

5 Innes, 'What Is Money?', 379–88.

6 Innes, 'Credit Theory of Money', 152.

Ultimately, the value of credit money comes from its capacity to redeem the debtor from his debt. People engage in economic activity as both sellers and buyers, and hence they appear as creditors as well as debtors. In Innes's account, the settlement of debt comes about when the original debtor is able to enter into other relations as a creditor. Debt is created as the result of an exchange of a commodity against credit between a seller and a buyer. Even the seller, who is now creditor, is sometimes the buyer of commodities. This agent may, for instance, be a manufacturing company that has to buy labour, raw materials or machinery in order to generate the output that is sold. Conversely, the buyer of the product is sometimes also a seller. This agent may, for instance, be a consumer who is also a labourer selling his labour power. Debt is settled as the original debt is offset against a new debt incurred by the original creditor. Innes provides an etymological account of this intricate circulation of debt and credit:

> The root meaning of the verb 'to pay' is: that of 'to appease', 'to pacify', 'to satisfy', and while a debtor must be in a position to satisfy his creditor, the really important characteristic of a credit is not the right which it gives to 'payment' of a debt, but the right that it confers on the holder to liberate himself from debt by its means—a right recognized by all societies. By buying we become debtors and by selling we become creditors, and being all both buyers and sellers we are all debtors and creditors. As debtor we can compel our creditor to cancel our obligation to him by handing to him his own acknowledgment of a debt to an equivalent amount which he, in his turn, has incurred. For example, A having bought goods from B to the value of $100, is B's debtor for that amount. A can rid himself of his obligation to B by selling to C goods of an equivalent value and taking from him in payment an acknowledgment of debt which he (C, that is to say) has received from B. By presenting this acknowledgment to B, A can compel him to cancel the debt due to him. A has used the credit which he has procured to release himself from his debt. It is his privilege.[7]

In the commodity theory of money, gold holds an exclusive position when it is assumed that everyone readily accepts gold in exchange

7 Innes, 'What Is Money?', 392–3.

for different kinds of goods. In Innes's credit theory of money, it is credit that holds this position. 'A first class credit is the most valuable kind of property . . . Credit and not gold or silver is the one property which all men seek, the acquisition of which is the end object of all commerce'.[8]

IT OWES YOU

The credit theory of money is a beautiful theory. It starts from the counterintuitive idea that money is not backed by any value residing beyond the money system itself. Once the reader has accustomed himself or herself to this idea, it seems almost impossible to go back to thinking about money in any other way. The simplicity of the theory makes it highly persuasive. The move from the commodity theory to the credit theory is comparable to the experience of looking at an optical illusion, such as the one simultaneously showing an old lady and a beautiful young woman. At first glance, you see the old lady, but as soon as your eye has caught sight of the young woman, it is difficult to go back to seeing the old lady again.

As we have seen, the commodity theory of money relies on a number of curious and less-than-convincing assumptions about the value of gold. Why would everyone accept pieces of an admittedly beautiful yet for most purposes useless metal in exchange for all kinds of useful commodities? In credit theory, the value of money does not seem to depend on the value of any material commodity. The theory does not have to make this kind of assumption. However, as philosophical scrutiny reveals, credit theory is not without its assumptions. In the following, we shall look at a number of these assumptions.

Despite obvious differences, commodity theory and credit theory share the idea that money emerges spontaneously from transaction between agents in the market. According to Innes, the evolution of economic organization beyond the state of barter comes about as merchants start trading commodities against credit. This is the story of the wooden tallies. But, we might ask, how was credit denominated on the first tally in the history of the world? Did it say: 'B owes to A two sheep'? If this were the case, the exchange would be nothing but a simple form of borrowing, insofar as B could only redeem the debt by

8 Ibid., 393.

paying back two sheep to A. In order for the tally to be a token of debt that could circulate beyond the immediate relation between A and B, it would have to be denominated in an abstract currency. It would have so say something like: 'B owes to A ten Crowns'. However, this also means that we cannot explain the origin of money from the immediate relation between a debtor and a creditor. The creation of money in this relationship presupposes the existence of an abstract standard of account.

The philosophical problem here is comparable to the one raised by Wittgenstein in his so-called private language argument.[9] Wittgenstein argues that an individual person cannot invent a private language because the criteria for the correct use of words and phrases presupposes an abstract set of rules that can only be maintained and sanctioned by a collective of language users. In a similar fashion, A and B require an abstract standard of account that allows them to express the value of the commodities (two sheep) in terms of a price (ten Crowns). This standard of value cannot be invented ad hoc in their immediate relation. The credit theory thus fails to explain the origins of abstract money of account.[10] As we shall see, this problem is not only relevant for the historical explanation of the evolution of money. It also has significant implications for our understanding of the general functioning of money.

What is lacking in the credit theory is of course the explanation of the role of government in the creation of money. As we have seen in our discussion of chartalism, when the state or another government power declares something to be money, it also provides an abstract unit of account. It provides the currency in which the value of specific commodities can be measured. This allows the market agents A and B to denominate the debt owed by B to A in terms of money rather than commodities. When credit theory states that money emerges as a credit between market agents, this is true only on the condition that there is already in place an abstract standard of account. This abstract standard provides the agents with the 'language' needed for them to state the debt in terms of money.

So far I have primarily presented credit theory in terms of its differences from commodity theory. The differences between credit

---

9 Wittgenstein, *Philosophical Investigations*, §. 243.

10 Ingham, 'The Emergence of Capitalist Credit Money', 181.

theory and chartalist theory are more subtle but no less important. In credit theory there is a symmetry not only between credit and debt but also between creditor and debitor. Credit is merely the inverse of debt. B incurs a debt to A in return for a commodity of an equivalent value. And conversely B satisfies this debt by exchanging a commodity in return for a credit of the equivalent value. A and B are principally equal agents in the market.

In chartalism, the relation between the two agents involved in the creation of money is asymmetrical. On the one side is the state and on the other side is the private user of money. Even though the individual fiat money object, such as a coin or paper note, represents a kind of credit against the state, this credit can only be redeemed as repayment of a more primordial debt which the state has enforced upon its citizens. This primordial debt does not refer to any original exchange of a commodity for money. The citizen is not obliged to pay taxes because he has originally received a specific quantity of commodities. The citizen is obliged to pay taxes because the law says so. The crucial point is here that, precisely because the primordial indebtedness of the citizen does not refer to a preceding commodity exchange, the state can immediately signify this debt in terms of an abstract standard of account.

In the credit theory, the denomination of credit in terms of money presupposes an operation whereby the value of the underlying commodity of the exchange is signified in terms of price. This creates the same paradox that we found in commodity theory. A system for the pricing of commodities has to be in place before agents in the market can start expressing the value of commodities in terms of price. In chartalism, however, money does not initially refer to the value of an underlying commodity. The operation of symbolization is short-circuited since fiat money merely refers to itself as an object. When the state issues money, it in effect says to the citizen: 'You owe me nothing. Hence, there is nothing you can repay me in order to redeem your debt. In the meantime, I shall be providing these objects, which you must use to pay regular instalments on your debt'.

In other words, the credit held by the individual bearer of a fiat money object is symbolic. It represents a specific amount, which immediately translates into a certain quantity of various commodities in the market. In opposition to this, the primordial indebtedness of the citizen against the state is real. We may recall here Žižek's description of the double move through which the real emerges:

> In a first move, the Real is the impossible hard core which we cannot confront directly, but only through the lenses of a multitude of symbolic fictions, virtual formations. In a second move, this very hard core is purely virtual, actually, non-existent, an X which can be reconstructed only retroactively, from the multitude of symbolic formations which are 'all there actually is'.[11]

The creation of fiat money can be described as the execution of these two moves, albeit in reverse order. In a first move, the citizen is interpellated as a debtor to the state, which represents society. This debt has the nature of a 'non-existent . . . X which can be reconstructed only retroactively, from the multitude of symbolic formations'. The only way to answer the question of what the citizen owes to the state is to add up the taxes, fines and other claims imposed on him by the state over the course of his life. And even though a person has dutifully paid his taxes all his life, there is still a sense that this has not freed him from his primordial debt to society. In a second move, money itself comes to incarnate a kind of real value – which we can confront only 'through the lenses of a multitude of symbolic fictions' – when it is exchanged in the market for a multitude of different commodities. The credit theory merely accounts for the second move insofar as it explains how commodities are exchanged for credit. But it fails to recognize how this operation presupposes the first move whereby the abstract standard of value emerges from the institution of an asymmetrical primordial debt. Geoffrey Ingham proposes a critique of Innes that amounts to a similar argument: 'Money has its origins in debt, as Innes maintained. And primordial debt is a debt to society, where we must assume money, in the sense of abstract value, originated'.[12] In the credit theory, money is originally an I Owe yoU, which corresponds to an equivalent yoU Owe Me. In chartalism, money is an It Owes yoU, which is founded upon a primordial yoU Owe It. This move from 'I' to 'It' is also captured by Simmel's formulation: 'This is the core truth in the theory that money is only a claim

11 Žižek, *The Parallax View*, 26.

12 Ingham, 'The Emergence of Capitalist Credit Money', 184.

upon society. Money appears, so to speak, as a bill of exchange from which the name of the drawee is lacking'.[13]

A BANK IS NOT (A) FAIR

The role of the state in the making of money is not the only thing credit theory downplays. In the following, we will see how the notion of banks implied in credit theory is too simple to capture their function in the creation of credit money. If we think of money as gold, it is natural to think of the bank as a place where people deposit their holdings of gold. In return, depositors receive notes confirming the amount of gold kept in the bank. These notes may then be used in exchange for commodities, and the ownership of the gold deposits may change hands as the notes are exchanged. In other words, the function of banks according to the commodity theory of money is to save people from the inconvenience of having to carry around gold.

The credit theory of money implies another way of thinking about banks. In connection with the historical account of the tally system, Innes explains how fairs where merchants would meet to settle their mutual debts and credits were regularly set up. These fairs, which were found in medieval Europe as well as other places around the world in different historical periods, served the function of clearinghouses. And just as the tally constitutes the original form of money in credit theory, so does the fair constitute the original form of the bank. Banks are essentially clearinghouses that facilitate the clearing of debts and credits:

> In practice it is not necessary for a debtor to acquire credits on the same persons to whom he is debtor. We are all both buyers and sellers, so that we are all at the same time both debtors and creditors of each other, and by the wonderfully efficient machinery of the banks to which we sell our credits, and which thus become the clearinghouses of commerce, the debts and credits of the whole community are centralized and set of against each other. In practice, therefore, any good credit will pay any debt.[14]

---

13 Simmel, *The Philosophy of Money*, 176.

14 Innes, 'Credit Theory of Money', 152.

We have already seen how private IOUs come to function as money when they are separated from the original credit and begin to circulate as liquid means of exchange. From this perspective, banks are merely facilitators of the circulation of credit money insofar as they provide practical arrangements that make the settlement of debts more convenient. However, I would argue that the function of banks in relation to credit money is not merely a matter of convenience.

One of the arguments raised by Innes in his refutation of commodity theory is that in ancient money systems based on precious-metal coins, the weight and purity of these coins was so uneven that the stability of the system could not possibly have been founded on the intrinsic value of their metallic content. Innes argues that even coins made of gold, silver or bronze are essentially tokens of credit.[15] However, a similar argument may be raised against his own credit theory of money. Imagine the following scenario: Merchant B buys from farmer A two sheep and incurs in return a debt of the amount of ten Crowns. Now B approaches beggar C, who is a poor man with no fortune. B offers C a simple meal in return for ten Crowns on credit. Even though this is far above the market price of a meal, C accepts the proposition since he is very hungry and does not have any money anyway. Now B goes back to A offering the credit on C as redemption of the original debt incurred in the purchase of the sheep.

Obviously, this scenario would not function in practice since A would never accept C's debt as redemption for B's debt, since the prospects of debt repayment are meagre given that C is a beggar. C is not in a position where he is likely to incur credits against any other agent. The general problem demonstrated in this scenario is that the value of debt depends on the creditworthiness of the debtor.

Indeed, Innes is well aware of this when he notes:

> The value of a credit depends not on the existence of any gold or silver or other property behind it, but solely on the 'solvency' of the debtor, and that depends solely on whether, when the debt becomes due, he in his turn has sufficient credits on others to set off against his debts.[16]

---

15 Innes, 'What Is Money?', 380–1.

16 Ibid., 394.

Innes, however, fails to follow the consequences of this insight. How is it possible to found a stable system of credit money if the underlying credit fluctuates with the solvency of the original debtors? How is it possible for debt to circulate beyond the immediate relation between the original debtor and creditor if the pricing of the debt requires intimate knowledge of the financial circumstances of the original debtor? How is it possible for someone to redeem his debt to a creditor by transferring a credit of a similar nominal amount held against a third party if the actual value of the two debts differ depending on the creditworthiness of the parties?

In the commodity theory of money, the crucial moment in the evolution from barter to monetary exchange is the 'setting apart' of gold from all other commodities. The above-mentioned problems with the credit theory of money derive from the fact that Innes fails to recognize how a similar moment is required in order for credit money to come about. This moment is the *setting apart of banks from all other debtors*. Innes's image of the bank as an advanced clearinghouse that functions to simply mediate the relations between debtors and creditors fails to recognize the crucial function of the bank as being itself a debtor. In other words, a bank is not a fair. Despite the obvious differences between the credit theory and the commodity theory of money, the role of the bank in the credit system of money is in a number of ways comparable to the role of gold in the commodity system of money. And, as we will see, the relation between banks and money is no less mysterious than the relation between gold and money.

Innes himself provides a scenario that allows us to examine the role of banks in the creation of money:

> In America today, there are in any given place many different dollars in use . . . Let us . . . suppose that I take to my banker in, say, New Orleans, a number of sight drafts of the same nominal value, one on the Sub-Treasury, one on another well-known bank in the city, one on an obscure tradesman in the suburbs, one on a well-known bank in New York, and one on a reputable merchant in Chicago. For the draft on the Sub-Treasury and for that on the bank in the city, my banker will probably give me a credit for exactly the nominal value, but the others will all be exchanged at different prices. For the draft on the New York bank I might get more than the stated amount, for that of the Chicago merchant, I should probably get less, while for

> that one on the obscure tradesman, my banker would probably give nothing without my endorsement, and even then I should receive less than the nominal amount. All these documents represent different dollars of debt, which the banker buys for whatever he thinks they may be worth to him. The banker whose dollars we buy, estimates all these other dollars in terms of his own . . . Everybody who incurs a debt issues his own dollar, which may or may not be identical with the dollar of any one else's money.[17]

First of all, the scenario illustrates the point that the value of a debt depends on the creditworthiness of the original debtor. The debt of a New York bank is worth more than the debt of an 'obscure tradesman'. Second, and more importantly, the scenario implicitly illustrates how the value of different debts is measured against a particular form of credit. The way Innes poses the scenario, the value of the different sight drafts is measured against the credit of his own banker in New Orleans. This means that this particular debtor is set apart from all the other debtors in order to function as a yardstick for the measurement of the value of the debts. The New Orleans banker becomes the 'gold standard' against which the value of all other debts is measured.

The composition of the scenario is slightly curious, as the New Orleans bank is apparently not the agent with the highest level of creditworthiness. The draft on the 'well-known bank in New York' is exchanged for a credit with the New Orleans bank at an amount higher than the nominal value, thus indicating that the credit of the New York bank is even better. The composition of the scenario seems to suggest that any one of the debtors could have been set apart as the standard against which the value of all the other debts could be measured. This is misleading.

Instead, I would argue that the evolution and functioning of a credit system of money presupposes the existence of a central agent with the capacity to issue debt that has an exchange value equivalent to the nominal value. This agent is a bank. We can characterize a bank as a debtor whose credit is generally accepted at nominal value in the exchange of commodities and the settlement of debt. Bank credit is endowed with extraordinary confidence from creditors. In a more

---

17 Innes, 'Credit Theory of Money', 154.

recent formulation of a credit theory of money, Parguez and Seccareccia define banks as distinguished debtors whose

> debts are accepted by all other agents in an economy as a means of payment to settle their own debt commitments. Banks are deemed to be so creditworthy that no holder of their debts would ever ask for reimbursement either in kind or in the debt of another agent.[18]

In other words, money in the bank is as good as money in the bank.

Again, we see how banks here are similar to gold in the commodity theory of money. Marx refers to gold as the 'Lord of commodities'. We can likewise refer to banks as the 'Lord of debtors'. The special quality which enables gold to qualify as money is that this particular commodity is ideally accepted by anyone, under any circumstances, in exchange for any kind of commodity. The value and liquidity of gold does not depend on the immediate hunger, thirst, cold or other idiosyncratic desire of the recipient. The value of gold is abstracted from the particular context of exchange. A similar quality applies to bank credit, as this form of credit is generally accepted at face value. The value and liquidity of bank credit is abstracted from the specific context of exchange. Ideally, the use of bank credit in economic transactions does not require close scrutiny of the financial circumstances of the bank, nor does it rely on an intimate knowledge of the moral constitution of the bank. Of course, empirical banks may in some instances deviate from these ideals, but there is a limit to how much they can deviate. If an actual bank deviates too much from the ideal of a bank, it stops being able to function as a bank. A bank that does not enjoy the full confidence of actual as well as potential creditors is no longer a bank.

We have seen above how the functioning of gold as money in commodity theory raised a particular paradox. On the one hand, gold is endowed with a particular exchange-value that enables it to function as the general equivalent for the measurement of the value of all other commodities. On the other hand, the real use-value of gold itself is highly elusive. Picking up from Marx, I have even argued that it is the uselessness rather than the usefulness of gold that is the basis

---

18 Parguez and Seccareccia, 'The Credit Theory of Money', 3.

for the setting apart of gold from all other commodities. Again, a similar paradox applies to the functioning of banks.

The creditworthiness of a particular agent depends not only on his current balance of debts and credits, but also on his ability to incur credits in the future. The creditworthiness of a worker depends on his ability to sell his labour power in the future. The creditworthiness of a company depends on the future productivity and profitability of the company. The creditworthiness of a merchant depends on his future ability to buy commodities at a low price and sell at a higher price. In the case of the worker, the company or the merchant, creditworthiness depends on the future ability to convert commodities (including commodities in the form of labour) into money. From this arises the paradox that the particular type of agent with the highest degree of creditworthiness is precisely the type of agent that produces absolutely nothing: banks. In the same way that gold is excluded from the sphere of commodities with immediate use-value, banks are excluded from the sphere of agents that produce use-value. Banks do not participate directly in the exchange and production of ordinary commodities. In turn, banks have the special capacity to produce money *ex nihilo*. Ordinary economic agents make money by producing use-value that is converted into exchange-value. Banks simply create exchange-value:

> Banking institutions enjoy, therefore, the capacity of freely issuing debt without it being subject to an exogenous resource constraint. This means that banks can create these debts *ex nihilo* when they grant credit to non-bank agents who must spend them to acquire real resources.[19]

According to Innes's credit theory, the creation of money is not an exclusive privilege of banks. All economic agents create money as they enter into relations of debt and credit. However, the money created in transactions between non-bank agents is merely a derivative form of money. Insofar as the debt of a non-bank agent is exchangeable only at a discount from the nominal amount corresponding to the risk of insolvency, the 'moneyness' of non-bank credits is incomplete. There is a minimal discrepancy between the price

---

19 Ibid., 103.

and the value of the credit. In contrast, bank credit is perfectly liquid in the sense that it is readily exchangeable at the nominal amount. The image Innes proposes of the bank as merely a sophisticated version of the ancient fair is thus highly misleading, since it fails to recognize the constitutional function of the bank in the system of credit money. Bank credit is the sublime form of credit money in which price and value coincide. This allows bank credit to function as the general equivalent of the credit system of money.

While the image of the bank as principally a fair where debts and credits are settled can be refuted on a theoretical basis, it may still hold some truth about the way banks function. In my earlier discussion of fiat money, we saw how the central bank can simply reject private bearers of bank notes who wish to redeem the value of these notes. This was illustrated by Kinsella's experiment. In the case of credit money, it is not so simple. Commercial banks cannot afford to reject bank customers who wish to withdraw their bank deposits by converting bank credit into another kind of money. Quite the contrary: it is crucial for the operation of the bank that customers believe this option to be open at any time. If this belief is put in doubt, it may trigger a devastating run on the bank, driving the bank out of business. The operation of banks is dependent on its customers entertaining the fantasy that the money in the bank is actually not credit money but in the last instance backed by another form of money. This is precisely the fantasy conveyed by the image of the bank as a fair.

At the fair there is a stub for every stock. Every amount of credit corresponds to an equivalent amount of debt. The fair merely functions to pair them with each other. If we translate this principle to the image of a bank, it would mean that the bank is merely a meeting place for people with excess money and people with insufficient money. Whenever the bank lends out $100 to a debtor, this money has been originally deposited with the bank by a creditor.

According to this image, banks do not make money. At the most, banks may temporarily convert commodity money or fiat money into credit money. This happens when banks issue promissory notes on creditors' deposits of gold or cash, which the creditor is then able to use for the direct exchange of commodities or for other kinds of payment. However, the value of these promissory notes is still principally backed by the value of the deposits made in commodity or fiat money.

The open secret of modern banking is of course that this is not the way contemporary banks conduct their business. If bank credit is good enough to function as a liquid medium of exchange, why would the banks waste their capital by having it tied up in reserves of gold or cash sitting idle in the vaults? Why would the banks lend out gold or cash to borrowers when these borrowers may fare just as well by having their loan paid out in bank credit? And why would the banks limit their lending capacity to the amount of deposits on their books if neither borrowers nor depositors are asking to have money paid out in gold or cash? The answer to all of these questions is the same: they wouldn't. The reason banks get away with issuing credit money *as if* it were ultimately backed by commodity money or fiat money is that they succeed in maintaining the fantasy that, ultimately, a bank is merely a fair.

By way of Kinsella's experiment, we saw how central banks function perfectly well even though they reject stubborn bearers of cash who demand to have the value of their fiat money redeemed. Private commercial banks do not have the same privilege with regard to credit money they have issued. The holder of bank credit is entitled to have this credit redeemed in another form of money, typically cash. Of course, there may be some restrictions as to how quickly this must happen. Some deposits may be encumbered with specific terms of notice. Still, the general principle is that bank credit is convertible into fiat money or, in some historic cases, commodity money. A private bank cannot refuse such conversion. If it does, the consequences can be devastating, as other creditors may come to fear for the solvency of the bank. This may result in a bank run, where all creditors simultaneously demand to have their deposits paid out in cash. Few if any banks are able to satisfy such demands unless they are backed by a larger conglomerate of banks or the state.

AS GOOD AS MONEY IN THE BANK

At the beginning of this chapter, we encountered the imaginary scenario of John the financial entrepreneur. Equipped with the credit theory of money, we are now in a position to unfold the logic of this scenario. Even though the scenario is purely fictitious, it serves to illustrate some of the ambivalences inherent in the process of making money. There was, firstly, a moral ambivalence in the scenario. On the one hand, John seemed to be nothing but a financial conman. He was a parasite on the local community of honest, productive, hard-working citizens, making his profits through sheer criminal activity. On the other hand, John's activities had a very positive impact on the economic life and prosperity of the local community. We might speculate that everybody would have been better off if John had not let his moral doubts put a stop to his lending practices. The termination of his business might even throw the imaginary community into a recession.

Secondly, the scenario also involved an economic ambivalence. At the end, John was in possession of one million real US dollars. Where did this profit come from? It came from the interest payments of the citizens. However, this interest was more than fully compensated for by the economic growth facilitated by the infusion of money. Even though the local citizens were initially deceived by the counterfeit money, everyone seemed to have benefited from the deception. Especially after the counterfeit money was exchanged for genuine money, it is difficult to point to anyone who lost out on the scheme. It could be argued that the infusion of extra money into the economy might result in inflation, thus devaluing existing savings and making savers the ones who ultimately pay for John's profit. We shall return to the discussion of inflation later.

Thirdly, we also find a theoretical ambivalence in the scenario. When we think of John as a counterfeiter, it is implied that he produces fake fiat money. In other words, he imitates the process by which governments create money. However, there is also another way of thinking about the process. In defence of John, it could be argued that the newly created money was not counterfeit fiat money, but simply receipts for a credit against John. When people were lending John's money out to other people, they were not lending cash. Instead, they were lending a promise that John would eventually redeem the notional amount on the notes in real cash. Arguably, the money produced on John's printing press was not fiat money in the form of an It Owes yoU. Instead, they were tokens of debt that functioned as credit money in the form of IOUs, with 'I' being John.

The scenario is, of course, purely a construction. John's activities do not immediately correspond to any actual institutions in society. Modern banks do not make money by printing counterfeit bank notes. However, if we imagine the following sequel to the scenario, we begin to see more clearly how it is analogous to actual banking:

> John is unable to make up his mind about what to do with his money. Besides generating a handsome profit, his lending business over the course of the past year has also given him great pleasure. Until he was overcome by moral scruples, he took pride in the respect he had earned from the people of the town. It was a constant source of satisfaction to see how his money brought prosperity to the community. So instead of spending his one million dollars on fast cars and women, John decides to use it to transform his business into a fully legitimate operation.
>
> John the financial entrepreneur announces to the town that he is once again open for business, offering loans 10 percent interest. This time, however, loans will not be paid out in counterfeit money but in real money. In the beginning, business is slow. People are suspicious of the operation. They have not forgotten how they were deceived before. But soon, word spreads that John's money is absolutely real. Within days he manages to lend out all of his funds.
>
> People keep coming to John for loans but he has to turn them down since he has no more money to offer. Fortunately, some of the initial borrowers have been very successful in their investments. They are already coming back to John to repay their debts with their newly earned profits. In order to meet the growing demand for new loans, John comes up with the idea of issuing IOUs to lenders instead of hard cash. Every time he receives \$100 in cash in repayments or interest on old loans, he issues IOUs at the notional value of \$1,000. He also finds a use for the old counterfeit money, which has been piling up in his office since his old scheme collapsed. John runs all the notes through the printing press, giving each of them a big red stamp that says, 'I promise to pay to the bearer on demand the sum of \$100', followed by his name and signature.
>
> Since John's reputation in town has gradually been restored, his IOUs begin to function as immediate means of exchange. With the new red stamp, there is no doubt that the notes are genuine Federal Reserve notes. In turn, people trust that the IOUs are backed by real money and they use John's IOUs as if they were indeed cash. The general acceptance of John's IOUs is further supported by the fact that more and more people in town have taken out loans with him.

> This means that there is a growing demand for IOUs to make repayments and interests.
>
> Whenever people in town need money to make transactions with people outside the town, they come to John to redeem enough IOUs to be able to make the payment in cash. John is careful to always keep on hand cash reserves equivalent to 10 percent of outstanding IOUs. This is sufficient to meet the demands for cash occasionally required for out-of-town transactions.
>
> Eventually, John has recovered the initial one million dollars in cash through repayments and interest. At the same time, his entire stock of IOUs at the notional value of ten million dollars is now circulating in the community, thus earning John an annual one million dollars in interest. As long as none of the borrowers defaults, this is equivalent to 100 percent profit on the initial investment.

What John has discovered here is nothing other than the principle of fractional reserve banking, which is at the core of modern banking. This principle allows banks to lend out funds against a reserve of money that constitutes only a fraction of outstanding loans. Reserves may come from deposits made by customers with excess funds, or they may simply constitute the equity of the bank. In the imaginary scenario here, John keeps reserves at the ratio of 1:10 to outstanding loans. In actual existing banks, reserve ratios are legally determined by regulations and practically determined by demands for cash from customers. Today it is not uncommon for banks to operate at reserve ratios as low as 1–2 percent.[20]

Fractional reserve banking is profitable insofar as banks are capable of getting their own credit money to circulate among the users of money as if it were indeed cash. If people needed cash for all of their economic transactions, the profitability of fractional reserve banking would be severely restricted. If loans were paid out in cash immediately upon issue, the issuance of a loan would automatically cause an equivalent decrease in bank reserves. In effect, the cashier would have to go into the bank vault and take out a wad of cash every time a loan was granted, and as soon as the vault was empty, no more loans could be granted. This was the way that John operated his business when he

---

20 Ryan-Collins et al., *Where Does Money Come From?*, 4.

was still paying out loans using his reserve of genuine Federal Reserve notes.

This is very far from the way that banks operate today. When a customer comes into the bank to take out a loan, typically the cashier does not pay out the loan in cash, nor does he have to go down into the bank vault. The whole operation can be executed on the cashier's computer screen. This operation consists of a double movement. In a first move, a book entry is made to register the customer as a debtor to the bank liable to pay principle and interest on the amount of the loan – say $100,000. In a second move, another book entry is made to register the bank owing the customer an equivalent amount. This amount is made available on the customer's transactional or checking account, where it is immediately accessible for use, for instance in an electronic bank transfer, a debit card purchase or the writing of a cheque. When someone uses a credit card to buy a commodity on credit, these two movements are executed at the moment of purchase. In this case, the money is only available on the customer's transactional account for a split second, since it is immediately transferred to the commodity seller's deposit account.

In the imaginary scenario, John's credit money circulates in the form of physical IOUs. This is not the case in actual contemporary society, where most of our transactions involving bank credit money are handled digitally. Still, the underlying principle and the economic mechanisms are the same. The only difference is that the digital arrangement is much more efficient and much more profitable, as it lowers the requirement for cash in monetary transactions. And, as we shall see further on, the digital nature of credit money further serves the ideological obfuscation of the difference between cash and credit money.

It is important to note two things here. First, if we define money as funds available for immediate use in exchange for commodities, the issuance of a bank loan is essentially the creation of money out of nothing. The bank lends out money that it does not have. Of course, this money corresponds to an equivalent liability on the part of the bank. When the bank makes the money available on the customer's transactional account, the bank should also be prepared to redeem this money when it comes back to the bank in the form of a demand for cash or a demand for a transfer of credit to another bank.

Second, as long as the money created through the loan does not come back to the bank for redemption in cash, the bank makes a profit equivalent to the difference in interest between the lending rate and the deposit rate. Since the annual lending rate on some consumer loans may be as high as 30 percent, while the deposit rate on some transactional accounts may be close to zero, this line of business has a very high profit margin. It is crucial to remember that this profit is made on the basis of money that the bank did not have in the first place. In brief, the bank makes money out of nothing and then profits on the interest margin for as long as the credit money is kept in circulation.

In the imaginary case of John, we saw how he has to use his reserves to redeem IOUs in cash every time one of his customers wants to use money in a transaction with out-of-town people who do not accept his IOU as an immediate means of exchange. Since the depletion of cash reserves restricts his ability to make new loans given the reserve ratio of 1:10, this kind of redemption restricts the profitability of his business. In actual banks, a similar thing happens when borrowers use the deposits in their transaction account to make a purchase from someone who is not a customer in the bank. If the person borrowing the above $100,000 goes straight from the bank to the car dealer and writes a cheque for $100,000 to pay for a new car, and the car dealer subsequently goes to the bank to have the cheque redeemed in cash, the loan has very quickly resulted in an equivalent decrease in the bank's reserves. The bank will still make money from the interest on the original loan for as long as it takes the borrower to repay it, but the profits will be partly offset either by the cost of acquiring new cash reserves (e.g. by raising new equity or attracting new cash deposits) or by lost profits brought about when the diminshed cash reserves curb the bank's ability to issue new loans. Once the credit money created through the issuing of the loan comes back to the bank as a demand for cash, the bank can no longer collect interest on money that it did not have in the first place. It can only collect interest on money that it actually does have. Although the latter may still be a good deal, it is not nearly as good as the former.

Fortunately (for banks), the aforementioned case where the purchase of a car led immediately to the dealer redeeming the credit money in cash, thus causing a reduction in the bank's reserves, is atypical. In the evolution of contemporary banking, we can identify a number of trends that function to increase the decoupling of the creation and circulation of credit money from the existence and possession of an underlying reserve of fiat money. These trends expand the ability of banks to collect interest on money they have created out of nothing. In chapter five, we shall return to the functioning of contemporary banking and review these trends. At the moment, let's look further into the philosophical properties of fractional reserve banking.

THE FANTASY OF FRACTIONAL RESERVE BANKING

The philosophical mechanism of fractional reserve banking hinges on the difference between two forms of money. On the one hand, there is the kind of money that constitutes the reserve. This may be fiat money in the form of government-issued cash, or it may be commodity money in the form of gold or another precious metal, or it may be a combination of the two. Reserve money may even be constituted by debt for which there is a stable and liquid market that allows for immediate exchange into cash – for instance, government bonds. On the other hand, there is the bank-issued IOUs. This is credit money. The precondition for the functioning of fractional reserve banking is that the difference between reserve money (in the form of fiat money, commodity money or liquid debt) and bank credit money does not make a difference to the users of money. The profitability of fractional reserve banking rests on the ability of the bank to make its credit money function *as if* it were indeed commodity money or fiat money.

In both of the scenarios involving John the entrepreneur, he makes a profit by getting his homemade money to function as if they were genuine money. In the first scenario, the difference between genuine Federal Reserve notes and counterfeit notes is veiled through simple deception. The scheme works because people actually think that the counterfeit money is genuine money. In the second scenario, there is no actual deception going on. People know full-well that the IOUs with the big red stamp are not actual Federal Reserve notes. Nevertheless, they still use this money *as if* it were indeed actual fiat money. The difference between John's IOUs and Federal Reserve notes does not make a difference to the users of the money. Instead of simple deception, the mechanism at work here is, of course, Žižek's concept of ideology. The following definition of the concept is appropriate here:

> Ideology involves translating impossibility into a particular historical blockage, thereby sustaining the dream of ultimate fulfillment – a consummate encounter with the Thing. On the other hand . . . ideology also functions as a way of regulating a certain distance with such an encounter. It sustains at the level of fantasy precisely what it seeks to avoid at the level of actuality . . . So ideology appears to involve both sustenance and avoidance in regard to encountering the Thing.[21]

The paradox of fractional reserve banking is that the reserves constitute only a fraction of the banks outstanding IOUs, while at the same time these IOUs circulate as if their value is fully covered by the reserves of the bank. The ideology of fractional reserve banking serves to manage this paradox by way of the double movement described in the above definition. Ideology translates the impossibility of the simultaneous redemption of all outstanding IOUs in cash reserve money as a practical matter. From the perspective of the individual depositor, there is little difference between commercial bank credit money and central bank money. Only when bank runs occur does the difference become manifest, as everyone wants to convert their commercial bank money into central bank money. The (ideo-)logic of banking goes something like this: 'We do not hold sufficient reserves to cover all outstanding customer deposits because there is no practical reason why we should do so. People do not need all this cash to perform their monetary transactions, so a 100 percent cash reserve would just sit idle in our vault anyway. Yet, we still hold enough reserves to serve customers that come to us with a demand for cash. If a person wants to, he can get his credit money converted into cash at any time'. Ideology sustains the fantasy that virtual credit money can be converted into real fiat money at any time. Simultaneously, this logic obviously serves to avoid the conversion of credit money into cash. By persuading depositors that they may convert their credit money into cash at any time, the bank is in effect making the conversion unnecessary. The ideology of fractional reserve banking sustains the fantasy of convertibility while at the same time avoiding convertibility at the level of actuality.

The philosophical relation between reserve money and commercial bank credit money corresponds to the relation between the real and the symbolic that we find in Žižek. It is not important whether

---

21 Žižek and Daly, *Conversations with Žižek*, 70–1.

the reserve is composed of commodity money, fiat money or even liquid debt, and we should not be confused by the fact that fiat money is itself a form of symbolic money. The important point is that the reserve money comes to function as the incarnation of real value, while the value of credit money seems to be merely derived from the value of the underlying reserve. From the individual depositor's perspective, credit money seems to be merely a symbolic representation of the underlying reserve of real money. The amount recorded as deposit seems to represent ownership in the underlying reserve of real money. However, it is in the very nature of fractional reserve banking that the amount of credit money greatly exceeds the amount of real reserves. The procedure by which credit money comes into being simultaneously produces a surplus in the order of the symbolic, which does not correspond to anything in the order of the real. Fractional reserve banking is constituted by a fundamental lack. This lack is veiled by the imaginary fantasy of convertibility. And as we know from Žižek, fantasy operates by producing precisely those effects in the real for which it serves to compensate. In the case of fractional reserve banking, the fantasy of convertibility produces the effect that credit money comes to function as if it were indeed real money endowed with real value, thus making the need for actual conversion redundant.

From this perspective, an ATM is truly an ideological apparatus. The ATM allows us to convert credit money from our deposit account into real tangible cash anytime and almost anywhere. The ease with which this conversion takes places works to persuade us that there is really no significant difference between the two forms of money, and hence there is no real reason to make the conversion in the first place. The ATM produces little 'answers from the real' that serve to reassure the users of money that their symbolic credit money is backed by the real value of cash.

As we have already touched upon, bank runs exemplify what happens when the ideological fantasy sustaining the value of bank credit money implodes. When ideology breaks down, the ontological difference between reserve money and credit money becomes manifest. In other words, bank runs occur when the ontological difference between reserve money and credit money indeed does make a difference.

We can also find this ideology at play in the way most people ordinarily think about money. If you ask a person on the street, 'What is money?', a typical response might be for this person to reach into his pocket and take out cash notes or coins. 'This is money.' Physical cash is perhaps the archetypal image of money today. This is paradoxical insofar as most people use cash only for a minor fraction of their total monetary transactions. Unless you are a drug dealer, a bank robber or a labourer that does a lot of moonlighting, a majority of your monetary transactions are probably made through the transfer of credit money to and from your bank account. As has already been mentioned, few people keep their savings in the form of paper money hidden under the mattress or in another safe place. The vast majority of money in contemporary society takes the form of bank credit money. (We shall return to this in chapter five.)

Nevertheless, we tend to think of this kind of money as being equivalent to physical cash issued by state governments. We tend to think that the amount of money we have saved up in our bank account ultimately represents a similar amount of money paid out in cash. And we tend to view the choice between cash or credit in our daily shopping transactions as nothing but a matter of convenience. A credit card is very handy because it obviates the need to carry around large sums of cash or visit the bank before going to the supermarket. We have already seen how commercial bank credit money and government issued cash is, *from a depositor's perspective,* equivalent. A similar thing applies when we look at money *from a consumer's perspective*. For the individual consumer, the standard question of 'cash or credit?' is merely a matter of convenience. Even though the vast majority of money in the world is bank-issued credit money, we still seem to think that in the last instance, money is cash. The system of bank credit money is a system of money without cash, but this system can only function under the condition that we still believe that money is essentially cash. *Cash is the sublime object of the ideology of credit money.*

The reduction of the difference between credit money and cash fiat money to a matter of convenience is found not only in commonsense thinking about money. It is also an inherent feature of the way neoclassical economics explains the evolution of money.[22] As we have

22 Tobin, 'Money'.

seen, mainstream economics tends to view money as primarily a convenient means of exchange that allows the exchange of commodities to proceed as efficiently as possible. This is the kind of explanation that starts with the image of the moneyless barter economy. A typical reference in this form of explanation is Jevons's classic idea of money as a solution to the 'problem of the double coincidence of wants'.[23] According to this notion, money is basically a means of coordinating the satisfaction of buyers and sellers, and whatever medium performs this function most efficiently becomes the prevalent form of money in a society. This theory may, for instance, be used to explain why at a certain time in history coins made of gold, silver and bronze were elevated to the status of money.[24] If we project this line of thinking to the present day, the explanation for the prevalence of credit money is that this kind of money is most convenient for handling our ordinary monetary transactions.

In the same way that the common-sense understanding of money is based on the perspective of the individual depositor or the individual consumer, neoclassical economics is inherently based on 'methodological individualism'.[25] This methodological individualism is part of the ideology that serves to veil the ontological difference between credit money and fiat money. But when we shift from the perspective of the individual depositor or the individual consumer to that of the collective economic community, crucial differences between government-issued cash and bank-issued credit money come to light.

Fractional banking is not a new thing. Ingham argues that this creation of credit money is one of the constitutive elements of capitalism itself. He claims that the origin of the principle may be traced back at least five hundred years to the use of transferable bills of exchange as payment in sixteenth century Latin Europe, as well as to the subsequent evolution of private deposit banking in seventeenth century Holland and England.[26] Thus, the existence of fractional reserve banking is in itself not a distinct characteristic of the contemporary paradigm of money. Still, the contemporary paradigm of

---

23 Jevons, *Money and the Mechanism of Exchange*, 51.

24 Ferguson, *The Ascent of Money*, 24–24.

25 Ingham, *The Nature of Money*, 23.

26 Ingham, 'Babylonian Madness'; Ingham, *The Nature of Money*, 107–33.

money, which comes into being with the collapse of the Bretton Woods system, implies a significant transformation of the conditions for fractional reserve banking – a transformation that allows this practice to proliferate almost exponentially. We shall explore this issue in depth in chapters five and six.

BELIEVER OF LAST RESORT

If we return to the imaginary case of John the financial entrepreneur, we can see that his capacity for supplying the economy of his town with his homemade IOU credit money is limited by a number of things: At all times, John has to keep enough genuine Federal Reserve notes to accommodate customers who come to him to redeem their IOUs. This means that he can only issue IOUs to the extent that they are backed by his reserve of cash, which is constituted by his initial investment and subsequent cash funds that have come in as payments of interest or repayments of debt. As we have discussed, this ratio between outstanding IOUs and cash reserves does not need to be 1:1. It is determined by the practical needs of the customers, which are in turn determined by the activity of the economy. In the illustration, John determined that a ratio of 1:10 was sufficient to serve these needs.

From a philosophical perspective, this limitation on John's capacity to issue new IOUs plays out at the intersection between the order of the real and the order of the imaginary. The redemption of credit money in cash fiat money not only serves the practical needs of bank customers. Cash money also functions as a 'piece of the real' that reassures the money-user that the value of credit money is basically the same as cash money. The real practical need for cash money – for instance, for payments to people from other towns – is intertwined with the ideological confirmation of the status of credit money. We can illustrate this by continuing the scenario:

> One Friday, an unusual amount of customers come to John to redeem their IOUs. There is going to be a big market in the neighbouring town that weekend and everyone wants real cash so they can trade and have fun there. There is even going to be a casino at the market, and some people are eager to gamble. As John accommodates their needs, his reserve of cash dwindles. He knows that on

> Monday, all the farmers who will have sold stock and produce at the market will come back with cash to repay their debts. Also, those who have been lucky at the casino will use their winnings to settle debts. This means that if only he can make it through the day, his business will survive.
>
> At five minutes before closing time, John pays out his last Federal Reserve note. Throughout the day John has managed to keep a pleasant demeanor, not showing any signs of worry to the customers. But now that he is out of money, he starts sweating and shaking. He alternates between looking at the clock and looking out the window for approaching customers. At one minute before closing time, the town gossip comes into John's office and insists on converting his $100 worth of IOUs into cash. Since he came clean on the counterfeiting scheme, John has promised himself that he would never again take advantage of anyone. So he presents the matter to the man as it is: He can't give the man any money because all the reserves have been withdrawn by the people going to the market. Instead, John reassures him that if only he can wait until Monday, there will be plenty of cash to pay out. The man seems to accept the explanation, but John is anything but calm as he leaves the office.

In this scenario, two things could happen. The problem of insufficient funds may remain just a practical problem in the order of the real. Even if the gossip decides to share his experience with other people in town, these people may choose to conceive of the problem as merely a temporary matter, just like they would if the grocery store was out of eggs one day because everyone had suddenly decided to make cakes. However, the incident might also evolve into a problem in the order of the imaginary. This would happen if people generally lost faith in the convertibility of John's IOUs – if the fantasy of convertibility broke down. This would, of course, trigger a bank run. On Monday morning, John would not be greeted by a few farmers and gamblers wanting to pay their debts. He would instead be met by a mob of angry people wanting their IOUs paid out in cash immediately.

Let us imagine that John survives. Let us imagine that no one cares to listen to the old gossip, either because they know he is a gossip or because they are too busy trading, drinking and gambling at the market to worry about boring banking matters. And let us imagine that come Monday, enough people return to pay their debts in cash such that John recovers a workable ratio of reserves. Still, the incident was a traumatic experience for John. He decides to take measures to decrease or even eliminate the risk of a bank run. Being an entrepreneur, John also thinks that, by the same token, he might be able to improve the profitability of his business. John has two ideas.

> Since the risk of the bank running out of cash was caused by his customers' need to take out money to spend in the neighbouring town, John first contacts the local banker in the neighbouring town. The bank has in fact set up a system that is in principle identical to John's, and the banker is thus experiencing the same challenges as John. Whenever there is a market in John's town, the people of the neighbouring town take out large amounts of deposits in cash to go and spend at the market. When this happens, the bank sometimes faces liquidity risk. The two bankers quickly make a mutually beneficial agreement. The neighbouring town bank agrees to accept John's IOUs at their nominal value as payment of debt or interest, or as deposits. In turn, John agrees to do the same with IOUs issued by the neighbouring town bank. Furthermore, the two bankers set up lines of credit with each other whereby their respective IOUs are balanced against each other as they are received. Once a year, the balance is reviewed and, if necessary, settled in a cash transfer from one bank to the other. When the terms of the agreement are resolved, the new cooperation between the two banks is made public. All bank customers in both towns are informed that they can now receive IOUs from the other town's bank in payment for goods or services, in full confidence that their own bank will redeem the IOU. The agreement is of course marketed as a sign of friendship and trust – everyone will prosper from increased trade and travel between the two towns.
>
> The effect of the agreement is that the next time there is a market in the neighbouring town, John does not experience any outflow of cash from his deposit. People no longer bother to convert their IOUs into cash, as all merchants in the neighbouring town – even the casino – are happy to accept John's IOUs at face value. Not only does the agreement seem to decrease the risk of a bank run, but it even allows John to issue more IOUs and increase his ratio of cash to outstanding debt to 1:20, since his IOUs now have a wider sphere of circulation.

> Seeing how the money-lending business has had a very positive impact on the prosperity of the town, the mayor becomes very favourable towards John's operation. Building on this goodwill, John is able to persuade the mayor that they have a mutual interest in consolidating the business. A collapse of John's business would not only be a catastrophe for John himself, but also for the town as a whole. Hence, the mayor agrees that the city council should support the maintenance of the liquidity of John's business. It is agreed that in the event that John is again about to run out of cash reserves, the city council will immediately provide a line of credit from which John may draw cash to satisfy customers who wish to redeem their IOUs.

In banking terminology, the city council comes to function as 'lender of last resort'. This is the role played by the Federal Reserve in the US and by the central banks of many other countries. In philosophical terminology, the city council comes to function as an 'Other of the Other'. When people in town use John's IOUs *as if* they were indeed money, they bring about a situation where the moneyness of the IOUs is maintained through the belief of the big Other. The crucial point of the sustainability of the system is not whether the individual users of money believe that the IOUs are money. Instead, the system is sustained through a form of generalized belief, which cannot be reduced to the belief of any individual money-user. The users of money need to believe that some imaginary other subject believes in the moneyness of the IOUs. As long as the individual user of money believes that any other subject will readily accept the IOU in exchange for commodities or as payment of debt, it does not matter whether he believes in the moneyness of the IOUs himself. In other words, the users of money merely needs to believe that the big Other believes in the moneyness of the IOUs.

The mechanism of bank runs is a perfect example of the functioning of Žižek's notion of ideology. Since ideology is not a distorting supplement to reality but an integrated part of reality as such, the implosion of ideology does not leave us with the reality 'as it actually is'. When creditors lose their faith in the solvency of the bank and run to the nearest branch to get their deposits paid out in cash, it is not as if they have finally discovered that the bank was actually insolvent. In fact, a certain kind of insolvency is the very founding principle of a bank. Crudely speaking, a bank with enough cash in reserves to cover all outstanding credits is not a bank. Only when the bank starts issuing credit that is not backed by cash on deposit is it truly a bank. In this sense, banks are *ontologically insolvent*. This means that bank runs do not necessarily happen when banks become insolvent. It is rather the other way around. Bank runs produce the very effects by which they seem to be motivated. In Heideggerian terminology, bank runs merely convert an ontological insolvency to an ontic insolvency.

We can understand the implosion of ideology involved in bank runs through Žižek's concept of the 'subject supposed to believe'. Žižek illustrates this concept by showing how the constant shortage of toilet paper in the socialist former Yugoslavia actually came about:

> Our hypothetical starting point is that there is an abundance of toilet paper on the market. But, suddenly and unexpectedly a rumour starts to circulate that there is a shortage of toilet paper – because of this rumour, people frantically begin to buy it, and of course the result is that there is real shortage of toilet paper. At first sight this seems to be a simple mechanism of what is called self-fulfilling prophecy, but the effective way in which it functions is a little more complicated. Each participant reasons as follows: 'I'm not naive and stupid, I know very well that there is more than enough toilet paper in the shops; but there are probably some naive and stupid people who believe these rumours, who take them seriously and will act accordingly – they will start frantically buying toilet paper and so in the end there will be a real shortage of it; so even if I know very well that there is enough, it would be a good idea to go and buy a lot!'[27]

In order to apply this illustration to bank runs, we need to invert it. Žižek demonstrates how the belief in the subject supposed to believe (that there is not enough toilet paper) creates a situation of shortage out of a situation of abundance. The starting point in bank runs is a situation of shortage. There is not enough cash in the bank to cover everyone's credits. However, this knowledge itself is not enough to trigger a run on the bank. Each creditor may know this, but since each creditor still believes that the other creditors believe in the solvency of the bank, the system is maintained; the creditors are able

27 Žižek, *The Sublime Object of Ideology*, 185.

to use the bank credit as a means of exchange and payment. We see here how belief in the subject supposed to believe (in the solvency of the bank) creates a situation of abundance (of credit money) out of a situation of shortage (of cash). What triggers the bank run is not that creditors stop believing in the solvency of the bank. Indeed, they may have never believed it in the first place. The reasoning goes as follows: 'I'm not naive and stupid, I know very well that there is more than enough cash in the bank; but there are probably some naive and stupid people who believe these rumours, who take them seriously and will act accordingly – they will start frantically cashing in their deposits and so in the end there will be a real shortage of money; so even if I know very well that there is enough, it would be a good idea to go and cash my deposits!' The decisive moment is when creditors stop believing that other creditors believe in the solvency of the bank. The implosion of belief in the subject supposed to believe now turns a situation of abundance into a situation of shortage.

Bank runs are symptoms of disintegration in the belief in the big Other. Depositors rush to the bank because they doubt that the big Other believes in the credit money of a particular bank any longer. When central banks act as lender of last resort for commercial banks, they demonstrate their unconditional belief in the moneyness of the credit money issued by these banks. While commercial banks merely have the capacity to issue credit money, central banks also have the capacity to create new fiat money to lend out to banks they support. (The imaginary scenario of the city council backing John's lending business is too simple insofar as the city council does not have the capacity to make new fiat money. The support of the city council would thus be limited to its deployment of existing cash reserves). In this sense, the central bank comes to function as an Other of the Other. The money system no longer just rests on the money-users' belief in the big Other's belief in the credit money issued by different commercial banks. As long as the belief in the big Other's belief in the moneyness of fiat money is maintained, this is enough to sustain the whole system. The big Other of fiat money comes to function as the support for the big Other of the credit system. In other words, the central bank comes to function as a believer of last resort for the credit money system.

DIRTY MONEY

> Money is such a routine part of everyday living that its existence and acceptance ordinarily are taken for granted. A user may sense that money must come into being either automatically as a result of economic activity or as an outgrowth of some government operation. But just how this happens all too often remains a mystery'[28]

This quote from a text on the basic functioning of modern money points to a seeming paradox of money. Money is immediately accepted and used by almost every member of our society, while at the same time few people are able to account for the way it is brought into the world. A first reading of this paradox may suggest that money works *despite* the lack of understanding among the vast majority of its users. While this reading is probably true on a immediate descriptive level, insofar as money does indeed work, there is perhaps a deeper analytic truth hidden in the paradox.

Having developed the theoretical concepts of commodity money, fiat money and credit money, it might be tempting to write a simplified history of modern money as follows: In Medieval Europe, the dominant form of money was commodity money insofar as most circulating means of exchange were coins of precious metal. The value as well as the general acceptance of these coins in exchange for commodities was sustained by their intrinsic value. With the evolution of central banks and the issuance of national currencies in the form of paper bank notes, commodity money was gradually replaced by fiat money. A key event in this development was the fusion of government power with private banking when, with the Bank Charter of 1844, the Bank of England was granted monopoly for the issuance of bank notes in England. Initially, this bank money was backed by a gold standard and hence convertible to precious metal. However, the reserve requirements of the Bank of England as well as subsequent central banks were gradually loosened, and in times of crisis even momentarily suspended. The history might conclude with the collapse of the Bretton Woods system in 1971, when the link between state money and gold was definitively severed as Nixon closed the so-called 'gold-window'. On the one hand, this event signifies the emergence of

---

28 Federal Reserve Bank of Chicago, *Modern Money Mechanics*, 3.

fiat money in pure form, freed of any ties to an underlying commodity value. On the other hand, the Bretton Woods collapse seems to have initiated an explosive growth in the volume of global financial markets. Insofar as this growth is fuelled by an equivalent growth in the issuance of private credit money, our contemporary economy seems to be subject to the laws of credit rather than fiat money.

Besides being a crude oversimplification of historical events, such an account is philosophically incorrect. In this chapter, we have seen how none of the three theories of money provides a coherent and comprehensive account of the constitution of money. Rather, each seems to capture no more than a few essential dimensions of the phenomenon of money. At the same time, the theories seem to be necessarily intertwined. Commodity money cannot come into existence without a symbolic standard brought about by fiat. Fiat money cannot exist without the fantasy of money as commodity. Both commodity money and fiat money seem to gesture towards credit systems, where the existence of real and symbolic money is doubled by the existence of imaginary credit money. In turn, credit money cannot exist in a pure form, as it has to rely on the fantasy that the value of credit money is ultimately backed by either commodity money or fiat money. And so on. This means that the history of money cannot be grasped as the succession of one form of money after another. The three forms of money always coexist in some kind of historically specific configuration. Money never exists in any theoretically pure form. Philosophically speaking, money is always dirty.

If most people do not know how money comes into existence or how money basically functions, it is not because they are stupid. Rather, it seems that the fundamental constitution of money is somehow *unknowable*. The constitution of money does not lend itself to intellectual comprehension in the form of a coherent theory. In this sense, the ontology of money is comparable to the ontology of quantum particles encountered in quantum physics. One of the fundamental enigmas of quantum physics is embedded in Niels Bohr's notion of complementarity, which states that a particle may have different properties that would seem to be mutually exclusive according to ordinary Newtonian physics.[29] The best-known example is the wave-particle duality, which implies that light may display both the

29 Nørretranders, *Det udelelige*, 101–4.

properties of waves and the properties of particles. Quantum physics constitutes a fundamental break from the paradigm of Newtonian physics, including Einstein's Theory of Relativity, insofar as it no longer conceives of nature as being in principle fully comprehensible by the human intellect. If we cannot understand the behaviour of quantum particles, it is not because we have not yet discovered the theories by which we may understand them. It is because they are simply beyond human comprehension. They do not lend themselves to a coherent theoretical account. Bohr is quoted as having once said about quantum mechanics: 'If you think you understand it, that only shows you don't know the first thing about it'.[30] The same thing could very well be said about money.

Of course, this is not to say that we cannot know anything about money. If this were the case, the whole ambition of this book would be futile. Furthermore, the purpose of the review of commodity theory, chartalist theory and credit theory in this chapter is not to definitively refute any of them. Each of the theories captures essential properties of money. By using Žižek's philosophy to review these theories, we have seen how each of them locates the foundation of money in a different ontological order. Commodity theory conceives of money as originally emerging from the intrinsic real value of commodities. Chartalist theory argues that money is created in the symbolic order of the law. And credit theory suggests that money is ultimately founded in the order of the imaginary insofar as it is based on the idea of debt and the future repayment of debt.

I have also used Žižek's theory of the subject as a model for the conceptualization of money. A key point in Žižek's theory is that we cannot reduce the subject to any of the three ontological orders. The subject cannot be explained as merely the outcome of neurochemical transmissions in the real of the brain. Nor is subjectivity just a social construction in the symbolic order of discourse. And certainly our individual imaginary fantasies of who we are should not be taken as true accounts of the constitution of subjectivity. Subjectivity can only be grasped as the continuous interplay and displacements among these three dimensions.

A constitutive part of being a subject is being unable to fully

30 Horgan, *The End of Science*, 91.

understand oneself. If the subject were to know completely who it was, it would no longer be a subject. Non-knowledge is a constituent component of subjectivity. A similar paradox is inscribed in the functioning of money. One of the most fascinating features of money is the way that people are able to use it in very sophisticated ways with very little and often even erroneous knowledge about the nature of money. Even small children are capable of sophisticated monetary transactions. We have already touched upon this in connection with the science of economics. It might be argued that the success of neoclassical economics, which has managed to institute itself as the hegemonic mainstream of the discipline, is founded on a basic ignorance or even misconception of the question of what money is.

Perhaps there is a truth about money hidden in the seeming paradox between the functioning and the non-knowledge of money, and perhaps the truth lies in the fact that there is no paradox at all. A fundamental feature of the functioning of money is precisely a lack of knowledge about its basic constitution. Money works not because we know how it works and how it comes into being, but rather *because we do not know* how it works and how it comes into being. We can use Žižek to summarize this point:

> The social effectivity of the exchange process is a kind of reality which is possible only on condition that the individuals partaking in it are *not* aware of its proper logic; that is, a kind of reality *whose very ontological consistency implies a certain non-knowledge of its participants* – if we come to 'know too much' . . . this reality would dissolve itself.[31]

In this respect, money resembles a number of other fundamental phenomena in life, such as language, love and thinking. We should thus not pose the question of what money is with the expectation that we will arrive at a formal theory of the thing. This is not only futile. It is misleading. The difference between mainstream economic thinking and the kind of monetary philosophy this book sketches out is not that the economist does not know what money is, while the philosopher does. The difference between the two positions is that the former

---

31 Žižek, *The Sublime Object of Ideology*, 20–1.

does not know that he does not know, whereas the latter knows that he does not know. Rather than reading the review of the three theories of money in this chapter as a conclusive answer to the question of money, I propose using it as an analytical framework for the understanding of monetary problems and phenomena in specific social and historical contexts. The purpose of the third and final part of this book is therefore to diagnose the monetary paradigm of contemporary financial capitalism.

Part Three:

The Age of Post-Credit Money

CHAPTER FIVE

Money without Cash

On 15 August 1971, US president Nixon announced the closing of the 'gold window', through which the US Treasury had hitherto guaranteed the convertibility of the US dollar into gold at a fixed rate. The event, subsequently dubbed 'the Nixon Shock', effectively ended the international Bretton Woods Agreement, which had regulated the exchange rate between all the major Western currencies (including the Japanese Yen) since World War II. The immediate result of the Nixon Shock and the Bretton Woods breakdown was that the currencies were left to float, and their relational values were determined by the foreign exchange markets.

From a longer historic perspective, the event also signified the final disconnection between money and gold. Indeed, this was not the first time that currencies existed without the support of some kind of gold standard. The British pound, for instance, which for more than a century was the dominant currency of the world, has a history of continuously suspending and re-establishing metallic convertibility. Yet, these suspensions were always regarded as exceptional arrangements justified by a state of emergency, typically in the form of war. When the US dollar and consequently all the other major currencies pegged to the US dollar was taken of the gold standard in 1971, this was not a temporary exception but rather the institution of a new permanent order. The collapse of the Bretton Woods system signifies a paradigm shift in the history of money.

The purpose of this third and final part of the book is to make sense of this paradigm shift and to investigate its implications for the constitution of contemporary money. In the aforementioned, I have posed the question of the ontology of money as: How *is* money? The following investigation is guided by an historical variant of this question: How *is* money today?

THE END OF MONEY WITHOUT GOLD

Keeping in mind the previous analysis of money and the different theories of money, we should be careful how we understand the philosophical meaning of the transition from Bretton Woods to Post-Bretton

Woods money. The straightforward interpretation is of course to suggest that the Bretton Woods breakdown signifies the ultimate end of commodity money and the incarnation of pure fiat money. However, the problem with this interpretation is that even when the US gold window was still in effect, money was, from a philosophical point of view, not commodity money, as its value was not sustained by the alleged intrinsic value of gold. In chapter three, we saw how the commodity theory of money is in itself aporetic, since it is not able to account for the intrinsic value of gold which supposedly sustains the value of the money. Furthermore, chartalism argues that the ultimate support of money is never its intrinsic metallic value but the legal proclamation of the money object by the state. And finally, with credit theory we can argue that even though the Federal Reserve guarantees the convertibility of US dollars into gold, this does not provide backing for the value of each and every US dollar in circulation. Even if the Federal Reserve did have enough gold reserves on hand to back every dollar in circulation (which it does not), the decisive point is still not the actual conversion of US dollars into gold, but the general belief that everyone else believes in the value of the US dollar and thus accepts it as a means of exchange, a means of debt payment and a store of value.

Of course, this is not to suggest that the Nixon Shock and the Bretton Woods breakdown have no importance. The point is rather that the importance of the events lies at the level of ideology. In order to understand the ideological implications of the transition to post-Bretton Woods money, we may resort to a joke from the 1939 movie *Ninotchka* by Ernst Lubitsch:

> A guy goes into a restaurant and says to the waiter: 'Coffee without cream, please'. The waiter replies: 'I am sorry sir, but we are out of cream. Could it be without milk?'[1]

Using the logic of this joke, we can conceive of money under the Bretton Woods Agreement as equivalent to coffee without cream – that is, 'money without gold'. Before we unfold the implications of this point, let us review the history of the Bretton Woods Agreement.

The Bretton Woods Agreement was a system for the regulation of the major currencies of the Western world, set up towards the end of

1 Retold in Zupančič, 'Reversals of Nothing', 173.

WWII.[2] The Bretton Woods Agreement was based on two principles. First, the currencies of member states were pegged to the US dollar, allowing for fluctuations only within a band of 1 percent variance. This peg was maintained through the strategic buying and selling of currencies in the world market by the central banks of the member states. The peg was further supported by capital controls that were imposed to prevent foreign exchange trading for speculative purposes. Second, the US dollar was pegged to gold at a certain fixed rate of convertibility. This peg was maintained by the gold window, where the US Treasury allowed, under certain conditions, the exchange of gold and US dollars at this fixed rate. Simultaneously, the price of gold on the world market was kept in check through the strategic buying and selling of gold by the central banks of the Bretton Woods member states. The major international institutions of the IMF and the World Bank were founded to oversee and undertake crucial functions within the Bretton Woods system.

During the nineteenth and into the beginning of the twentieth century, Britain was the central power of the world economy. The Bank of England played a key role in the functioning of the global monetary system. The British pound issued by the Bank of England was initially backed by a gold standard, guaranteeing convertibility between money and gold. Just like several other central banks, the Bank of England suspended convertibility on a number of occasions in the nineteenth century, usually in times of war and economic crisis.[3] On each of these occasions convertibility was restored once business was back to normal. The same thing happened with the outbreak of WWI, only this time the economic turbulence caused by the war was so severe that the British monetary system would never fully recover. Following a brief return to the gold standard in 1925, the convertibility of the British pound was permanently suspended in 1931.

The Bretton Woods Agreement marked a shift of economic world power from England to the United States. The system placed the US dollar at the centre of the world economy. This was the currency through which the entire system was linked to gold, and it was the US Treasury that administered the gold window. But even though Bretton Woods was dominated by the US, the system signified the

2 Eichengreen, *Globalizing Capital*, 91–133.

3 Smithin, *Controversies in Monetary Economics*, 85.

internationalization of a system which was previously maintained by individual nation-states. In Bretton Woods, stabilization of the economy was viewed as the collective responsibility of the states involved.

Although Nixon's decision to close the gold window did indeed come as a surprise to the other members of the Bretton Woods system (they were not consulted beforehand, hence the Nixon *Shock*) it was hardly a spontaneous sovereign decision on his part. The decision should rather be regarded as the culmination of a crisis which had been unfolding within the Bretton Woods system for a long time. Over the course of the 1960s, a growing deficit in the US balance of payments was gradually eroding international confidence in the dollar and its continued convertibility into gold. This trend was further exacerbated by increasing US spending on the Vietnam War. Consequently, open world market prices for gold were exceeding those offered through the convertibility of US dollars, thus compounding the risk of a run on gold.[4] Furthermore, capital control restrictions were relaxed in 1958, which made it more difficult to contain foreign exchange fluctuation within the 1 percent peg.[5] Pressure on the Bretton Woods system from international flows of speculative capital was amplified by the emergence and proliferation of the so-called Eurodollar market over the course of the 1960s.[6] Eurodollars are dollar-denominated credits issued by banks in offshore locations. The Eurodollar market, which was, and still is, first and foremost located in London, allows for the issuance and circulation of credit money beyond the control of onshore banking regulations. In other words, this market allowed for banks and speculators to evade the capital controls of Bretton Woods, thus planting the seed for the voluminous foreign exchange markets that determine currency prices today.

In 1970, the US Treasury experienced a severe outflow of gold that threatened to deplete the reserves, as private investors as well as other states were losing faith in the sustained value of the dollar. The Nixon Shock was a kind of solution to the crisis whereby the Bretton Woods system was effectively scuttled. A brief attempt at continued management of foreign exchange rates was made when the fluctuation band was widened from 1 to 2.25 percent. This merely postponed

---

4 Eichengreen, *Globalizing Capital*, 122.

5 Ibid., 112–14.

6 Shaxson, *Treasure Islands*, 66.

the ultimate breakdown, and by 1973 all currencies that were part of the agreement were floating, with their relative exchange rates determined by the financial markets. The floating of currencies coincided with the ascendance of neoclassical finance and the development of theoretical models of financial markets that described these markets as efficient and thus reliable in terms of returning accurate prices on the value of money.

The Bretton Woods system, especially viewed in light of its own collapse, illustrates some of the contradictions of grounding the value of money in gold. According to commodity theory, gold is the incarnation of an intrinsic value which functions as an extrinsic anchor for the money system. The value of symbolic money is ultimately grounded in the metallic value of gold. In the case of the Bretton Woods system, the relation between money and gold is mediated by the US Treasury. The gold window is, in Žižek's terminology a *point de capiton*, where the real is weaved into the symbolic order of the money system. The exceptional role of the US dollar in the Bretton Woods system is instituted by the fact that this is the one particular currency which is directly convertible into gold. Whenever the value of the US dollar is disputed, the Treasury will come up with gold as an *answer of the real* testifying to the value of the dollar.

Marx argues that gold becomes money as 'all other commodities *set it apart* from themselves as equivalent'. A similar mechanism is at play in the Bretton Woods system when all the other currencies of the system set the US dollar apart from themselves as an equivalent. The US dollar is the standard against which the value of all other currencies is measured, and the value of the US dollar itself is measured against gold. In other words, this arrangement institutes the US dollar as the master signifier of the system of currencies, thus making the dollar 'as good as gold'. The contradiction here is that the price at which the dollar is valued against gold does not spontaneously emanate from the material matter of gold itself. Gold does not come into the world with a price tag in dollars attached. The price of the dollar in terms of gold under Bretton Woods was dictated by the US Treasury, and throughout the duration of the system it was fixed at \$35 per ounce. In other words, the gold standard of the US dollar was instituted by fiat, that is, by a declaration from the state. The true foundation of the value of the US dollar was not the intrinsic value of gold but rather the commitment of the US government and other key agents in the Bretton Woods system to maintaining convertibility at the fixed price of $35.

This commitment was further complicated by the fact that not only is the price of gold in dollars not given a priori, but the price of gold itself becomes a symptom of the state of the money system itself. Again, gold is not an unambiguous external anchor, as the price of gold is first and foremost the result of mechanisms within the symbolic order of the money system. This makes the whole system vulnerable to a self-perpetuating mechanism. When doubts about the sustainability of the system arise, agents in the system may convert their reserves of dollars into gold in the anticipation of a future devaluation. This automatically leads to an increase in the open market price of gold, which creates a further incentive to convert dollars to gold at the fixed rate guaranteed by the US Treasury. The net result is an outflow of gold from the reserves of the Treasury, ultimately sowing doubt about the continued sustainability of the system.

We have already seen how Žižek explains the intricate mechanisms at play in the maintenance of an object as the answer of the real that supports the symbolic structure:

> While it is true that any object can occupy the empty place of the Thing, it can do so only by means of the illusion that it was always already there, i.e., that it was not placed there by us but *found there as an 'answer of the real'*. Although any object can function as the object-cause of desire – insofar as the power of fascination it exerts is not its immediate property but results from the place it occupies in the structure – we must, by structural necessity, fall prey to the illusion that the power of fascination belongs to the object as such.[7]

Over the course of Bretton Woods it becomes increasingly difficult to sustain 'the illusion that it [gold] was always already there', i.e., that it was not placed there by us but *found there as an 'answer of the real'*. In 1961, for instance, eight members, including the US, pooled some of their gold reserves together in the London Gold Pool. The purpose was to strategically intervene in the open gold market in order to prevent open market prices of gold from deviating from the fixed rate set by the US Treasury. This was a neurotic attempt at

7 Žižek, *Looking Awry*, 32–3.

controlling not only the fixed price of gold through the gold window, but also the 'free market' price of gold. The effort, which was in place only until 1968, clearly illustrates how the price of gold does not reflect the intrinsic properties of gold but rather 'results from the place it occupies in the structure'. The idea of a price of gold which is 'always already there' is a fantasy that conceals the role of the symbolic structure in the determination of this price. Rather than a gold window, it is perhaps more appropriate to speak of a 'gold mirror' insofar as gold does not provide a stabilizing connection to a form of value that is outside of the money system. Instead, gold merely becomes a reflection of the state of the system itself.

In this way, the Bretton Woods collapse and the Nixon Shock did not signify the loss of an external anchor for the money system. This anchor was never there in the first place. Of course, the Bretton Woods system did sustain the illusion that the value of money was backed by the intrinsic value of gold. This is how we should understand money under the Bretton Woods era as 'money without gold'. The Lubitsch joke revolves around the non-identity between 'coffee without cream' and 'coffee without milk'. The difference between the two is constituted not by their positive properties – both are strictly speaking just plain coffee – but by the thing which is absent from their being. When Nixon announced the closing of the gold window, he was effectively saying: 'I am sorry sir, but we are out of gold'. Or in other words: 'I am sorry sir, but we are no longer able to offer money with the illusion that its value is backed by gold'. The closing of the gold window did not lead to the collapse of money as such. The dollar still existed as a functional means of exchange on 16 August 1971. This seems to suggest that the US was able to offer something else instead of money without gold. Being unable to offer coffee without cream, the waiter in the joke makes the following proposal: 'Could it be without milk?' If money under the Bretton Woods is money without gold, then how should we understand money after the collapse of Bretton Woods? If gold did not support money under Bretton Woods, then what does not support money today?

The short answer is that the Bretton Woods collapse marks the beginning of the era of money without cash. So the monetary paraphrase of the joke becomes: 'Sorry sir, but we are out of gold. Could it be without cash?' We will explore what this means over the course of the remaining parts of this chapter and the next.

THE EXORBITANT PRIVILEGE OF THE DOLLAR, OR, $ AS *OBJET PETIT A*

While the suspension of the convertibility of the British pound in the beginning of the twentieth century signified a weakening of the position of the pound in the international monetary order, the complete opposite seems to be the case with the suspension of the convertibility of the US dollar. When Nixon closed the gold window he effectively liberated the Federal Reserve to supply the commercial banks of the reserve system with unlimited funds. Under the gold standard, the issuance of US dollars was itself restricted by a kind of fractional reserve system. If the amount of circulating US dollars became too large, users of the money might start worrying about the continued convertibility of the currency and thus also about its exchange rate. Such worries might trigger a run on the reserves of gold backing the currency. In the context of private commercial banks, fiat money functions as the reserve backing the issuance of credit money. In the context of the gold standard of Bretton Woods, the issuance of fiat money in the form of US dollars was itself backed by the gold reserve. The gold reserve provided a commodity-based backing of fiat money.

Obviously, the relation between the amount of outstanding US dollars and the amount of gold reserves is not one to one. Just as private commercial banks are able to issue credit money far exceeding their reserve of fiat money, so the Federal Reserve is able to issue fiat money far exceeding the US reserve of gold. As we have already noted, Bretton Woods was not merely an international mutual agreement among equal member states. Given the key role attributed to the US dollar, the system served to consolidate the position of the US as the centre of the international post-war economy. This means that the US dollar is no longer just the currency of the US. The US dollar is at the same time the currency of the world. The US dollar functions as the preferred means of exchange in international trade, and it is also kept as a reserve by central banks of other countries.[8] This situation gives the US the special status that former French finance minister Valéry Giscard d'Estaing referred to as an 'exorbitant privilege'.[9] It means that the US is able to profit immensely by making the money that is

8 Eichengreen, *Globalizing Capital*, 111–15.

9 Eichengreen, *Exorbitant Privilege*.

used all over the world. In other words, the exorbitant privilege provides optimal conditions for the practice of fractional reserve banking by the US Federal Reserve.

In Žižek's terms, the currencies of the Bretton Woods system constitute a series of principally equal elements: £, DM, ¥, €, F, $, ₱, etc. Each of these elements denotes the form of valuation for a specific country. However, one of these is not just an individual element in the series. It is at the same time also the master-signifier that fixes the whole system of signification. This is, of course, the $. We can understand this through the Hegelian notion of 'concrete universality', which Žižek explains this way:

> The paradox of the proper Hegelian notion of the Universal is that it is not the neutral frame of the multitude of particular contents, but inherently divisive, splitting up its particular content: the Universal always asserts itself in the guise of some particular content which claims to embody it directly, excluding all other content as merely particular.[10]

In the context of the Bretton Woods system, this paradox plays out insofar as the US dollar is on the one hand just a particular element in the series of nation-state currencies, and on the other hand the universality that structures the series. The US dollar is sent into circulation by the Federal Reserve, just as the French franc is sent into circulation by the Banque de France. But at the same time, the US dollar is also the universal benchmark against which the value of all other currencies is measured, and it is the preferred currency for international transactions. It is the exorbitant privilege of the US to make the money that the other countries of the world use whenever they want to transcend the sphere of their own nation-state. While all other currencies are national, the US dollar is simultaneously national and *inter*national. In Hegelian terms, the US dollar is the concrete embodiment of universal money.

It is interesting to note that Keynes originally conceived the Bretton Woods system as centred on a wholly new currency, the bancor.[11] This currency would function as a credit issued by an inter-

---

10 Žižek, *The Ticklish Subject*, 101.

11 Eichengreen, *Exorbitant Privilege*, 45–7.

national Clearing Union. The idea of the bancor was, however, rejected by American negotiators, who insisted that the US dollar become the key currency of the system. Perhaps this was an instance of Hegelian concrete universality defeating a Kantian system of purely transcendental universality.

We can understand the closing of the gold window and the subsequent collapse of Bretton Woods as the result of a kind of bank run. Despite the US's exorbitant privilege of supplying the reserve currency of the world, private investors as well as foreign governments started to doubt the sustained ability of the US to maintain the gold convertibility of the dollar. As a result, increasing amounts of dollars flowed into the US for conversion, putting pressure on US gold reserves. When Nixon finally succumbed to the pressure and closed the gold window, one might have expected this to be the end of US monetary hegemony. Indeed, the event brought about a devaluation of the US dollar relative to the deutschmark and other European currencies. But in terms of eliminating the exorbitant privilege of the US and changing the status of the dollar as the international currency par excellence, the Nixon Shock had no significant transformative effect.

In fact, we might argue that the Nixon Shock served to eventually strengthen the role of the dollar in the world economy. When the gold standard was still in place, it had the double effect of persuading the users of US dollars in the world that the value of the dollar was ultimately backed gold, thus giving the dollar its exceptional status. At the same time, this restrained the money-making capacity of the Federal Reserve, as an excessive creation of dollars would eventually result in a run on gold. The closing of the gold window enabled the Federal Reserve to retain the former effect while being freed from the latter. The gold standard was a crucial element in the initial establishment of the US dollar as the hegemonic world currency. At the end of WWII, the US had 60 percent of the world's gold reserves. This was one of the arguments for placing the dollar at the centre of the Bretton Woods system. But once the post-war world economy had been organized around the hegemonic dollar, the gold standard could be removed without shifting the pivot-point of the system.

Nixon's closing of the gold window was not a sign of American monetary impotence, but rather a display of hyperpotence. This change of logic can be illustrated by way of Hans Christian Andersen's tale 'The Emperor's New Clothes,' which turns on the climax where the little boy cries out the obvious fact that the emperor is naked. The cry of the boy does not reveal new knowledge insofar as everyone in the crowd is already aware of the emperor's nakedness. However, the effect of the cry is to transform this from individual knowledge on the part of each of the subjects, to knowledge which is shared by everyone. The cry of the boy serves to make the big Other aware that the emperor is not wearing anything.

The imperial status of the US today has moved one step further than the (ideo-)logic of Andersen's tale. The closing of the gold window exposes the fact that the value of the US dollar is not backed by gold. It exposes the nakedness of the US dollar as pure fiat money. But instead of bringing about a state of embarrassment, this confirms the superiority of the US insofar as it shows that the US can do without the illusion of a gold standard. The logic is no longer: 'We are entitled to a superior position because we have the largest amount of gold'. After the closing of the gold window, the logic is turned around: 'We are so superior that we do not even need the support of a gold standard to maintain our exceptional position'. After Bretton Woods, the status of the US dollar is maintained by the mere fact that is has already been established as the dominant currency of the world. We may conceive of this as a shift from a political to a post-political foundation of the dollar.[12]

The hegemonic status of the US dollar today is comparable to the hegemonic status of Microsoft Windows. Although there are numerous alternative operating systems which are better, cheaper and more reliable, this is still the most widely used operating system in the world. The dominant position of Microsoft is not justified by the quality of its software. Instead, a completely circular logic is at play. The reason that Windows is the system that most people use is that Windows is the system that most people use. In other words, the big Other uses Windows.

The liberation of the Federal Reserve from the restraints of the gold standard expands the scope of its ability to make new money. The Federal Reserve no longer has to worry about the money coming back in the form of demands for conversion into gold at a fixed price. Of course, this does not mean that the Federal Reserve can just make infinite amounts of money. The Nixon Shock may have enabled the

12 Žižek, *In Defense of Lost Causes*, 268.

Federal Reserve to ignore the price of the dollar relative to gold, but it still needs to pay attention to the price of the dollar relative to other currencies, as well as to all other commodities. The unrestrained creation of money will eventually create inflationary effects whereby the buying power of the money will deteriorate. However, there are a number of conditions that serve to keep such potential inflationary effects in check for now.

Such conditions include the fact that the US dollar is widely used by foreign central banks as the preferred reserve currency. US dollars or US-dollar-denominated treasury bonds are perceived as the 'ultimate store of value'.[13] Major central banks holding large amounts of US dollar reserves and US debt include those of China, Japan, the United Kingdom and Brazil. The US dollar is also the preferred currency in international trade.[14] This creates a steady demand from companies for dollars to settle their obligations with international trading partners, and it makes the US dollar the dominant currency in foreign exchange markets. It is also important to note that since the 1970s, OPEC countries have priced their petroleum exports in US dollars, and any attempts to go against this line have been meet with strong resistance.[15] Furthermore, the US still has the largest and most important financial markets in the world. This creates another important outlet for the use and circulation of US dollars.

But perhaps the most important condition for the maintenance of the exorbitant privilege of the US dollar is the absence of alternatives. Eichengreen argues that the euro lacks the level of political integration in the eurozone to constitute an actual alternative. The Chinese renminbi is not integrated into the global financial system and has only limited use in international trade and speculation. Finally, the IMF's establishment of the Special Drawing Right (SDR) has so far only had a minor impact on the global monetary order, and it can only be used for the settlement of intergovernmental debt obligations or debt to the IMF.[16] As long as the US dollar retains the privilege of being not only the national currency of the US but also the de facto international currency of the world, this confers enormous powers on

---

13 Graeber, *Debt*, 365.

14 Eichengreen, *Exorbitant Privilege*, 123.

15 Graeber, *Debt*, 367.

16 Eichengreen, *Exorbitant Privilege*, 121–52.

the US Federal Reserve. In this connection, it is important to note that, despite its name, the Federal Reserve is not actually a government agency. It is part of a consortium of privately owned banks, while at the same time enjoying the public privilege of being able to create new money.[17] This arrangement confers some of the benefits of the 'exorbitant privilege' of the US dollar on the private banking corporations that are affiliated with the Federal Reserve. As we will see, the collapse of Bretton Woods not only led to a reconfiguration of the relations between nation-state currencies. It was also followed by a transformation in the conditions for the production of credit money by commercial banks.

BANKING BEYOND THE MONEY MULTIPLIER

While the Bretton Woods system put the state and fiat money at the centre of the creation of money, in the four decades following the its collapse we have seen that the centre of gravity of the monetary system has shifted to the creation of credit money by private banks. In chapter four, we looked into the way banks make money, and we also explored the philosophical properties of fractional reserve banking. The purpose of the imaginary scenario involving John the financial entrepreneur was to illustrate some general principles of the relation between cash issued by a central bank and credit money issued by a private commercial bank. The main point was to show how the difference between cash fiat money and commercial bank credit money does not seem to matter from the perspective of the individual user of money, and how bank runs come about as the ideological image of the bank is put into question. This fictitious illustration leaves open a number of questions related to the way fractional reserve banking is put into practice in actual banking. This is what we will look at in the following. I will argue that the Bretton Woods collapse not only marks a shift in the way different sovereign currencies relate to each other on a macroeconomic level. The collapse also happens at an historical moment where we can identify a shift in the practice of commercial banking and in the way private banks make money.

---

17 Graeber, *Debt*, 364–5.

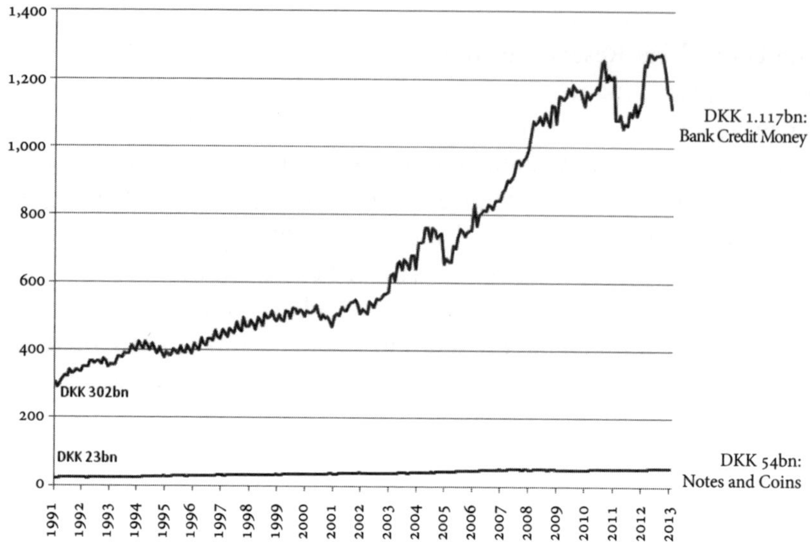

Source: Danmarks Nationalbank. Bank credit money is measured as the difference between the money aggregate M3 and cash money in the form of notes and coins.

Figure 3: Denmark Money Supply 1991–2013

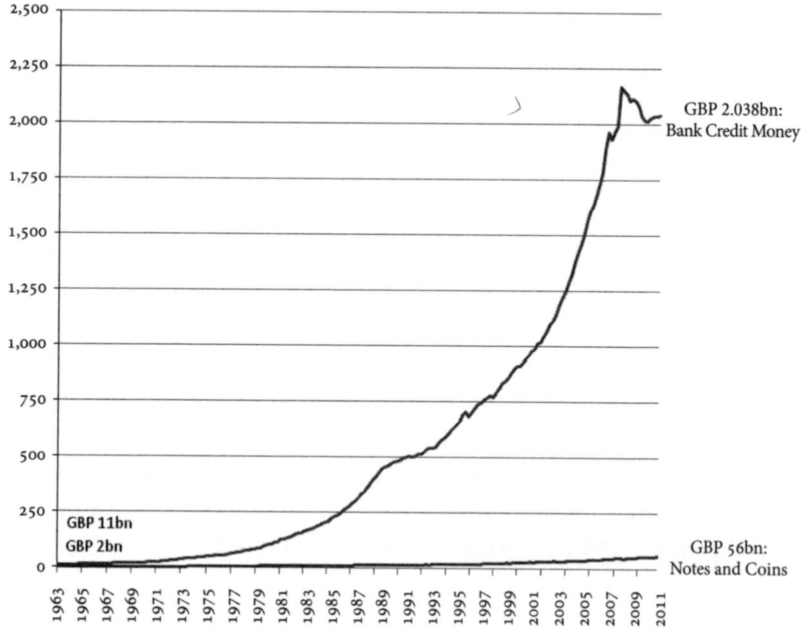

Source: Bank of England. Bank credit money is the difference between the money aggregate M4 and cash money in the form of notes and coins.

Figure 4: United Kingdom Money Supply 1963–2013

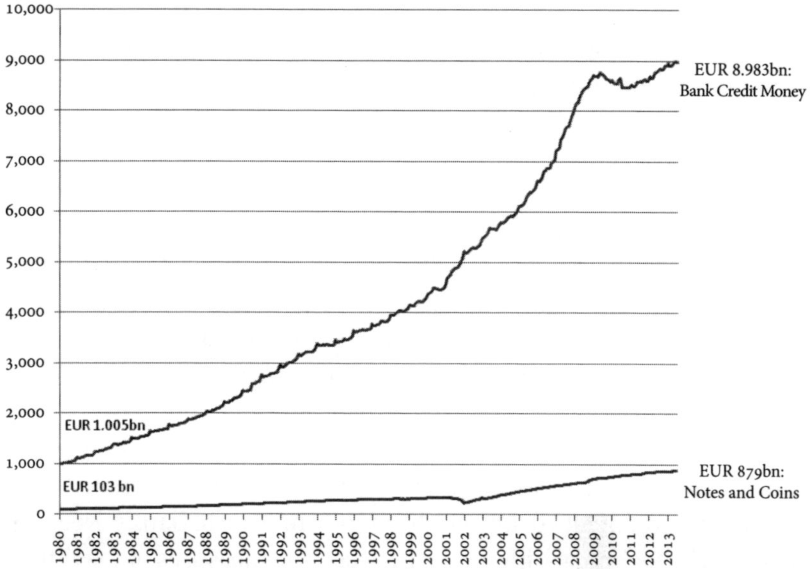

Source: European Central Bank. Bank credit money is measured as the difference between the money aggregate M3 and cash money in the form of notes and coins. Data preceeding the actual implementation of the euro is ECB experimental data.

Figure 5: Eurozone Money Supply 1980–2013

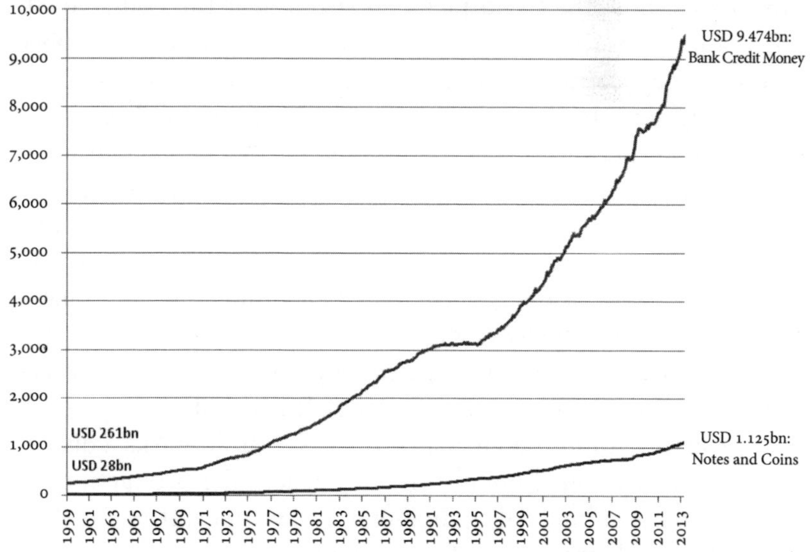

Source: Federal Reserve Bank of St Louis. Bank credit money is measured as the difference between the money aggregate M2 and cash money in the form of notes and coins.

Figure 6: United States Money Supply 1959–2013

Figures 3 through 6 show the historical transition of the composition of the money supply in Denmark, the UK, the eurozone and the US. It is important to note that the diagrams are based on data from different central banks with different standards for categorizing and measuring the money supply. The diagrams also differ according to the periods for which data are available. Despite these technical differences, it is possible to detect a general trend across the four different economic entities. First of all, we see that the amount of state-issued physical money in the form of notes and coins makes up only a very small portion of the total stock of money. The vast majority of money circulating in the economy exists in the form of commercial bank credit money. In the Danish economy, the ratio between the two forms of money is 5 percent state-issued cash versus 95 percent electronic credit money in private banks. Keeping in mind the technical differences between the measures of the different central banks, the comparable ratio is 3 percent vs. 97 percent for the UK, 10 percent vs. 90 percent for the eurozone, and 12 percent vs. 88 percent for the US. Another important similarity among the four diagrams is the significant growth in the amount of commercial bank credit money. This trend is most obvious in the UK and US diagrams, as these have data going back several decades. We can see how the trend picks up speed over the course of the 1960s and 1970s. In all four diagrams we can see how the supply of credit money continues to grow exponentially. In the UK, for instance, private banks created £1.358bn worth of credit money in the ten-year period between 2000 and 2010, which constitutes almost a tripling of the total supply of money. Writing in the context of the US, Benes and Kumhof of the IMF note that 'it is privately created deposit money that plays the central role in the current US monetary system, while government-issued money plays a quantitatively and conceptually negligible role'.[18] This remark can be used to summarize a transition of the money system that is noticeable across a number of Western economies. This transformation of the money supply is not merely a quantitative shift. It marks a qualitative shift in the constitution of money, where the production and circulation of commercial credit money is decoupled from the state's production and circulation of fiat money.

18 Benes and Kumhof, *The Chicago Plan Revisited*, 10.

The standard textbook account of banks and the relation between central bank money and private bank credit money presents two different images of a bank.[19] The first image is that of a piggy bank. This kind of bank takes deposits but makes no loans. The bank functions merely as a safe storage place for people's cash money, and it does not create any new money. The second image is that of fractional reserve banking. The functioning of this kind of banking is explained through the model of the money multiplier. The fractional reserve bank not only accepts deposits but also extends loans. In order to make loans, the bank has to use some of the cash money that was deposited for safe-keeping by depositors. This means that the bank will no longer hold 100 percent of its deposits in reserves. Instead, the bank holds only enough reserves to service depositors' immediate needs for cash. In the aforementioned example from Mankiw's classic textbook, these needs require the bank to keep 20 percent of deposits. This allows the bank to lend out 80 percent of all of its deposits. If a customer deposits €1,000 in cash, the bank keeps €200 in the vaults and lends out €800 to another customer in need of cash.

The principle of the money multiplier comes into play because the borrower of the €800 will not typically just stash this money away under his mattress. The borrower may take this money and deposit it with another bank or (more realistically) he will use the money to pay for a product or service, and the receiver of the money will take it back to his bank for deposit. This allows the process to be repeated once again in the second bank. The €800 in cash is deposited with the bank. Twenty percent of this money, or €160, is kept in reserve and the remaining €640 is lent out to a third customer. Again this borrower spends the money on a product or service from yet another person, who takes the money to deposit in his bank. The process is repeated in a third bank where the €640 deposit results in a €128 reserve and another €512 available for lending. Every time the process is repeated, more money in the form of borrowed credit money is added to the total supply of money. In principle the process can be iterated infinitely, but since the amounts eventually approach zero, this does not result in the creation of an infinite amount of money. After a certain number of rounds, the process stops having any real effect. In Mankiw's example, the original deposit of €1,000 in cash generates

19 Mankiw and Taylor, *Macroeconomics*, 563–7.

altogether €5,000 in credit money through the money multiplier. When the loans are repaid, this additional stock of money is destroyed and disappears from circulation.

This account of the principle of fractional reserve banking through the money multiplier does indeed allow for multiplicative creation of credit money in relation to state-based fiat money, yet it still insists on a certain relation between the two forms of money. Even though the ratio is far from 1:1, the central bank may ultimately control the supply of credit money created by private banks by limiting the amount of cash and central bank reserves that are put into circulation, or by changing the reserve ratio that is required by law. However, closer scrutiny of the money multiplier account of fractional reserve banking suggests that it makes a number of assumptions that overemphasize the role of cash in the contemporary monetary system. This leads to an equivalent overestimation of the role of the state and an underestimation of the independent power of private banks in the creation of credit money. Critique along these lines is put forward by Ryan-Collins, Greenham, Werner and Jackson. They summarize the argument as follows:

> Economists and policymakers following a simple textbook model of banking will assume that:
>
> 1) Banks are merely intermediaries and have no real control over the money supply of the economy.
> 2) Central banks can control the amount of money in the economy.
> 3) There is no possibility the growth in the money supply can get out of control because it is mathematically limited by the reserve ratio and the amount of base money.
>
> Unfortunately this textbook model of banking is outdated and inaccurate and, as a result, the assumptions will be untrue.[20]

In the example given by Mankiw, it is assumed that loans granted by private banks are paid out in cash to customers. Today this is the exception rather than the rule. If a bank customer is granted a loan, the amount borrowed is typically just entered into his current account

20 Ryan-Collins et al., *Where Does Money Come From?*, 21.

rather than paid out in cash. And even when the customer starts spending the money to purchase goods or services, he does not need to convert his credit money into cash beforehand. He can execute the transaction using a debit card, a cheque or a bank transfer. This means that cash is not needed in order for money to be moved from the first bank to the borrower, from the borrower to the seller of a product, and from the seller of a product to the second bank. Instead, the money is just moved between different accounts within the same bank or between different accounts in different banks. When someone uses a credit card to pay for a product, all of these three transactions are made simultaneously: A loan is debited with the credit card user's bank; a credit is issued with the credit user's bank; this credit is transferred to an account at the bank of the receiver of the payment. Cash is not needed in order to perform these transactions.

Furthermore, the money multiplier account assumes that the bank has to wait for a cash deposit to be made in order for the process of credit money creation to begin. However, an implication of the aforementioned is that deposits are made in the same movement as a loan is issued. As we have already seen, when a bank customer takes out a loan, an equivalent amount is instantly entered into his current account as a deposit. Just as credit money does not have to be transformed into cash in order to leave the bank, neither do deposits have to enter the bank in the form of cash. Deposits and loans are merely two sides of the same coin. Or rather, deposits and loans are merely two sides of the same double entry bookkeeping operation. Along these lines, Benes and Kumhof suggest a break with the usual understanding of contemporary banking prevalent in modern-day macroeconomics:

> The critical feature of our theoretical model is that it exhibits the key function of banks in modern economies, which is not their largely incidental function as financial intermediaries between depositors and borrowers, but rather their central function as creators and destroyers of money. A realistic model needs to reflect the fact that under the present system banks do not have to wait for depositors to appear and make funds available before they can on-lend, or intermediate, those funds. Rather, they create their own funds, deposits, in the act of lending . . . Bank liabilities are money that can be created and destroyed at a moment's notice. The critical importance of this fact appears to have been lost in much of the modern

macroeconomics literature on banking, with the exception of Werner,[21] and the partial exception of Christiano et al.[22]

The crucial point here is the same one we have already touched upon in the imaginary scenario of John the financial entrepreneur. Credit money is not merely a stand-in for real cash money. Under certain conditions, credit money itself comes to function as a means of exchange and payment. Obviously, the scenario involving John differs radically from the practice of actual contemporary banking because John's private bank issues physical tokens to represent its credit money. While actual private banks today do not issue such physical tokens, the evolution of increasingly effective and pervasive systems for electronic payment and transfer of credit allows these banks to function in a way that is, in principle, similar to John's bank. Just like John's homemade IOUs, credit money issued by private banks functions as if it were indeed money, which effectively makes it money.

Based on the understanding of banks as creators of money and credit, Werner provides an alternative to the textbook version of the money multiplier.[23] Instead of dividing an initial deposit of €1,000 into €200 that is kept as reserve and €800 that is extended as a new loan, the bank may keep the entire sum of €1,000 as a reserve on the basis of which credit may be extended to a borrower in the form of an entry in the borrower's account. If we assume reserve requirements to be 20 percent, the bank is instantly capable of issuing €4,000 worth of credit money. The bank simultaneously records a debt by the borrower of €4,000 and a credit in the borrower's drawing account of €4,000, which is immediately available for use. However, if the economy is based on an efficient credit payment system, where most payments are carried out through electronic credit transfers, the practical need to keep cash reserves will be much lower. As we shall see later, this is indeed the case in most developed economies today, which is also reflected in legal reserve requirements set by banking authorities that range between 0 and 2 percent in most Western countries. In Werner's

21 *New Paradigm in Macroeconomics.*

22 Christoiano et al., *Financial Factors in Economic Fluctuations*; Benes and Kumhof, *The Chicago Plan Revisited*, 9.

23 Werner, *New Paradigm in Macroeconomics*, 177–87.

example, he assumes reserve requirements of 1 percent, which allows the bank to issue €99,000 on the basis of the initial €1,000 deposit. He summarizes the argument like this:

> The crucial question is: 'Where did the €99,000 come from?' The money was not withdrawn by the bank from other uses. It was not diverted or transferred from any other part of the economy. Most of all, although it is shown as a deposit, it was not actually deposited by anyone. The bank simply created the money by writing the figures into its books and the customer's account book. In effect, the bank pretends that its borrower has made a deposit that was not actually made. Unlike the textbook representation, we see that each individual bank can thus create money when it extends a loan. *Showing this truth in textbooks would not only be more memorable, but it would also teach students about what banks really do: they create money out of nothing. The bank just pretends it has the €99,000, credits someone's books with them, and nobody knows the difference.*[24]

From the perspective of the individual consumer, credit cards, debit cards, internet banking and other electronic payment systems offer a convenient alternative to cash payments. However, these systems are also, from a macroeconomic perspective, a crucial component of a significant shift in the ontological constitution of money. The monetary infrastructure provided by these electronic systems is the condition of possibility for credit money to circulate, not merely as a representation of reserves of real cash money, but rather as money in and of itself. The increase in the share of private credit money relative to notes and coins in the total stock of money between the 1960s and today (illustrated in figures 3 to 6) signifies a shift in the economic power relations between, on the one hand, the state and the central bank, and on the other, private banks. While this shift has significant implications for the users of money, it is not immediately visible from the perspective of the individual consumer.

In the imaginary case of John, the growing importance of the bank is immediately visible to the users of money since they observe John's IOUs constituting a growing proportion of their payments and

---

24 Ibid., 178.

stock of money. Of course, they may still think of these monies as merely stand-in representations of real Federal Reserve notes. But in our society, the virtual and hence almost invisible nature of credit money means that the changing proportion between state-created cash money and private bank credit money is much less tangible. Ingham reflects on the discrepancy between the actual proportion of cash in circulation and the ideological importance of cash in the general image of money:

> 'Cash' – portable things that we take to be money – is still used in 85 per cent of all transactions [2000 figures], but now amounts to only 1 per cent of the total value of monetary transactions . . . In other words, actual media of exchange are now a relatively insignificant element of most monetary systems; but consciousness of money is still formed to a significant extent by the small-scale transactions.[25]

The money multiplier account of fractional reserve banking seems to reproduce this popular view of money. While it indeed admits the fact that the proportion of private credit money outweighs the proportion of cash, the money multiplier account still maintains the image of credit money as 'in the last instance' cash. This ontological assumption is also implied in the usual distinction between base money (central bank money) and broad money (private bank money). The account allows that a deposit of cash may serve as the source of credit creation many times over, thus producing multiple amounts of credit money. But it still maintains that cash is required in order to make actual payments, whether in the form of exchanges between money-users or balance settlements between banks. As systems evolve to execute both of these kinds of payments without the involvement of central banks, the money-multiplier assumption that credit money depends on cash becomes increasingly problematic.

THE INTERBANK MONEY MARKET

The evolution of credit cards, debit cards, internet banking and other electronic payment systems is only one of the conditions of possibility for the circulation and proliferation of credit money as money. The

25 Ingham, *The Nature of Money*, 5–6.

other is the interbank money market. When credit money is used directly as a means of payment, it involves the transfer of money from the payer's account to the payee's account. If payer and payee are customers in the same bank, this transfer is done simply by debiting the account of the former and crediting the account of the latter. If the two parties are customers in different banks, there are a number of ways to make the transfer. As a first option, we might imagine bank 1 debiting the account of payer A and then having a clerk physically bring the appropriate amount of money in cash from bank 1 to bank 2. Upon receipt of the cash, bank 2 would then credit the account of payee B and the transfer would be complete. Obviously, this is a very impractical way of making interbank credit transfers. The impracticality of the method lies not only in the inconvenience for the bank clerks of having to run back and forth between different banks. It also requires banks to keep a substantial amount of cash on hand in order to make payments to other banks, which, in turn, limits their capacity to create credit.

A second and more realistic method is for each bank in a particular economic community to keep an account with a central bank. When customer A in bank 1 makes a payment to customer B in bank 2 using his credit card, bank 1 debits payer A's account and then simply sends a request to the central bank for a transfer of credit from its own central bank account to the central bank account of bank 2. This operation is made through simple bookkeeping by the central bank. Once bank 2 receives notice of the transfer, it credits the account of customer B. This whole transfer can be done electronically, with no running bank clerks involved.

However, this second option still requires the commercial banks to allocate a certain amount of their assets as central bank reserves in order to service interbank credit transfers. Commercial bank deposits in the central bank may come about in several ways: Commercial banks may physically transfer the cash deposits of bank customers to the central bank. Commercial banks may also simply borrow the funds from the central bank at the so-called discount rate. And finally, the central bank may purchase financial assets from the commercial banks. These assets may consist of various forms of debt, such as government bonds, treasury bonds or high-quality commercial bonds. Repurchase agreements, or repos, are a combination of loans and central bank purchases of financial assets. Under a repo, the central bank purchases financial assets from a commercial bank for cash or central bank reserves, with the agreement that the commercial bank will buy back the assets after a certain period of time. This creates, effectively, a collateralized loan from the central bank to the commercial bank.

When commercial banks use central bank deposit accounts for interbank credit transfer and clearance, the creation of credit money is still to some extent restricted by the supply of central bank money. We are, in other words, still within the conventional model of the money multiplier. However, there is a third option for credit transfer, which has the effect of decoupling the two forms of money and relaxing the restrictions on credit money creation. Instead of instantly making a request for a credit transfer through the central bank, when customer A in bank 1 makes a payment to a customer B in bank 2, the two banks may decide to keep a record of the current balance of payments between the two banks. Perhaps customer A makes the payment to customer B in the morning and then in the afternoon customer B makes an equivalent payment to customer A. Instead of going through the central bank, bank 1 and bank 2 may simply clear the balance between themselves by the end of the day.

This is, in principle, how interbank money market credit clearance works. We may recognize the underlying principle from Innes's writings on the function of medieval fairs as clearinghouses. Just as the evolution of an efficient and pervasive system for electronic payments through credit cards, debit cards, internet banking, etc. gradually liberates commercial banks from the need to keep cash, so an efficient interbank money market partly liberates the commercial banks from the need to keep reserves with the central bank to service interbank payments. The interbank market partly sets free the creation of credit money from the supply of central bank money.

As we have seen in the discussion of the credit theory of money in chapter four, the creation of stable credit money presupposes a central debtor, whose credit is generally accepted at the nominal value. The credit issued by this debtor constitutes the abstract standard of value against which all other credits are measured. I have also referred to this as the 'Lord of debtors'. Therefore, the interbank money market cannot function without the participation of the central bank.

Transfers of credit between commercial banks thus function as a combination of options two and three presented above.[26] Efficient interbank money markets exist to facilitate the transfer of credit money between commercial banks, but central banks still play a crucial role in the maintenance of the markets. When possible, commercial banks clear credits among themselves, but they sometimes resort to central bank clearance. We shall return to the relation between the two forms of clearance.

The extent to which the network of commercial banks in the interbank money market is able to clear their mutual balances among themselves without having to resort to their accounts in the central bank determines the extent to which these banks are able to create more credit money without being limited by their reserve of central bank money. In other words, the efficiency of the interbank money market reduces the reserve ratio of the commercial banks. But the practical reserve ratio of individual banks may also differ according to their size and position in the network. Large banks with large shares of the market carry out a higher rate of payments where each party is a customer of the same bank. This means that they do not even have to resort to the interbank market to clear the payment. Smaller banks will have to clear a larger share of their payments in the market and are thus required to hold larger reserves with the central bank relative to outstanding credits.

The interbank money market not only functions as a place to clear outstanding balances. It is also a market where banks borrow from and lend to each other. This allows commercial banks to fine-tune their holdings of reserves in accordance with legal and practical requirements. Banks with excess reserve holdings may choose to lend these out to banks with too little reserve holdings. This enables the individual bank to find the optimal and most profitable way of financing operations. Excess funds may be lent out at the optimal interest rate and required funds may be borrowed at the cheapest rate possible. The existence of a liquid interbank money market adds liquidity to the various forms of debt and securities that are traded in the market. Instead of holding non-interest-bearing cash in reserve, banks may hold interest-bearing debts and securities because the interbank market makes it possible to immediately convert these

---

26 Ryan-Collins et al., *Where Does Money Come From?*, 52–76.

assets into cash or whatever form of credit the bank needs in order to carry out its operations.

On the one hand, the interbank money market is a 'market' just like any other market where things are bought and sold according to prices that are more or less subject to supply and demand. The 'things' that are bought and sold in the interbank money market are assets with different levels of liquidity. The price of liquidity is expressed through the interbank rate of the particular market, such as the LIBOR (UK), the EURIBOR (eurozone) or the federal funds rate (USA). If there is a shortage of liquidity, the prices go up, and if there is an excess of liquidity, prices go down. On the other hand, the interbank money market is very different from most other markets. While banks may indeed make profits buying and selling different kinds of money in the interbank market, this is not their primary motivation for participating in the market. While each individual bank may have an interest in getting the best financing they can get in the interbank market, they have a much stronger collective interest in the efficient functioning of the market itself.

An efficient interbank market has the ideological function of effacing the difference between commercial bank credit money and state-created fiat money. The unconditional willingness of the central bank to exchange central bank money for commercial bank credit money at the nominal value enables commercial bank credit money to circulate in the general economy is if it were indeed central bank money. The effacing of the difference between credit money and fiat money is established through the myriad ways in which the central bank accepts different kinds of credit and securities in exchange for central bank money. When the interbank market functions most efficiently, the central bank does not even have to actually perform these transactions. The mere commitment to doing so if needed is enough. The central bank's commitment to accepting credit money at the nominal value from any of the banks in the interbank network allows the banks to exchange credit among themselves at nominal value without considering the creditworthiness of each individual bank. As we have already noted, the central bank functions as a 'believer of last resort', which allows each of the individual commercial banks to believe unconditionally in each other.

We see here how the 'thing' – liquidity – which is traded in the interbank money market does not obey the same laws of supply and demand as conventional commodities. The efficiency of the market, the sustained commitment of the central bank, and the sustained belief of the commercial banks in the creditworthiness of each other add general liquidity to the market in a way that benefits all of the market participants. This is because it allows the credit money issued by individual commercial banks to be treated as liquid cash. The interbank money market for liquidity is almost the opposite of a zero sum game. This becomes obvious when the market is pressured in times of crisis. Davies and Green show how this happened in 2009 following the financial crisis:

> The interest rates at which individual banks could fund themselves became a function of confidence in individual names in the interbank market, regardless of the price at which the authorities supplied funds . . . The lack of trust between banks started to make the central bank in effect a systematic central counterparty for the private banks, and the central intermediary in the money market. Instead of lending to each other, they managed their liquidity increasingly by borrowing from and lending to the central bank.[27]

In this situation, the ideology that veils the difference between fiat money and credit money – thus allowing the two to be exchanged at par – erodes. Instead of a general interbank interest rate, credit is now traded at different prices depending on the 'individual name' of the issuer. The crisis reveals the difference between commercial bank credit money – the value of which is ultimately dependent on the ability of the issuing bank to redeem the credit – and state-based fiat money – the value of which is backed by the existence and power of the state.

Invoking the thinking of Giorgio Agamben, we can characterize the nature of the interbank money market as a 'zone of indistinction'.[28] Just as the difference between credit money and fiat money is effaced in the interbank market, so is the distinction between the state and private-market agents. The interbank market is a place where private agents trade liquid assets in order to make profits. But it is also a

27 Davies and Green, *Banking on the Future*, 41.

28 Agamben, *Homo Sacer*.

market where the central bank plays a key role by using its monopoly in issuing fiat money on behalf of the state. This monopoly is not only used to service the interests of private banks; it even undermines itself by granting private banks the de facto capacity to issue credit money that functions as if it were indeed fiat money. When the central bank extends privileges to private banks, such as discount window access, lender of last resort guarantees and deposit insurance, the very distinction between the state and private-market agents becomes extremely blurry.

This is perhaps most pertinent in the case of the US Federal Reserve. The Federal Reserve is in fact owned by the private banks that are part of the US banking system, although its actions are in principle subject to congressional control and oversight. The Federal Reserve refers to its own status as 'an independent entity within government'.[29] The ambiguity of this phrase is probably best interpreted as a symptom of the fact that the political role of the Federal Reserve is an ongoing point of contention rather than an evident triviality. Or, as one critic puts it: 'The US Federal Reserve is no more federal than Federal Express'.

Agamben is concerned with the legal paradoxes involved in the state of exception. When the sovereign declares a state of exception, it uses its legal power to suspend the very power of the law:

> If the state of exception's characteristic property is a (total or partial) suspension of the juridical order, how can such a suspension still be contained within it? How can anomie be inscribed within the juridical order? And if the state of exception is instead only a de facto situation, and is as such unrelated or contrary to law, how is it possible for the order to contain a lacuna precisely where the decisive situation is concerned? And what is the meaning of this lacuna? In truth, the state of exception is neither external nor internal to the juridical order, and the problem of defining it concerns precisely a threshold, or a zone of indifference, where inside and outside do not exclude each other but rather blur with each other.[30]

---

29 Board of Governors of the Federal Reserve System, 'FRB: Who owns the Federal Reserve?'.

30 Agamben, *State of Exception*, 23.

The interaction between the central bank and commercial banks in the interbank money market is an ongoing negotiation and coordination of the capacity to create money. On the one hand, the sovereign state holds a distinct monopoly on the capacity to create new money. On the other hand, its monopoly is de facto handed over to private agents which issue credit money that functions as money. Agamben refers to the place where the law opens up the possibility of its own suspension in the state of exception as a 'lacuna'. In the monetary system, the central banks seem to be the institutionalization of such a lacuna. The central bank is the place where the state uses its sovereign power to create new money to enable a network of private banks to create new money. When the system of private bank credit money creation is threatened, the central bank resorts to exceptional measures to ensure the survival of the system. The current period of financial and monetary crisis provides ample illustrations thereof. This includes central banks acting as lenders of last resort to bail out financially distressed banks, supplying liquidity to the market by purchasing bad debt ('troubled assets'), or extending the discount window even to investment banks. In Agamben's terms, the actions of the central bank and the functioning of the interbank money market 'concerns precisely a threshold, or a zone of indifference', where the creation of state money and the creation of credit money 'do not exclude each other but rather blur with each other'.

MONEY OUT THE DISCOUNT WINDOW

The emergence of efficient credit payment systems as well as interbank money markets decreases the demand for cash and central bank reserves, thus removing the practical limitations on commercial banks' capacity to create credit money. But there are other limitations on this capacity. Governments and central banks impose a number of policies and legal requirements on private banks to control the supply of money. Such measures include credit rationing, legal reserve requirements and discount rate variations. In the same year that the Bretton Woods system collapsed, the Bank of England introduced the 1971 Competition and Credit Control reform of the UK banking system. The aim of the reform was to promote competition within the UK banking sector, not only between different banks but also between banks and other agents in the financial sector.[31] The Competition and Credit Control reform was merely one tiny part of a much more comprehensive trend involving the deregulation and liberalization – and, in effect, also the financialization and globalization – of the banking sectors of our economies. The reform is notable, however, insofar as it included a number of measures that are exemplary of a more general shift in the banking policies of comparable Western countries. In this sense, we can see the reform as a symptom of a broader paradigm shift.

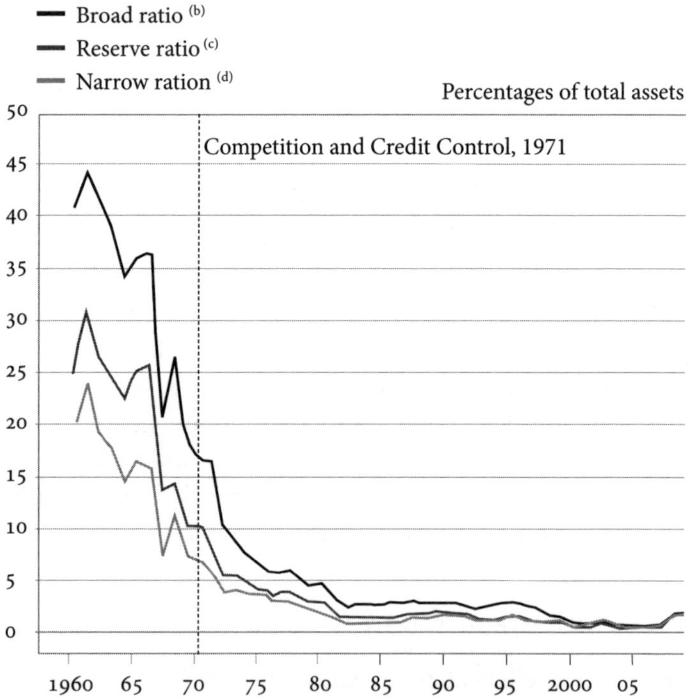

Sources: Bank of England, Bankers Magazine (1960–68) and Bank calculations.

(a) Data before 1967 cover only the London clearing banks.
(b) Cash + Bank of England balances + money at call + eligible bills + UK gilts.
(c) Bank of England balances + money at call + eligible bills.
(d) Cash + Bank of England balances + eligible bills.

Figure 7: Sterling liquid assets relative to total asset holdings of the UK banking sector

31 Davies and Richardson, 'Evolution of the UK banking system'.

A key measure of the reform was the relaxation of legal liquidity requirements from 28 percent to 12.5 percent of eligible liabilities. In subsequent decades, these requirements were gradually decreased even further, to the point where the holding of reserves by UK banks is entirely voluntary today. Other countries still have some legal liquidity requirements, but this gradual relaxation represents a general trend in Western economies. Of course, the causal relationship between deregulation and actual historical developments is oftentimes a chicken-or-egg scenario, but in any case the relaxation of liquidity requirements in the UK banking system was accompanied by a parallel decrease in actual holdings of liquid assets. Davies and Richardson provide the above figure to illustrate this point:[32]

> In philosophical terms, the figure shows the relation between fiat money and credit money. It illustrates how banks are able to create more and more credit money with less and less state-issued fiat money in the form of either cash or central bank deposits. Since the 1960s, actual as well as legal liquidity ratios have decreased steadily, thus signifying a shift from the central bank to private banks as de facto controllers of the making of money.

During the period of Bretton Woods, many central banks imposed direct credit controls on private banks, setting specific ceilings on the amount of money banks were permitted to lend out. However, the 1960s saw the emergence of parallel credit markets, where credit money was created outside of a currency's home jurisdiction.[33] This was especially true in the Eurodollar market, in which London-based banks issued US-dollar-denominated-credit, thus evading American as well as British credit controls and other banking regulations. With the emergence and growth of these parallel credit markets, direct credit controls became increasingly ineffective in regulating the total supply of money. The Competition and Credit Control reform can be viewed as a pragmatic response to this development, as another one of its key measures was the abolition of direct quantitative credit rationing. Instead of setting explicit limits on the issuance of credit

32 Ibid., 328.

33 Davies and Green, *Banking on the Future*, 26–7.

money in private banks, the central bank would now use variations in central bank interest rates (discount rate) as the primary tool for controling the money supply.[34]

While liquidity requirements and quantitative credit rationing are relatively direct ways of controling the money supply, variations in the discount rate have a more indirect impact on the total supply of money, as the effects are mediated through the market. It is assumed that the demand for credit is a function of the price of credit, and this allows the central bank to determine the demand for credit by setting a particular price. In this sense, the shift from the former to the latter kind of money-supply control measures represents a financialization of central bank policy. The role of the central bank is no longer to curtail the market forces and to appropriate these in the pursuit of politically defined goals. Instead, the facilitation of efficiently functioning markets has become a political goal in itself. Rather than imposing politically determined limits on the supply of credit, the central bank commits itself to supplying whatever amount of credit the market demands at a certain price.

The shift from credit rationing to discount-window guidance is part of a more general ideological shift in central bank policy. As we have already touched upon, the Bretton Woods system was to some extent crafted according to the ideas of Keynesian economics, where nation-state governments have the capacity and the responsibility for regulating and stimulating key economic variables. Hence, the collapse of Bretton Woods was not just the collapse of an actual monetary system. It was also the collapse of an ideology, marking a shift from Keynesianism to monetarism as the dominant approach to macroeconomics and the operation of central banks.[35]

While monetarism has a long history dating back even to the writings of David Hume in the eighteenth century, its contemporary formulation is typically attributed to Milton Friedman.[36] The basic point is that the determination of the price of money is subject to the general laws of supply and demand. In a simple form, this is expressed by Irving Fisher's classic equation of exchange below.[37] Friedman takes

---

34 Ryan-Collins et al., *Where Does Money Come From?: A Guide to the UK Monetary and Banking System*, 48.

35 Graeber, *Debt*, 375.

36 Smithin, *Controversies in Monetary Economics*, 40–62.

37 Fisher, *The Purchasing Power of Money*, 26.

this as his starting point; his achievement is to develop a more elaborate and sophisticated version of the formula:[38]

$MV = \Sigma pQ$
M is the nominal amount of money in circulation
V is the velocity of the turnover of money
Σp is the average price level of goods
Q is the quantity of purchased goods

The two sides of the equation represent money and goods. A fundamental implication of the formula is that an increase in the supply of money (M) merely results in a decrease in the average price of goods (p). When this implication is reversed, it becomes an explanation for the phenomenon of inflation as the result of an increase in the nominal supply of money.[39] The monetary policy implication of monetarism is that the primary purpose of the central bank is to provide a supply of money that creates a low, steady and predictable rate of inflation. The stimulative effect of introducing extra money into the economy is absorbed by inflation, so the combined effect is merely to create instability and insecurity in the market, which has a negative effect on productivity. Hence, the primary purpose of central banking is to provide a stable monetary framework within which the free market system may function to provide efficiency, productivity and prosperity.

While central banks do in fact see their role in light of a range of policy issues, the past four decades has witnessed a growing consensus that inflation targeting is the primary objective of the central bank.[40] The increasing adoption of monetarism in central bank policy after the collapse of Bretton Woods involves a curious paradox. While the Nixon Shock and the closing of the gold window can be seen as the culmination of a gradual decoupling of the value of money from a commodity standard, the basic assumption of monetarism is that money obeys the general laws of supply and demand which apply to ordinary commodities. The paradox of the adoption of monetarist central bank policy after the Bretton Woods collapse is thus, according to Graeber, that

38 Friedman, 'A Theoretical Framework for Monetary Analysis'.
39 Ibid., 3.
40 Davies and Green, *Banking on the Future*, 31.

even though money was no longer in any way based in gold, or in any other commodity, government and central-bank policy should be primarily concerned with carefully controlling the money supply to ensure that it acted *as if* it were a scarce commodity. Even as, at the same time, the financialization of capital meant that most money being invested in the marketplace was completely detached from any relation to production of commerce at all, but had become pure speculation.[41]

When central banks design their policies based on a theory insisting that even in a world where most money is electronic credit money that circulates in global and virtual financial markets, money still basically behaves as if it were a commodity, it is perhaps no wonder that the financial crisis of 2007–8 and the consequences of the ensuing credit crunch came as a surprise to most monetary policy makers. Based on their experiences in central banking, Davies and Green note:

> It is striking that much of the discussion of monetary policy in the last decade and more has said very little about what is happening in the financial system and how that impinges on both inflation and activity. Although in earlier years the focus was on controlling credit or money, the discrediting of the targeting of credit expansion, or of monetary aggregates, as a direct route to price stability seems to have had the consequence that the analysis of the flow of funds in aggregate, and as between sectors, which was a core feature of some central banks analysis some decades ago, almost faded from view . . . Even as recently as 2006 it was possible to read reflections on the conduct of monetary policy by well-respected central bankers that contained no reference whatsoever to the possibility that the behavior of the financial system might have some influence on the economy or vice versa.[42]

The adoption of monetarism in central banking leads to a regime of monetary post-politics. Post-politics, according to Žižek, is 'a regime whose self-legitimization would be thoroughly "technocratic",

41 Graeber, *Debt*, 375–6.

42 Davies and Green, *Banking on the Future*, 35–6.

presenting itself as a competent administration'.[43] This definition seems to be perfectly in line with the trend towards central bank independence which has in recent years increased to an extent suggesting a 'veritable revolution'.[44] Apparently, the management of the stock of money in sovereign nation-states is such a straightforward matter that we are perfectly safe leaving it to independent entities populated by technocrats, whose dispositions are only to a limited extent subject to political control by democratically elected officials in the same way as ordinary government entities. Once the primary objective of the central bank has been specified as inflation targeting, the execution is merely a matter of technocratic administration. In the US, the matter is even so simple that it may be left in the hands of an entity that is part of the private banking system.

FROM CREDIT TO POST-CREDIT MONEY

In this chapter, I have identified four aspects of the transformation of the monetary system after the collapse of Bretton Woods: Sophisticated credit payment systems allow bank credit to circulate as means of payment without being exchanged into cash. An efficient interbank money market allows commercial banks to clear payment balances among themselves with only minimal requirements for central bank money and cash. Deregulation of the banking sector lowers the legal requirements for commercial banks to hold cash and other liquid assets as reserves. The shift from credit rationing to discount rate variability as the primary aim of central bank policy removes politically determined limits on the supply of credit money. I want to argue that these trends all signify a monetary paradigm shift towards a regime of post-credit money. The quantitative aspect of this shift is illustrated in figures 3 to 6, which show an exponential increase in the ratio of credit money relative to fiat money. However, this is not merely a quantitative but also a qualitative shift.

We can understand the shift as a transformation of the relationship between state-created fiat money and private bank credit money. A simple way of thinking about credit money is as a merely symbolic representation of another underlying form of money, such as fiat

43 Žižek, *In Defense of Lost Causes*, 268.
44 Cukierman cited in Davies and Green, *Banking on the Future*, 141.

money. This is the kind of thinking that we find in the money multiplier model. In this model, the initial credit is created as a customer deposits €1,000 of cash fiat money in the bank. In other words, the depositor's credit with the bank is created when the bank borrows this amount of fiat money from him. The credit is a symbolic representation of the fact that the bank 'holds' the real cash for the customer. In the next step, the bank lends out €800 in cash fiat money. The credit of €800, which is now entered in the books of the bank, is a symbolic representation of the fact that the borrower now 'holds' the real cash, which actually belongs to the bank. The borrower now deposits this money with his own bank, thus creating another €800 worth of credit money. This money is then used to issue another loan to another customer and, as we have seen, the procedure may be iterated a certain number of times, each time creating an additional amount of credit money in the form of bank deposits.

In order to understand this philosophically, we shall return, for the third time, to Žižek's double conception of the real:

> In a first move, the Real is the impossible hard core which we cannot confront directly, but only through the lenses of a multitude of symbolic fictions, virtual formations. In a second move, this very hard core is purely virtual, actually, non-existent, an X which can be reconstructed only retroactively, from the multitude of symbolic formations which are 'all there actually is'.[45]

The relation between cash fiat money and credit money as conceived in the money multiplier model is captured by the first move of the real. In this model, cash is the 'impossible hard core' of credit creation. When this money is deposited with the bank, the bank turns around and uses it for the basis of the creation of a loan. The original real cash fiat money has now become a credit the depositor holds with the bank. Since the bank now only holds a fraction of the initial deposit in its vaults, it has become a form of money, which the depositor 'cannot confront directly'. The depositor's insistence on 'confronting' his money 'directly' would result in a run on the bank, whereby the system would collapse. Since the initial €1,000 of real cash money has now become the basis of up to €5,000 worth of credit money, it

45 Žižek, *The Parallax View*, 26.

can only be confronted 'through the lenses of a multitude of symbolic fictions, virtual formations'. Customer 1, 2 and 3 may simultaneously read in their account statements that they hold €1,000, €800 and €640 respectively in their deposit accounts. These statements constitute the 'multitude of symbolic fictions, virtual formations'. Even though the money multiplier model admits to a certain overdetermination insofar as the initial amount of real cash generates multiple symbolic representations, there is still an insistence that in the last instance, credit money is merely the symbolic representation of an underlying base of real fiat money cash.

As we have seen, the money multiplier model is inadequate when it comes to accounting for the way credit money is created in contemporary banking. Admittedly, we do not live in a completely cash-free society. However, I would still argue that the function of cash in contemporary society is first and foremost ideological rather than practical. The four trends identified in this chapter all serve to minimize the need for cash in the creation, circulation and exchange of credit money. When credit money is created though the simultaneous issuance of a loan and entering of a deposit to one and the same customer, there is no need for actual cash to change hands or to even be present. When the borrower uses his deposit to make payments with a debit card or another form of electronic payment, neither is there a need for cash. And when the two banks involved in the transaction use the interbank system to clear the balance, this can also be done without the use of cash.

The relationship between the real and the symbolic is different than what is implied in the money multiplier model. Credit money is not the symbolic representation of the movement of real cash fiat money. It is the other way around. The creation of credit money through the simultaneous issuance of a loan and entering of a deposit creates the image that there is somewhere a sum of real cash money which backs the whole transaction. This is captured by the second move in Žižek's account. The real cash was never there in the first place. It is 'purely virtual, actually, non-existent'. This is not to say that the role of cash is insignificant. For the system to function, it is crucial to maintain the fantasy that the cash is there to ultimately back the value of the credit money. However, the efficiency of the credit payment system and the interbank clearance system means that the cash does not need to be there in any physical form. The belief in the ultimate backing of cash means that the cash works even though it is purely virtual. This is the crux of central bank policy. As long as the central bank demonstrates its unconditional commitment to backing the commercial banks, it does not have to do anything to back the system. Credit money is 'all there actually is.' As central banks abandon quantitative credit rationing in favour of discount rate variability, they commit themselves to supplying whatever amount of liquidity is demanded by the commercial bank system. In this sense, the central banks provision of liquidity in response to demands created by commercial banks' issuance of credit is the 'retroactive reconstruction' of an 'X', which is required for the 'multitude of symbolic formations' of credit money to function even though they are 'all there actually is.'

When we apply the difference between the first and the second move in Žižek's account of the real to the creation of credit money in the banking system, we see the difference between credit money and post-credit money. This difference refers back to the notion of money without cash that was presented at the beginning of this chapter. Post-credit money is money without cash.

CHAPTER SIX

The Financialization of Money

It is obvious that the moon revolves around the earth. The gravitational pull of the earth exerts a force that has an effect on the moon's path of movement. Less obvious is the fact that the earth in a sense also revolves around the moon. The moon has a gravitational force of its own, which pulls the earth slightly away from the path it would otherwise follow. But because the mass of the earth is some eighty-one times bigger than the mass of the moon, the effects of the earth's gravitational pull on the moon are much larger than those of the moon's gravitational pull on the earth. The combined result is that both earth and moon orbit around the so-called 'barycentre', which constitutes the centre of gravity of the earth-moon system. Given the relative difference of the mass of the two bodies, the moon's orbit around the barycentre has an average radius of about 384,000 km, while the equivalent radius of the earth's orbit is merely 4,700 km. If we imagine some kind of cosmological event whereby the proportional relation between the mass of the two bodies were changed, this would also change the course of their movements around each other. If the moon was to become larger than the earth, this would cause the earth to start moving in a much larger orbit around the moon, while the moon would be positioned much closer to the barycentre of the system.

While such a major cosmic event does not seem to be immediately forthcoming, we can nonetheless use it as a metaphor for the shift that has occurred in the world of money and finance. In this chapter, we will see how money is not merely the medium of financialization. Today, the logic of financial markets pertains to the very constitution of money itself.

'DEBT IS THE OXYGEN OF FINANCIALIZATION'

A central implication of the Bretton Woods collapse is that today, the price of money is no longer determined within the political sphere of sovereign nation-states. This applies to gold prices, foreign exchange rates, interest rates and rates of inflation. As the volume of trading in financial markets has grown exponentially over the last four decades, the pricing of money has become increasingly difficult to determine and control politically. Markets for financial derivatives play a crucial role in this development:

> The gargantuan size of the derivatives market, especially for derivatives devoted to interest rates and currencies, creates a culture of circulation in which no nation-state, not even the United States, can regulate the exchange value of its currency, the character of its reserve assets, or the transnational movements of capital.[1]

The total notional value of outstanding derivatives contracts in 2010 was estimated at $1.2 quadrillion, which is twenty times larger than the total value of the annual productive output of the entire world economy.[2] (The latter figure stands at a mere $60 trillion.) In a sense, this represents a 'financial moon' that has grown twenty times bigger than the 'productive earth', with the consequence that the movement of the price of money, even in the productive economy, is determined by the 'gravitational pull' of financial markets rather than the other way around. Of course, the astronomical figure of $1.2 quadrillion should be taken with a grain of salt, as the notional value of a derivative refers to the notional value of the underlier even though the contract does not involve actual possession of this underlier. The actual exchange of money involved in the issuance and execution of the contract typically represents only a fraction of the notional amount. This is especially true in the case of interest rate swaps, which constitute a major portion of the total amount of derivatives contracts. But even if we are only talking about a fraction of $1.2 quadrillion, the main point still holds true: That's a lot of money!

In a radio interview, ex-trader Satyajit Das made the following succinct statement: 'Debt is the oxygen of financialization'. It refers to the fact that trading in financial markets is to a large extent carried out with borrowed money. This is done, for instance, by way of leveraged investments, which we will return to. The point is that the extent of financialization we have witnessed over past four decades, along

---

1 LiPuma and Lee, *Financial Derivatives and the Globalization of Risk*, 48.

2 DailyFinance, 'Big Risk'.

with the corresponding exponential growth in financial trading, have been made possible only through an excessive influx of credit money. The creation of this credit money has in turn become possible only through the transformation of the banking system described in the previous chapter. In brief, the monetary paradigm shift towards the regime of post-credit money also contains the condition of possibility for financialization.

But the causal relation between the creation of post-credit money and the growth of financial trading volume also works in the other direction. In the previous chapter, I identified four trends that constituted the conditions of possibility for the creation of post-credit money. The combination of these four trends allows banks to supply credit money in almost unlimited quantities as long as there is a demand for this money at the going price. If credit money was demanded only by companies wanting to invest in new initiatives to expand their capacity for productive output, this demand would be limited by the growth capacity of the productive economy. If this were the case, we would probably not have seen such extreme growth in the supply of credit money. However, the demand for credit money in contemporary capitalism is not restricted to productive investments. Much of the credit money that is created is used for activities whose productive output is questionable. This includes simple consumption but also speculation in financial markets, which is what will be concerned with here. One image of financial markets suggests that they serve to allocate excess capital in the economy towards investment opportunities that are the most productive, and thus the most profitable. While this is certainly one aspect of financial markets, it also seems reasonable to argue that they contain an element of unproductive speculation. The distinction between investment and speculation is at the heart of much debate about financial derivatives. We shall return to this issue.

For now, it suffices to note that the growth in the volume of financial markets also generates a growing demand for credit money insofar as financial trading is primarily carried out in credit money. Trading in financial markets is not just about the redistribution and circulation of existing money. As trading volumes grow, financial markets themselves generate their own demand for more money to come into being in order to service transactions in the market. This means that not only is debt and credit money the oxygen of financialization, but the growth in financial trading also leads to a financialization of money itself. In this chapter we will see how this financialization of money pertains not only to the price of money, such as commodity prices, foreign exchange rates and interest rates, but even to the very nature of money. The disproportionate volume and power of financial markets relative to sovereign nation-states and to producers and consumers of real goods means that the very question 'What is money?' is settled in these markets.

There are two main aspects to the following analysis of financial markets in general and financial derivatives in particular. The first aspect relates to the pricing of money in financial markets. The second aspect relates to a shift in the very constitution of money brought about by financialization. With Heidegger, the move from the first to the second aspect signifies a move from the sphere of the ontic to the sphere of the ontological. The idea is that not only do derivatives markets have an impact on the pricing of money, but the growing volumes signify a transformation in the ontological constitution (what Heidegger calls 'Seinsverfassung') of money. Bryan and Rafferty perform a comparable shift when they move beyond the speculation-hedging discussion and instead pose the question of whether derivatives are in themselves a wholly new form of money.[3] While I concur with the methodological shift in their inquiry, I want to propose a different interpretation of the meaning of derivatives for the ontology of money. Derivatives do not constitute a new form of money, although they do constitute a crucial component in a new system for the creation of money. While we should be careful how far we stretch Heideggerian terminology in our exploration of money – since this terminology was originally devised for the investigation of Dasein – it is tempting to conceptualize derivatives as an existential in the Being-in-the-world of money in contemporary financial capitalism. Heidegger unfolds his investigation of the meaning of Being as an investigation of the relationship between Being and time: 'The primordial ontological basis for Dasein's existentiality is temporality.'[4] A key point in the investigation is that Dasein is constituted as Being-towards-death.[5]

3 Bryan and Rafferty, 'Financial Derivatives and the Theory of Money', 135.
4 Heidegger, *Being and Time*, §. 45.
5 Ibid., §. 53.

As we have seen, derivatives are constructed through a peculiar configuration among past, present and future. Derivatives express a present price that represents a specific anticipation of the future, which is derived from the past volatility of the underlier. As these instruments come to play an increasingly central role in the functioning of financial markets where the supply and price of money is determined, they bring about a reconfiguration of the temporal horizon of money itself. Translating Heidegger into the study of money, we can say that 'the primordial ontological basis for the existentiality of money is temporality'. This means that the reconfiguration of the temporal horizon of money itself, created by the proliferation of derivatives trading, is a reconfiguration of the ontology of money itself.

$1,200,000,000,000,000

If the Bretton Woods collapse marked the end of a particular monetary paradigm, it was succeeded by another event that marked the beginning of a new paradigm. This event was the founding of institutionalized markets for trading in financial derivatives. In 1972, the Chicago Mercantile Exchange (CME) opened a market for currency futures, and in 1973 the Chicago Board of Trade (CBOT) began organized trading in stock options.[6] The opening of these two markets can be conceived of as the institutional counterpart to the innovations in financial theory that I described in chapter two. Black, Scholes and Merton had discovered a way to calculate the price of an option, and now there was a place where these financial products could be traded systematically. The idea of organized trading in derivatives was not in itself new. Since the nineteenth century, futures contracts on various agricultural products and other physical commodities had been traded in both of these exchanges. The novelty of the idea was the creation of derivatives in which the underlying assets were not physical commodities but rather financial products themselves.

It is almost impossible to overestimate the significance of the innovation of financial derivatives for the economic development of the world over the following decades. In hindsight, it is ironic to read

---

6 MacKenzie, *An Engine, Not a Camera*, 147–50.

Merton's reflections on the importance of options in the introduction to his theory of rational options pricing from 1973:

> Because options are specialized and relatively unimportant financial securities, the amount of time and space devoted to the development of a pricing theory might be questioned.[7]

Since then, the volume of trading in financial derivatives has increased exponentially. In 1970, the outstanding amount of derivatives was only a few million dollars. As derivatives trading started picking up, this sum grew to about $100 million in 1980. In 1990 the number was nearly $100 billion, and then nearly $100 trillion in 2000.[8] The Bank for International Settlements valued the outstanding notional amount of over-the-counter (OTC) derivatives at $632,679 trillion by the end of 2012, while some experts, as noted above, estimate the total outstanding amount of derivatives to be as much as $1.2 quadrillion.[9]

The emergence and evolution of financial derivatives trading signifies a new paradigm for the making of money. It is important to note here the double meaning of 'making money', as financial derivatives play a crucial role with regard to both the appropriation of shares of the existing pool of money in the world and the process by which new money come into the world. While the first role is perhaps reasonably easy to see, the latter is less obvious. We can distinguish between the two roles by invoking Heidegger's distinction between the ontic and the ontological domains, as discussed earlier in this chapter.

Looking backwards from the perspective of contemporary finance, the Bretton Woods Agreement essentially functioned as an open-ended American call and put option. (An American option gives the holder the right to exercise the contract at any time between issue and expiry. This differs from the European option, which can only be exercised at the exact time of expiry.) By guaranteeing the convertibility of the US dollar to gold, the US Treasury was effectively

7 Merton, 'Theory of Rational Option Pricing', 164–5.

8 LiPuma and Lee, *Financial Derivatives and the Globalization of Risk*, 47.

9 BIS, *Semiannual OTC derivatives statistics at end-December 2012*; DailyFinance, 'Big Risk'.

offering anyone 'the option but not the obligation' to exchange US dollars for gold, or vice versa, at a given strike price at any given time in the future. In a similar fashion, the pegging of the currencies of a number of other Western nations to the US dollar can also be conceived as a series of options. These 'options' were essentially offered for free. As long as the Bretton Woods member states and the US in particular were able to exert control over the financial markets by limiting the price fluctuations between different currencies and controlling the price of gold, the actual value of these options was also close to zero, since the volatility of their underliers was kept in check.

An immediate way of understanding the emergence of financial derivatives and their explosive proliferation is to see them simply as a response to demand in the market. A hallmark in the development of modernity is the principle of the division of labour. We find this idea in Adam Smith as well as all in the founding fathers of modern sociology, Durkheim, Weber and Simmel. With post-industrialism, this principle extends beyond the borders of the nation-state, as entire regions of the world specialize in different elements of the production process. We can refer to this as the multinationalization of capitalism. As the invention, production, marketing, sale and financing of products become dispersed over different nation-states, companies become vulnerable to price fluctuations between different national currencies. The collapse of Bretton Woods signifies the inability of (Western) nation-states to provide monetary stability in a globalized world. While Bretton Woods was an *inter*national system, the markets for financial derivatives comprise a truly global system. Some commentators argue that derivatives constitute an entirely new form of money that fulfills the functions no longer provided by state-based money.[10] Here is how Bryan and Rafferty account for the shift:

> It is in the context of this rather different monetary system, where money cannot be explained by reference to the state – where volatile shifts in exchange rates are inexplicable and beyond state regulatory capacity – that derivatives, particularly interest-rate and cross-currency interest-rate swaps, have come to the fore. Derivatives

10 Bryan and Rafferty, 'Money in Capitalism or Capitalist Money?'; Bryan and Rafferty, 'Financial Derivatives and the Theory of Money'; Pryke and Allen, 'Monetized time-space: derivatives – money's 'new imaginary'?'

provide what nation-state fiat money could not provide on a global scale: they secure some degree of guarantee on the relative values of different monetary units.[11]

Since nation-states of the Bretton Woods system no longer offer free 'options' on the price of gold and the fluctuations between currencies, private agents in the derivatives markets take over the task of providing financial products that serve the equivalent purpose. Instead of money being grounded in an asymmetrical relation between the market and the state, money is now regulated in symmetrical relations between different actors within the market. Trust in money is based on the imagination of a network of mutual insurance that disperses the damaging effects of fluctuations in the money market over a great number of actors, thus minimizing the effects on the individual actor.[12] In this understanding, derivatives markets emerge because they have a superior capacity for risk management in a globalized world. Derivatives offer the opportunity for multinational companies and other agents in the market that are exposed to the price volatility of financial assets to hedge their exposure to financial risks.

An example of this way of thinking may be found in Chicago Board of Trade's own account of the function of derivatives trading. In the publication *Action in the Market Place*, CBOT presents the following notion of risk:

> Price risk exists throughout business. In agriculture, for instance, a prolonged drought may affect a farmer's crop supply as well as the income he receives. The drought also may affect the price paid by grain companies for corn, wheat, soybeans, and oats. Those prices, in turn, may directly impact consumer prices for cereals, cooking oils, salad dressings, bread, meat, and poultry. For manufacturers, diminished supply – caused by an extended labor strike or embargo of a raw material – could result in a sharp price increase of a specific manufactured product. These economic factors may directly affect the price manufacturers and consumers pay for an array of commodities, ranging from gasoline and home heating oil to jewelry. For a

11 Bryan and Rafferty, 'Money in Capitalism or Capitalist Money?', 87.

12 Bryan and Rafferty, 'Financial Derivatives and the Theory of Money'.

> bank, savings and loan, or other financial institution, an interest rate change affects the rate the institution pays on certificates of deposit. This, in turn, influences its lending rates. There is no escaping the varying degrees of price fluctuation, i.e. risk, in every sector of today's economy. Hedging in the futures markets minimizes the impact of these undesirable price changes.[13]

Just as in the example illustrating the introduction of money into a barter economy, we once again encounter here the figure of the farmer. In this case, the farmer functions to show that particular notions of risk and time are governed by the predictability and unpredictability of nature. The farmer's demand for a futures contract comes from the fact that his production process is determined by the rhythm of the seasons and the time it takes for his crops to grow. There is a 'naturally' determined delay from the time of investment to the time when the crops can be harvested and sold. This period of delay exposes the farmer to the risk of price fluctuations in the markets where his crops are eventually sold. These risks also seem to have their origin in nature insofar as prices in the markets for agricultural products fluctuate with supply volumes. These volumes are determined by the weather conditions during the period when crops are grown and harvested. Invoking the image of the farmer performs a kind of 'naturalization of risk'.

The CBOT account also gives examples of the kind of risks faced by manufacturers and banks. It is interesting to note how the account takes the form of a listing of principally equivalent examples. The impact of a drought on crop prices is equivalent to the impact of a strike on goods prices, which is equivalent to the impact of interest rates on lending rates. It seems that similar types of risks exist in farming, manufacturing and the pricing of money itself. In other words, the account presupposes continuity between markets for the buying and selling of physical products, markets for the buying and selling of human labour, and markets for the buying and selling of money. The aforementioned naturalization of risk pertains to all kinds of markets.

In light of the functioning of contemporary financial markets, this account of derivatives is at best romantic and at worst downright

13 Chicago Board of Trade, *Action in the Marketplace*, 10.

misleading. Agricultural and other commodity futures may have been the historical predecessor of financial derivatives, but today, trading in commodity-based derivatives makes up less than 1 percent of the total market.[14] Derivatives markets are through and through dominated by trading in derivatives where the underlier is some form of financial indicator with a highly abstract relation to the actual productive economy. Such indicators are interest rates, currency exchange rates, different forms of price indexes, default rates, etc. It should perhaps be added that even the image of farming in the example is romantic. In order to stay competitive, many farmers today have increased their production capacity through heavy expansion and expensive investments, turning their farm into industrial agricultural factories. As these initiatives have been financed largely through debt, the most significant risk to the sustained profitability of many farms is not posed by the whims of Mother Nature but rather by the possibility of increased interest rates in global financial markets. These farmers have been subject to the phenomenon of financialization.

The difference between commodity-based derivatives and financial derivatives is not merely one of quantity. There are also significant qualitative differences which are easily overlooked when the image of the agricultural future is used as a model for derivatives in general. The farmer example invokes the image of an asymmetrical exchange between a financial agent (the trader selling the future contract) and a non-financial agent (the farmer buying the future contract). In this image, the future functions in a way similar to private insurance. Just as insurance provides a form of security to the buyer, allowing him to concentrate on other things in life without having to worry about possible accidents in the future, so does the future contract allow the farmer to concentrate on his core (non-financial) activity – farming – without having to worry about possible price fluctuations in the market.

Prior to the 2007–8 financial crisis, the largest bank in Denmark, Danske Bank, ran a series of commercials built around the slogan 'Do what you do best'. The message of the campaign was that the bank would take care of the customer's (boring) financial matters, thereby setting the customers free to use their talents in their real

---

14 LiPuma and Lee, *Financial Derivatives and the Globalization of Risk*, 118.

(non-financial) life. The campaign was terminated at the onset of the financial crisis. This campaign and the farmer example imply an image of financial markets and financial products as essentially a service to the real productive economy, or simply to real life. Financial products, and financial derivatives in particular, are sophisticated risk-management tools which allow the transferring of particular forms of risk to those parties best suited to absorb these risks. This image is at the heart of modern finance, and we can trace it back to Markowitz's initial ideas about portfolio selection. As we have seen, proper portfolio selection allows the investor not only to manage risk but even to make risk disappear through diversification. When this image is applied to derivatives, they are seen as tools for hedging and for the maintenance of efficiency in financial markets. They come to benefit the general economy. This image was propounded, for instance, by Federal Reserve Board Chairman Alan Greenspan in a now infamous remark made in 2003:

> Although the benefits and costs of derivatives remain the subject of spirited debate, the performance of the economy and the financial system in recent years suggests that those benefits have materially exceeded the costs . . . The use of a growing array of derivatives and the related application of more-sophisticated methods for measuring and managing risk are key factors underpinning the enhanced resilience of our largest financial intermediaries. Derivatives have permitted financial risks to be unbundled in ways that have facilitated both their measurement and their management . . . As a result, not only have individual financial institutions become less vulnerable to shocks from underlying risk factors, but also the financial system as a whole has become more resilient.[15]

RISK AS REAL

In the analysis of financial markets in chapters one and two, we saw how risk can be framed through Žižek's notion of the real. Financial derivatives are a sophisticated way of calculating, pricing and essentially symbolizing a wide variety of risks, which then allows these

15 Greenspan, 'Corporate Governance'.

risks to be exchanged for money. The philosophical point here is that the process of symbolization is not merely a neutral recording of events in the order of the real. The real also emerges as the very product of the process of symbolization. Let us invoke once again Žižek's account of this double movement:

> In a first move, the Real is the impossible hard core which we cannot confront directly, but only through the lenses of a multitude of symbolic fictions, virtual formations. In a second move, this very hard core is purely virtual, actually, non-existent, an X which can be reconstructed only retroactively, from the multitude of symbolic formations which are 'all there actually is'.[16]

This is a very precise account of the relation between risks and financial derivatives. In a first move, risk appears in the form of unpredictable price fluctuations in a particular financial market that may have severe consequences for agents dependent on selling and buying assets in the market. Price fluctuations in the oil market may, for instance, have severe consequences for a commercial airline. Only those events that involve an element of unpredictability have the nature of risks. This means that by definition, 'we cannot confront' these events 'directly'. One of the crucial consequences of the Efficient Market Hypothesis is precisely that price fluctuations in financial markets can be regarded as random. Any predictable future event that is relevant to assets in the market is always already incorporated into the current price. Prices only change when something unpredictable happens. Under this assumption, we cannot predict future oil prices with absolute certainty. We can, however, confront them through probability theory. Using historical data on oil prices, we can calculate the probability of a 10 percent price increase within a given future period of time. Calculations of different probabilities constitute Žižek's 'multitude of symbolic fictions', and the implied image of the long run constitutes a 'virtual formation'. On the basis of these calculations, oil futures may be priced and offered in the market as insurance against the risk of price increases.

In a second move, the particular pricing of futures and options in the derivatives markets projects certain expectations onto the

---

16 Žižek, *The Parallax View*, 26.

underlying market from which the derivative is derived. If the price of oil futures goes up, this is a signal that instability in the market for oil is expected. This signal is not only read by agents trading in the derivatives markets, but also agents trading in the underlying market for oil. In many cases, agents trade simultaneously in both markets. The trading behaviour in the underlying market is highly influenced by trading in the corresponding derivatives market. This means that if oil prices do begin to spike or fall radically, it is impossible to determine whether this is a reflection of changes in the supply and demand of actual oil, or whether it is merely the result of endogenous mechanisms in the market. In this second move, the price fluctuations become 'purely virtual' and their causes 'can be reconstructed only retroactively, from the multitude of symbolic formations'. In other words, the price fluctuations can only be explained in terms of changes in the symbolizations within the market itself.

The famous stock market crash of October 1987, sometimes referred to as Black Monday, provides the classic illustration of the way that exogenous and endogenous risks in financial markets can become reciprocal to the point of being indistinguishable. The crash happened on a day when there were no significant or abnormal events reported in the financial news. Nevertheless, financial markets all over the world experienced sudden drastic declines, with the Dow Jones falling by 22.61 percent. This is still the largest relative one day decline in the history of the Dow Jones Industrial Average. The fact that no consensus about the actual cause of the crash has been reached is itself an indication of the way that the real 'can be reconstructed only retroactively, from the multitude of symbolic formations'.

Donald MacKenzie, among others, has suggested that the widespread use of so-called portfolio insurance played a key role in the crisis.[17] Portfolio insurance is a trading strategy devised by Hayne Leland in the 1970s. It is built on Black, Scholes and Merton's theory of options pricing.[18] The idea is to offer clients an insurance against losses to their portfolio of stocks if stock prices fall below a predefined floor. Clients pay a premium for this service, which allows the insurer to make a profit. The provider of portfolio insurance hedges his own

---

17 MacKenzie, *An Engine, Not a Camera*, 179–210.

18 Bernstein, *Capital Ideas: The Improbable Origins of Modern Wall Street*, 269–94.

position by building a so-called replicating portfolio of stocks and cash that mirrors the payout of a put option on the client's portfolio. The replicating portfolio is continuously adjusted according to relevant price fluctuations so that whenever stock prices fall, the insurer moves from stocks to cash, and whenever the same prices increase, he moves back from cash to stocks. If stock prices fall below the predefined floor, the insurer will have realized all his stocks in cash and will be able to compensate the client out of the profits he has made on the way down.

At the time, stock options were not systematically traded in a way that made it feasible for the client to just buy options on his entire portfolio directly. This created a market for the provision of portfolio insurance through the creation of these 'synthetic' put options. In 1982, the Chicago Mercantile Exchange established an organized market for trading futures on the S&P 500 index. These futures allowed for a much simpler and more efficient implementation of the strategy of portfolio insurance. The insurer could substitute the buying and selling of stocks with the buying and selling of index futures, as long as the portfolio under insurance was correlated with the index. By 1987, the provision of portfolio insurance had become big business, covering an estimated $100 billion worth of stocks.[19] Since all providers of portfolio insurance were using similar theories to adjust their replicating portfolios, their buying and selling of assets would tend to happen in sync with each other. The hypothesis for what happened on Black Monday is that minor price declines in the market triggered the simultaneous selling of stocks by a range of portfolio insurance providers, which in turn further lowered prices, thus triggering further selling, and so on. One of the preconditions for the functioning of portfolio insurance is that market prices move continuously so that the insurance provider has sufficient time and opportunity to adjust his portfolio. However, the simultaneous acting of several agents in the market caused prices to jump instantaneously in a discontinuous fashion. Again, this would add to the self-propelling mechanisms of the market, producing endogenous effects that drive down prices.

Even though this theory explains the acceleration of the crisis by endogenous factors, it does not deny that there might have been

---

19 MacKenzie, *An Engine, Not a Camera*, 182.

exogenous events that set the crisis in motion in the first place. This is further supported by the fact that the crisis started in Hong Kong, where portfolio insurance and programme trading was not practiced at the time. While the initial cause of the crash may have been some exogenous real event in Hong Kong or some other place on the planet, in retrospect the impact of this event is indistinguishable from endogenous mechanisms in the symbolic order of the market.

The account of risk in terms of Žižek's notion of the real reveals the ambivalent relation between derivatives and risk. We have already seen how some accounts project the image of derivatives as tools for risk-management that provide stability in financial markets by offering agents the opportunity to hedge. In contrast to this image, critics argue that derivatives are themselves the cause of significant price fluctuations in financial markets. According to this argument, derivatives produce and perpetuate the very same risks they allegedly serve to manage:

> At the core of the process is a self-generating and self-perpetuating circularity . . . Corporations doing business transnationally employ derivatives to offset the repercussions of currency volatility; the provision of sufficient market liquidity requires the participation of speculative capital which tends to amplify volatility; the amplification of volatility both increases the need for the corporations to hedge their currency exposure and the profit opportunities for speculatively driven capital. From this perspective, financial derivatives do not simply exploit price fluctuations around the mean (as conventional economics would have us believe) but actively create them; thus they do not simply express economic reality but are central to the creation of circulatory capital. Historically, financial derivatives markets have expanded so globally and exponentially because they produce the conditions of their own necessity.[20]

We see here that there may indeed be an initial (real) demand for financial derivatives from actual businesses in the productive economy who want to hedge their exposure to currency exchange risks or other kinds of financial risks. But when this demand is met by the provision of derivatives in financial markets, this is not merely a

20 LiPuma and Lee, *Financial Derivatives and the Globalization of Risk*, 38–9.

symbolic reflection of the initial real demand. The provision of derivatives creates a kind of overdetermination, and the end result is a situation where the initial demand becomes indistinguishable from the demand created by the effects of derivatives trading itself. In fact, the ambivalence of the situation reaches a point where it can be argued that the initial demand was never there in the first place. The demand for derivatives as means to hedge against the risks and volatility produced by the very same derivatives is 'all there actually is.'

ARBITRAGE AND MARKET EFFICIENCY

Related, albeit not identical, to the issue of hedging vs. speculation and stability vs. instability is the issue of arbitrage. As we saw in chapter two, the emergence of financial derivatives opens up the possibility of exploiting a whole array of new arbitrage opportunities. Derivatives markets have the status of a kind of meta-market in relation to the markets where the underlying assets are traded. This means that arbitrage opportunities may appear not only when similar assets are traded at different prices in different markets, but also when the pricing of a derivative does not correspond to the market behaviour of the underlying asset. I have referred to the former as horizontal arbitrage and the latter as vertical arbitrage. The emergence of financial derivatives has multiplied the ways in which traders can compare, connect and combine different markets in order profit from arbitrage.

It is uncontroversial to note that derivatives may be used to exploit arbitrage opportunities. The initial success of the hedge fund Long Term Capital Management is often referred to as an example of arbitrage exploitation through the use of derivatives. The fund was founded in 1994 and it is remarkable not only for its sophisticated use of financial theory but also for the actual inclusion of Robert C. Merton and Myron Scholes as partners in the company. One of the strategies applied by LTCM was so-called swap-spread arbitrage, which exploited price discrepancies between the rate of interest on US government bonds and the price of US dollar interest-rate swaps.[21] The swap allows one party to pay a fixed rate of interest in return for a floating rate of interest, while the counter party takes the opposite

21 MacKenzie, *An Engine, Not a Camera*, 291–2.

position. LTCM would buy bonds yielding a fixed rate of interest, finance the purchase through a repo – where the bonds are held by a creditor as collateral against a loan – and pay a fixed interest rate on the swap while receiving a floating rate of interest on the swap. The arbitrage consisted in the spread between the interest rate on the swap and the interest rate on the bond. This is an example of vertical arbitrage between the price in the derivatives swap (meta-)market and the price in the underlying bond market. Even though this spread was minimal at the time when LTCM initiated the trade, the fund was able to leverage the deal and earn a profit of $35 million dollars.[22]

The concept of arbitrage is related to the idea of market efficiency. In an efficient market, arbitrage is by definition impossible. Absence of the kind of risk-free profit inherent in arbitrage is the very criterion for market efficiency. As we have seen, the Efficient Market Hypothesis plays an ambivalent role in finance theory. In Kantian terminology, it can be understood as an analytic proposition about the characteristics to which an empirical market would have to conform in order to qualify as efficient. The EMH can also be understood as a synthetic proposition about the actual state of empirical financial markets.

The status of the EMH is at the core of the dispute between neoclassical finance and behavioural finance. Proponents of neoclassical finance defend the EMH not only as an analytic proposition, but also as a synthetic proposition that has significant validity as a description of actual markets.[23] Experiments in behavioural economics show that actual human beings rarely conform to the ideals of fully rational agents suggested by neoclassical economics, and that agents in financial markets are subject to various kinds of cognitive bias such as overconfidence,[24] overreaction,[25] loss aversion,[26] etc. While recognizing the validity of such experiments, neoclassical proponents of the EMH may argue that, even though some agents act irrationally, their behaviour is outweighed by other rational agents in the market, who take advantage of their 'erroneous' trading through arbitrage, thereby bringing prices in the market back to a state of efficiency.

---

22 Ibid., 219.

23 Fama, 'Market Efficiency, Long-Term Returns, and Behavioral Finance'.

24 Gervais and Odean, 'Learning to Be Overconfident'.

25 Bondt and Thaler, 'Further Evidence on Investor Overreaction and Stock Market Seasonality'.

26 Kahneman and Tversky, 'Prospect Theory'.

Against this view, proponents of behavioural finance argue that the element of irrationality in markets may exceed what can be arbitraged away. This leads to the suggestion that actual empirical markets do not conform to the definition of market efficiency.[27]

Even though authors in the field of behavioural finance are critical of the EMH as a synthetic proposition about empirical markets, their approach still retains the notion of market efficiency as a true analytic proposition. Behavioural finance relies on notions of market efficiency and rationality as benchmarks against which the behaviour of actual markets and agents can be measured. Hence, the philosophical depth of the ongoing dispute between neoclassical finance and behavioural finance is not as significant as it might immediately seem. In the words of Robert Shiller: 'In an important sense both maximizing finance and behavioral finance were born together; they are sisters'.[28] Behavioural finance does not dispute the notion that it makes sense to speak of market efficiency as an ideal state to which actual markets could in principle conform. The approach only questions the extent to which actual markets do in fact conform to the ideal. The two sisters may differ with respect to the status of the EMH as a synthetic proposition, but they stick together when it comes to defending the status of the EMH as a sensible analytic proposition. With Žižek, we can say that the controversy between neoclassical finance and behavioural finance is merely a superficial dispute that ultimately serves to maintain the idea of market efficiency as an ideological fantasy.

The crucial issue, which is suppressed by the controversy between neoclassical finance and behavioural finance, is the extent to which trading in financial markets has the capacity to produce certain effects in the underlying economy, which may then subsequently be exploited. The EMH and the related components of neoclassical finance theory are modelled on a certain image of the stock market. These ideas are the products of an era when financial markets had significantly different characteristics than today. As noted by Fox:

> The efficient market hypothesis, the capital asset pricing model, the Black–Scholes option-pricing model, and all the other major

27 Shiller, 'From Efficient Market Theory to Behavioral Finance'.

28 Shiller, 'Tools for Financial Innovation', 2.

> elements of modern rationalist finance arose toward the end of a long era of market stability characterized by tight government regulation and the long memories of those who had survived the Depression. These theories' heavy reliance on calmly rational markets was to some extent the artifact of a regulated, relatively conservative financial era – and it paved the way for deregulation and wild exuberance.[29]

In other words, the fantasy of the efficient market paved the way for the transformation, deregulation and exponential expansion of financial markets that has taken place since the 1970s. It may very well be that at the time of its inception, the EMH did indeed make sense as a benchmark against which the state of empirical financial markets could be measured. However, the relationship between financial markets and the underlying economy today has become so much more complex that even the idea of measuring whether 'prices 'fully reflect' available information' is a gross simplification, if not highly misleading. Let us review once again Fama's original statement of the Efficient Market Hypothesis:

> The primary role of the capital market is allocation of ownership of the economy's capital stock. In general terms, the ideal is a market in which prices provide accurate signals for resource allocation: that is, a market in which firms can make production-investment decisions, and investors can choose among the securities that represent ownership of firms' activities under the assumption that security prices at any time 'fully reflect' all available information. A market in which prices always 'fully reflect' available information is called 'efficient'.[30]

When Fama wrote this passage in 1970, markets for financial derivatives were virtually non-existent. Today, their volume is expressed in sixteen-digit dollar figures. This transformation is not just one of quantity. The evolution of financial derivatives markets implies a qualitative transformation of the ontology of financial markets themselves. We can see what this means by looking into the

29 Fox, *The Myth of the Rational Market*, 320.
30 Fama, 'Efficient Capital Markets', 383.

philosophical implications of the notion that 'prices 'fully reflect' all available information'.

According to Black, Scholes and Merton, the price of a derivative in the form of an option expresses the volatility of the underlying asset – for instance, a stock, a bond, or a currency exchange rate. The efficiency of a derivatives market is hence determined by the extent to which the prices of the derivatives 'fully reflect' all available information about the volatility of the underlying asset. In other words, the price of a derivative is a symbolic expression of the risk of price fluctuations in the underlying asset. The question is whether this risk of price fluctuation in the underlying assets is independent from the very act of symbolization performed in the pricing and trading of the derivative. It is obvious that the price of the derivative is *derived* from the characteristics of the underlier. But is it reasonable to assume that the causality runs only one way?

If we think of derivatives and risk management through the image of the farmer hedging against unpredictable weather conditions, it makes sense to think of derivatives prices as merely a reflection of the risk of price fluctuations in the underlier. The pricing and trading of corn futures do not have any immediate impact on the probability of drought. The problem arises, however, when this conception of risk as a natural phenomenon is extended to the pricing of financial derivatives, where the underlier is itself subject to the social interaction between agents in a market. LiPuma and Lee comment on this issue:

> For the most part, those who base their calculations and global strategies on this conception of risk, both in financial circles and in much of the academy, see it simply as the contemporary elaboration of a universal confrontation with uncertainty. The idea is that humans everywhere, from time immemorial to the present day, have sought to master and manage risk, attempting to offset uncertainty and forecast the future to increase the chance of economic success . . . The epistemological premise underlying this perspective is that though risk is inherently connected to a time and a place and inherently circumscribed by the here and now, it is an acultural and ahistorical species of knowledge . . . This view of risk derives from the natural sciences. So it assumes that the financial community can grasp risk by using natural science models, such as, literally, the equations that capture the collisions of atomic particles. This natural

> science view of risk is extremely appealing because it allows for the use of mathematical statistics, which, in turn, allows the financial community to price derivatives precisely. But precision is very different from accuracy, and however appealing the natural science model may be, using it is a disabling mistake.[31]

If the price of a derivative were to 'fully reflect' all available information about the underlying asset, it would have to reflect not only the asset's inherent risk of price fluctuation, but also the potential impact of the very pricing and trading of the derivative on the price of the underlying asset. Given the volume of contemporary trading in financial derivatives, it is naive to think that this trading can take place without any effects on the markets for the underlying assets. There are myriad ways in which causality can run from derivatives markets to the underlying market, rather than the other way. Let us review just a few examples:

As oil prices hit a record high in 2004, it became apparent that 60 percent of the positions in oil derivatives markets were held by non-oil interests, that is, traders and investors with no use for physical oil.[32] These speculators were merely trying to make a profit in the anticipation of prices going even higher. This speculation had an impact on the actual prices of oil, as the positions in the derivatives markets created a kind of virtual or speculative demand for oil, thus upsetting the laws of actual demand and supply in the market. Traders would buy up oil in order to settle or hedge derivatives contracts, thus increasing the demand for and also the price of oil. In other words, trading in derivatives markets served to bring about and exacerbate those very same arbitrage opportunities that traders were aiming to exploit. And by the same token, the oil derivatives trading created the kind of risk and price volatility in the underlying market which the derivatives were allegedly created to manage in the first place.

A key feature of derivatives is their inherent capacity to enable traders to take leveraged positions. With a relatively low investment it is possible to make a relatively large profit. The holder of a stock will receive a 10 percent return on the initial investment if the price of the stock increases 10 percent. The holder of a stock option can, however,

---

31 LiPuma and Lee, *Financial Derivatives and the Globalization of Risk*, 54.

32 Das, *Traders, Guns, and Money*, 30.

earn several hundred percent on the initial investment (depending on the specifics of the contract) if the price of the underlying stock increases 10 percent. However, if the stock price does not increase, the holder of the stock will have lost no money, whereas the entire investment of the stock option holder is lost. Leverage not only multiplies the ratio between investment capital and risk incurred. It also multiplies how much a given amount of capital can impact market prices. If the aim is to move prices in a market by buying and selling large positions, the derivatives market offers a much 'cheaper' way of doing this than simply trading in the underlying market. The impact of $100m worth of oil futures on oil prices is several times larger than the simple purchase of $100m worth of oil. The ratio between investment capital and market impact is even greater when speculative positions are financed with borrowed money.

This technique of leverage through financing is one of the defining characteristics of hedge funds. These funds use investor capital as collateral for borrowing money at amounts several times greater than the initial investment. Combined with their willingness to take speculative positions in derivatives markets, hedge funds employ this leverage technique to bring about capital movements that are large enough to move prices in certain markets. Through leverage, some hedge funds may gain control of enough speculative capital to take on entire nation-states in struggles to move the price of a currency.[33] The classic reference here is George Soros's Quantum Fund, which played a key role in bringing about the devaluation of the British pound in 1992 and the Thai baht in 1997.[34] In both cases, the fund made large transactions selling and shorting the currencies prior to their devaluations, thus precipitating the price fluctuations from which it then made profits of an estimated $1 billion and $750 million respectively.

Derivatives markets not only reflect underlying economic indicators. These markets have become in themselves crucial market indicators that are used to inform not only economic but also political decisions. This means that price fluctuations in derivatives markets can drive economic events in the underlying economy. LiPuma and Lee have analyzed this phenomenon:

---

33 LiPuma and Lee, *Financial Derivatives and the Globalization of Risk*, 49.

34 Mallaby, *More Money Than God*, 153–67; 198–206.

For an example of how this works we need look no further than the Brazilian presidential election of 2002. When it became clear that Luiz da Silva of the Workers' Party stood a reasonable chance of being elected – to underline its identity, the American press referred to it exclusively as the socialist or leftist Workers' party – the principal players in the Latin American financial markets began to sell and short the Brazilian currency. By the time da Silva was elected, the reale had depreciated by more than 30 percent against the dollar and euro. The secretary of the U.S. Treasury, Paul H. O'Neill (the retired CEO of a corporation that participated in the derivatives market), predicted that the derivatives markets would continue monitoring da Silva's performance until he could 'assure them that he is not a crazy person', hell bent on economic redistribution and social justice (quoted in the New York Times, 29 October 2002, 3). During the electoral campaign, da Silva's opponents cited the reaction of the derivatives markets as a compelling reason to vote against him.[35]

Da Silva was in fact elected despite the opinion of the derivatives markets. Still, his economic room for maneuvering was severely restricted when he came into office, since much of the funds that he might have used to bring about social and economic reforms had to be used to meet foreign debt obligations, which had increased due to the depreciation of the reale. In this sense, the negative expectations towards da Silva represented by price fluctuations in the derivatives markets in themselves had a severe impact on the Brazilian economy. This means that when politicians and voters evaluate a political programme, they have to take into account not only the direct effects of the economic initiatives, but also the indirect effects of the financial markets' perceptions of the effects of the programme. It does not matter whether the financial markets are right or wrong, since the dominant beliefs held in the market will have an immediate effect on interest rates, currency exchange rates and other crucial indicators, with direct consequences for the nation's economy. These beliefs held by the market thus serve as a self-fulfilling prophecies.

---

35 LiPuma and Lee, *Financial Derivatives and the Globalization of Risk*, 58–9.

UNKNOWN KNOWNS OF DERIVATIVES MARKETS

The claim that the price of a particular derivative 'reflects' information about the underlying market to which the derivative refers is basically a claim that derivatives markets incorporate knowledge about the underlying market. The debate between neoclassical finance and behavioural finance can be understood as a debate about the extent to which this knowledge incorporates 'all available information' in a rational fashion. Regardless of the outcome of this debate, it still leaves another more fundamental question untouched. This question concerns the epistemology of the knowledge incorporated into financial derivatives markets.

Warren Buffett has famously referred to derivatives as 'financial weapons of mass destruction'.[36] This analogy may serve as an occasion to invoke what Žižek refers to as 'Rumsfeldian epistemology' in order to understand the kind, or perhaps rather the kind*s*, of knowledge incorporated into financial derivatives. In 2002, Donald Rumsfeld held a press conference where he tried to justify the American invasion of Iraq despite the absence of evidence that Saddam Hussein was developing weapons of mass destruction. Rumsfeld made a distinction between different kinds of knowledge, which Žižek subsequently picked up. This is Žižek quoting and commenting on Rumsfeld:

> 'There are known knowns. These are things we know that we know. There are known unknowns. That is to say, there are things that we know we don't know. But there are also unknown unknowns. There are things we don't know we don't know.' What he Rumsfeld forgot to add was the crucial fourth term: the 'unknown knowns', things we don't know that we know – which is precisely the Freudian unconscious. If Rumsfeld thought that the main dangers in the confrontation with Iraq were the 'unknown unknowns', the threats from Saddam the nature of which we did not even suspect, what we should reply is that the main dangers are, on the contrary, the 'unknown knowns', the disavowed beliefs and suppositions we are not even aware of adhering to ourselves.[37]

36 Buffett, 'Chairman's Letter'.

37 Žižek, *In Defense of Lost Causes*, 457.

The brilliance of the Black and Scholes formula for option pricing is that it enables the pricing of derivatives on the basis of known knowns. All the five variables going into the formula are things we know that we know. These variables have already been listed in chapter two: (1) The strike price, i.e. the price at which the stock can be bought at the expiry of the option (X). (2) Time to expiry of the option (τ). (3) The current price of the underlying stock (S). (4) The risk-free interest rate (r). (5) The variance of the stock price (σ). The crucial variable is of course the fifth variable, the variance of the price of the underlying asset. But even this variable can in principle be calculated purely on the basis of know knowns since it is derived from a sequence of historic price fluctuations.

At the heart of derivatives pricing is a distinction between known knowns and known unknowns. The brilliance of Bachelier consisted first and foremost in establishing this distinction. As we have seen, Bachelier states: 'At a given instant the market believes neither in a rise nor in a fall of the true price'.[38] In other words, the market knows that it does not know if a price is going to go up or down. The direction of future price movements is unpredictable. But at the same time, it is precisely this knowledge of the ignorance of the market that enables the calculation of the probability of price fluctuations of different sizes. This is what Bachelier refers to as 'a priori probability'. Knowing what we do not know about the future allows us to use what we know that we know about the present and the past to calculate the probability of different events in the future.

Obviously, there is a paradox involved in designating the unknown unknows of financial derivatives markets. The unknown unknowns of derivatives markets only appear after the fact, after the crisis. They are the kind of events that are not even imagined when the pricing of a derivative takes different risks into account, but they nevertheless have profound consequences for the market when they do happen. Before they happen, they are not a risk because they are not even considered by the market. The market does not even know that it does not know about the possibility of such events. These events only become risks when they are observed in retrospect as the market itself tries to understand what caused a particular crisis. Financial crises are caused by the occurrence of unknown unknown events. When

38 Bachelier, *Theory of Speculation*, 26.

the market 'learns' from a crisis, this means that it starts taking into consideration the possibility of the particular type of event that caused the crisis. It incorporates the probability of a recurrence of such an event into the pricing of derivatives. The unknown unknown is transformed into a known unknown. A retrospective view of the 1987 stock market crash may serve as an example of this kind of transformation.

As we have already seen, the 1987 stock market crisis happened because the simultaneous selling of particular stocks by multiple traders involved in portfolio insurance created discontinuity in the price fluctuations in the market. The result was a case of what Mandelbrot refers to as 'financial turbulence',[39] where reciprocal endogeneous mechanisms are triggered, thus upsetting the 'normal' functioning of the market. The distinction between 'normal' and 'abnormal' is defined by the assumption that price fluctuations are 'normally distributed'. This assumption is an intrinsic component of the Black and Scholes formula for options pricing. According to this assumption, price declines on the scale of what happened on 19 October 1987 were considered so unlikely as to be nearly impossible. Prior to 19 October 1987, options were priced in a way that did not take into account the possibility of a 22.61 percent decline in the Dow Jones Index. This event was an unknown unknown.

However, the event has had profound and permanent consequences for the pricing of options. After the 1987 crash, a phenomenon known as 'The Volatility Skew' emerged. The Volatility Skew refers to the relation between, on the one hand, the implied volatility of an option and, on the other, the difference between the strike price and the current price. Implied volatility is the volatility that corresponds to a given market price of the option. Implied volatility is calculated by using the options pricing model – i.e. Black and Scholes – to calculate backwards from actual market price to assumed volatility. Implied volatility is the market's assessment of the volatility of the underlying asset. If derivatives were traded at prices that were identical to the theoretical prices calculated on the basis of the Black and Scholes options pricing model or a similar model, all options would have the same implied volatility regardless of the strike price. In other words, a stock index put option with a strike price of $105 on an index

39 Mandelbrot and Hudson, *The (Mis)Behaviour of Markets.*

with a current level of $100 would have the same implied volatility as a put option with a strike price of $80 on the same index.

Before 1987, it was indeed the case that options with different strike prices were traded at market prices implying the same level of volatility. But after the crash, this was no longer the case. Index stock put options with strike prices well below current prices became relatively more expensive than puts at or above current index prices. This produced the aforementioned Volatility Skew, since the relatively more expensive options have a higher implied volatility. MacKenzie draws the following conclusion regarding the emergence of the post-1987 Volatility Skew:

> The level and pattern of option prices might reflect not just the empirical distribution of changes in index levels or in index-future prices but the incorporation into option prices of the possibility of a catastrophic but low-probability event that did not in fact take place. In other words, prices might have incorporated the *fear* that the 1987 crash would be repeated.[40]

The point here is that after 1987, sudden significant price drops have come to be regarded as less improbable by the market than they were before the crash. Before 1987, the risk of such price drops were an unknown unknown. After 1987, they have become a known unknown.

The transformation of unknown unknowns into known unknowns implies the ability of the market to learn from past crises. After every significant crisis emerges a heightened awareness and sensitivity to a new type of risk which is perceived to have been the cause of the crisis. A retrospect view of the collapse of Long Term Capital Management in 1998 may serve as another illustration. The collapse had major repercussions in the whole of the financial system, and it resulted in growing awareness of the liquidity risk involved in the kind of leverage used by hedge funds. LTCM used Black, Scholes and Merton's options pricing theory to identify vertical arbitrage opportunities, and it used derivatives to build the kind of hedged portfolios needed to exploit them. In order to profit from these arbitrage opportunities, LTCM relied on the rest of the market to

40 MacKenzie, *An Engine, Not a Camera*, 205.

gradually 'correct' seeming inefficiencies, thus causing prices to revert to the levels predicted by the EMH and the theoretical options pricing models.

The event sometimes identified as the initial instigator of the collapse was Russia's default on its ruble-denominated bonds.[41] LTCM had only limited exposure to the Russian market and thus suffered only insignificant direct losses from the default. However, the event came as a shock to a number of other investors who had been expecting Russia to default on its foreign currency bonds rather than its domestic currency bonds. In order to retain liquidity, some of these investors started getting out of the same positions that LTCM held. This, in turn, caused the spreads that LTCM was betting on to widen rather than close, as suggested by the EMH. Even though this theoretically opened new arbitrage opportunities, it also put severe strain on LTCM. Not only did LTCM's own investors start putting pressure on the fund to cut losses, but doubts about the survival of the fund spread throughout the market, causing other investors to get out of positions similar to the ones held by LTCM, as they feared that LTCM would have to liquidate these positions and dump their assets into the market. These doubts about the survival of LTCM acted as self-fulfilling prophecies, causing the prices of the fund's assets to drop. Eventually, LTCM ran out of credit to cover increasing demands for collateral from counter parties and clearinghouses to maintain their positions. The fund was liquidated in a kind of 'controlled demolition' orchestrated by a consortium of major banks and the Federal Reserve Bank of New York. Even though LTCM was carefully hedged against conventional market risks – indeed, the basic trading strategy of the fund was based on perfect hedging – the fund had not anticipated the kind of liquidity risk that ultimately prevented other investors from coming in to close the 'inefficient' gaps in the market. LTCM's positions might have been extremely profitable in the long run, but the fund was confronted with the problem noted by poker player Rick Bennet: 'The short run is longer than most people know'.[42]

Derivatives are sophisticated devices for the calculation and transfer of risk. In Žižek's terminology, derivatives function to symbolize the real. This symbolization transforms unpredictable

---

41 Ibid., 229.

42 Bennet, *King of a Small World*, 270.

future events into risks designated by statistical probabilities. But as we know, the real does not readily lend itself to symbolization. Every symbolization is incomplete and inevitably gives rise to the return of the real as 'that which resists symbolization'. Derivatives may enable the control and management of risk, but they also seem to produce new forms of risk. We can distinguish three-plus-one different types of financial risk: 1) Market risk is the immediate risk of price fluctuations in the market. 2) Credit risk is the chance that the counter party to a contract – for instance, a future contract – might fail to fulfill his obligation. 3) Liquidity risk is the risk that someone will be unable to meet the payments required to maintain a position (e.g. post additional collateral when the exposure on a position increases) or will be unable to find liquid markets to buy or realize assets (e.g. buy assets to close a short position).

As we have seen in the examples from 1987 and 1998, these three forms of risks are not absolutely distinguished, and can in fact be highly correlated. Using derivatives to hedge against one of these risks may simply produce exposure to another type of risk. For instance, using stock index futures contracts to hedge against the market risk of price declines may create exposure to the credit risk that the counter party will not be able to service his end of the contract. And if there is a widespread uncertainty about credit risk in the market, it may promote a so-called 'flight to quality', where investors move capital to relatively safer assets, thus depleting liquidity in markets for risky assets. This lack of liquidity in turn causes a decrease in prices, thus increasing immediate market risks.

These concepts not only refer to different sources of risk in financial markets, but the interrelatedness of the risks itself constitutes a source of risk. This brings us to the final type of risk: 4) systemic risk. According to the definition proposed by Kaufman and Scott, systemic risk

> refers to the risk or probability of breakdowns in an entire system, as opposed to breakdowns in individual parts or components, and is evidenced by comovements (correlation) among most or all the parts.[43]

43 Kaufman and Scott, 'What Is Systemic Risk, and Do Bank Regulators Retard or Contribute to It?', 371.

Rather than a positive designation of a particular type of event that presents risk in financial markets, the notion of systemic risk seems to be a residual category that captures everything that does not fit into any of the other categories. This refers first and foremost to the kind of risk generated by the proliferation of risk management. Marx's idea of revolution must be the ultimate example of systemic risk. While market risk, credit risk and liquidity risk refer to events – the probability of which can be calculated with some degree of precision and in principle hedged away – systemic risk refers to events that we can hardly imagine but that nevertheless have the potential to severely upset the profitability of our engagement in financial markets.

The logic by which the management of market risk, credit risk and liquidity risk itself becomes a source of systemic risk is similar to the logic at work in the following joke about former Croatian president Franjo Tudjman and his large family, who are in a plane above Croatia:

> Aware of the rumors that a lot of Croats lead miserable unhappy lives, while he and his cronies amass wealth, Tudjman says: 'What if I were to throw a cheque for a million dollars out of the window, to make at least one Croat, who will catch it, happy?' His flattering wife says: 'But Franjo, my dear, why don't you throw out two cheques for half a million each, and thus make two Croats happy?' His daughter adds: 'Why not four cheques for a quarter of a million each, and make four Croats happy?' and so on, until finally, his grandson – the proverbial innocent youth who unknowingly blurts out the truth – says: 'But Grandpa, why don't you simply throw yourself out of the window, and thus make all the Croats happy?'[44]

While derivatives may be constructed to hedge against market risk, credit risk and to some extent even liquidity risk, the most efficient way to get rid of systemic risk is perhaps to get rid of derivatives markets themselves.

It is tempting to apply the same logic to monetary policy. One of the key proponents of free market ideology, Milton Friedman, once famously proposed dropping money from a helicopter as a means of

44 Žižek, *The Fragile Absolute*, 53–4.

combating price deflation.[45] Given the historical experiences of implementing Friedmanite policies in their pure form in Chile, Bolivia, Poland, Russia, and South East Asia, we might speculate that an even more effective remedy for monetary instability would have been to simply drop Milton Friedman from the helicopter.[46]

Market risk, credit risk and liquidity risk emerge in the relation between known knowns and known unknowns. Systemic risk marks the limit of present knowledge in the market. Systemic risk is the unknown unknown of financial markets. As the market learns from a previous crisis and develops new risk-management tools to calculate and hedge against the probability of the kind of events that are perceived to have caused the crisis, previous systemic risks are translated into particular market, credit or liquidity risks. Unknown unknowns are transformed into known unknowns. In turn, these new risk-management tools produce yet new risks that may become the cause of future crises. The transformation of unknown unknowns into known unknowns produces new unknown unknowns. We can paraphrase Žižek's definition of the real in order to conceive of systemic risk as 'that which resists risk management'.

In the aforementioned, Žižek blames Rumsfeldian epistemology for failing to take into account a fourth category of knowledge: the unknown known. This is the category of the Freudian (or perhaps rather Lacanian) unconscious, which is 'knowledge that doesn't know itself'.[47] We may follow Žižek even further by suggesting that the 'main dangers' of an system of global capitalism which relies increasingly on the circulation of money in financial markets is not the confrontation with the unknown unknowns – events unanticipated and oftentimes even perpetuated by financial markets – but rather the unknown knowns of these markets, that is, 'the disavowed beliefs and suppositions' that agents in these markets are 'not even aware of adhering to' themselves. So what are the unknown knowns of financial markets?

A shorthand account of the recent financial crisis might say that on the one hand, there was a hoard of financial scholars and financiers who had blind faith in the models of neoclassical finance built

---

45 Friedman, *The Optimum Quantity of Money*, 4.

46 Klein, *The Shock Doctrine*.

47 Žižek, *How to Read Lacan*, 52.

on the assumption of market efficiency. On the other hand, there were the financial markets, marked by irrational exuberance and other forms of inefficiency. The financial crisis was merely the inevitable outcome of a growing mismatch between the models and the markets. Even though this account is not entirely wrong, it misses a crucial point in the functioning of financial markets. The account assumes a dichotomy between those who believe in the efficiency of the market – i.e. the uninformed and uncritical agents of financial markets – and the informed critics who have recognized the true nature of financial markets and no longer believe in their efficiency. However, this notion of belief is much too simple to capture the post-ideological foundation of contemporary financial markets.

Perhaps the most radical critique of modern neoclassical finance theory and the inherent notion of market efficiency has been proposed by Benoit Mandelbrot. Mandelbrot goes to the very heart of the theory by separating the assumption that price fluctuations in financial markets behave in a random fashion from the assumption that these fluctuations are normally distributed. Mandelbrot concedes that prices may indeed be random in the sense of being unpredictable, but he goes on to distinguish between 'mild' and 'wild' randomness.[48] The first is the kind of randomness that conforms to the assumptions of Gaussian probability theory: prices follow to the bell curve–shaped normal distribution and each individual price movement is independent from preceding movements. Mild randomness is what you get when you toss a coin multiple times. The second kind of randomness, however, does not conform to these assumptions. Wild randomness can, for instance, give rise to the phenomenon of turbulence as found in the behaviour of wind or rivers. Turbulence occurs when laminar motions of matter exceed a certain threshold and begin to interact in a mutually reinforcing way, thus producing new and more complex patterns that cannot be reduced to the effects of the initial motions. Turbulence produces sudden and very violent fluctuations on a scale that is significantly larger than the fluctuations that appear when the matter is in a more regular state. In other words, turbulence marks a radical break with the 'ordinary' volatility of a situation. Compared to the normal distribution, wild randomness produces far more 'abnormal' events. Unlikely events are much less unlikely.

---

48 Mandelbrot and Hudson, *The (Mis)Behaviour of Markets*, 32.

The gist of Mandelbrot's critique is of course that prices in financial markets follow the pattern of wild rather than mild randomness. Hence, the frequent occurrence of crisis, where prices fluctuate far beyond the expectations of the market, should come as less of a surprise, since these instances of 'financial turbulence' are intrinsic moments in the very functioning of the system. 'The market is very risky – far more risky than if you blithely assume that prices meander around a polite Gaussian average'.[49]

Mandelbrot grounds his argument in a combination of theoretical reflections on probability theory and empirical studies of historic price series. Not only is he widely recognized as a mathematical genius, but he also presents his argument in a simple and extremely convincing fashion. In this light, it is interesting to note the reaction to his critique from mainstream financial theorists. This is Mandelbrot's own summary:

> Such is the weight of evidence against the assumptions in the standard model of modern finance theory that it is no longer reasonable to ignore entirely. Indeed, forty years after I started a battle on the subject, most economists now acknowledge that prices do not follow the bell curve, and do not move independently. But for many, after acknowledging those points, their next comment is: So what? Independence and normality are, they argue, just assumptions that help simplify the math of modern financial theory. What matters are the results. Do the standard models correctly predict how the market behaves overall? Can an investor use Modern Portfolio Theory to build a safe, profitable investment strategy? Will the Capital Asset pricing Model help a financial analyst, or a corporate finance officer, make the right decision? If so, then stop arguing about it.[50]

This quote provides an insight into the way ideology and belief function with regards to financial markets. In order to explore this, we may invoke Žižek's account of an anecdote regarding Niels Bohr:

> Surprised at seeing a horseshoe above the door of Bohr's country house, the fellow scientist visiting him exclaimed that he did not

49 Ibid., 169.
50 Ibid., 100.

> share the superstitious belief regarding horseshoes keeping evil spirits out of the house, to which Bohr snapped back: 'I don't believe in it either. I have it there because I was told that it works even when one doesn't believe in it at all.' This is indeed how ideology functions today: nobody takes democracy or justice seriously, we are all aware of their corrupted nature, but we participate in them, we display our belief in them.[51]

A similar point applies to financial markets and perhaps even to capitalism in general. Who really believes that financial markets function to effectively and efficiently allocate capital resources in order to provide the highest level of productivity and prosperity? Especially after the 2007–8 financial crisis, true believers in the unconditional benefits of free-market financial capitalism are becoming rarer and rarer. Even Alan Greenspan was pressed in congressional hearings to concede that he had found a 'flaw' in his 'ideology' that assumed 'that free, competitive markets are by far the unrivalled way to organize economies'. The optimistic interpretation of the growing scepticism towards the efficiency and benevolent nature of financial markets is that we are at an historical turning point where the trend of liberalization and deregulation that defined the past forty years is going to be reversed. The more gloomy interpretation is that financial markets have now evolved into a state where they no longer require people to believe in them in order for them to function as the key determinant of the circulation and distribution of money in the world. The whole of our economy has been organized around the notion that markets are efficient and that they generate the best estimates of the true prices of different assets, securities and money itself. This organization has become so encompassing that the belief of the individual is no longer needed. It works even though we do not believe in it.

This is what the Mandelbrot quote pointedly illustrates. Even finance professionals do not believe in the EMH or the accuracy of the conglomerate of models that constitute modern neoclassical finance. Still, they keep adhering to these models because the models work regardless of the disbelief of their users.

Mandelbrot's distinction between mild and wild randomness is a distinction between a kind of randomness which lends itself to

51 Žižek, *First as Tragedy, Then as Farce*, 51.

probabilistic calculation and risk management and another kind of randomness which is essentially unmanageable. In Žižek's terms, mild randomness may be symbolized, whereas wild randomness is a 'return of the real' in the sense that it is a form of financial volatility that 'resisting symbolization'. Accepting the theory that financial markets are prone to wild randomness means that we also have to accept the fact that the riskiness of financial markets is ultimately unmanageable. Insofar as the central objective of modern finance is coming up with new and evermore sophisticated tools for risk management, such a concession would be detrimental. It would be an admission of basic impotence. In this light, it is interesting to review one of the earliest reactions to Mandelbrot's theory, which was formulated by Paul Cootner:

> Mandelbrot, like Prime Minister Churchill before him, promises us not utopia but blood, sweat, toil, and tears. If he is right, almost all of our statistical tools are obsolete – least squares, spectral analysis, workable maximum-likelihood solutions, all our established sample theory, closed distribution functions. Almost without exception, past econometric work is meaningless. Surely, before consigning centuries of work to the ash pile, we should like to have some assurance that all our work is truly useless.[52]

Mandelbrot's critique of modern finance theory is radical because it touches the unknown knowns which constitute the basic framework for thinking about financial markets and risk management. Žižek invokes Kant to elaborate on the nature of the unknown knowns: 'what is the Kantian transcendental a priori if not the network of such "unknown knowns", the horizon of meaning of which we are unaware, but which is always-already here, structuring our approach to reality?'[53] In chapter one, we explored the relationship between Kant and Bachelier. With Bachelier, modern finance was founded as the study of the a priori probabilities of the market. As we have seen, he concludes his thesis by saying that 'the market, unwittingly, obeys a law that rules it: the

52 Cootner, *The Random Character of Stock Market Prices*, 114.

53 Žižek, 'Philosophy, the "Unknown Knowns", and the Public Use of Reason', 137.

law of probability'.[54] This is the unknown known of financial markets: the notion that prices in financial markets behave in a way that makes them subject to probabilistic reasoning. This form of reasoning in finance presupposes the distinction between known unknowns (the direction of future price movements) and known knowns (the historic price volatility of an asset). The unknown known is the very distinction between these two categories of knowledge. The unknown knowns of financial markets provide the 'horizon of meaning' . . . 'structuring our approach to reality'.

We have also seen how the EMH can have the status of an analytic proposition or the status of a synthetic proposition. The dispute between neoclassical finance and behavioural finance plays out only at the level of the EMH as a synthetic proposition. At stake is merely the question of whether and to what extent actual empirical markets conform to the theoretical definition of market efficiency. But underlying this dispute is the EMH as an analytic statement. Only insofar as we accept the EMH as a meaningful theoretical concept does it make sense to discuss whether empirical markets conform to this concept or not. In this sense, the EMH as an analytic proposition constitutes an unknown known. This is why Mandelbrot's argument is so disturbing. It does not just dispute the known knowns and the known unknowns of neoclassical finance theory and all the risk-management models derived from this theory. It disputes the validity of the unknown knows underlying the whole edifice. Critique of the kind proposed by Mandelbrot not only argues that current models of risk management are incomplete or insufficient. It implies that the whole idea of managing risk in financial markets is flawed.

The unknown know is the unconscious, and according to the famous Lacanian slogan, 'The unconscious is structured like a language'.[55] In financial markets, the unknown know is structured like the language of probability theory. Satyajit Das gives an example of this structure when he makes the following observation about so-called 'quants', that is, the scholars who build financial risk models on the basis of highly sophisticated quantitative finance theory:

54 Bachelier, *Theory of Speculation*, 77.
55 Lacan, *The Four Fundamental Concepts of Psychoanalysis*, 34.

> In credit markets, you cannot empirically validate any proposition. If you ask what the risk of Company X defaulting is, then it hasn't defaulted – you can't look at history to determine the probability. The data paradox did not trouble the geeks. Their training was not in dialectics. They started each paper with the familiar greeting to fellow quants, 'Assuming the following, we can show that'.[56]

The aim of probability theory is precisely to make simplifying assumption which allow for the statistical comparison of different hypothetical situations. The initial statement of the assumptions which are necessary in order for a particular argument or calculation to make sense serves to indicate that the author of an academic paper or the constructor of a risk model is very realistic; he is well aware that empirical reality does not necessarily conform to the properties of the model. The statement is an admission of the known unknowns of the financial model in question. At the same time, the statement of such assumptions is also a confirmation of the underlying unknown knowns of the model: 'I know very well that this model does not conform to the nature of actual reality, nevertheless I shall proceed as if the model did in fact conform to reality'. In other words, the knowledge that the model does not conform to the nature of actual reality is not incorporated into the model itself. It remains an unknown known.

MONEY AND DERIVATIVES

The significance of the emergence of financial derivatives and the exponential increase in the volume of the markets in which they are traded lies not only in the transformation of the structure and functioning of financial markets. Derivatives serve also to drive financialization. According to Epstein, 'financialization means the increasing role of financial motives, financial markets, financial actors and financial institutions in the operation of the domestic and international economies'.[57] Epstein says that financialization has been taking place over the last thirty to forty years. Comparing this to the evolution of financial derivatives, it seems obvious that the two are related.

---

56 Das, *Traders, Guns, and Money*, 293.

57 Epstein, *Financialization and the World Economy*, 3.

If we think of derivatives as tools for the pricing of risk, we can see how they present an eminent vehicle for linking prices in otherwise distinct financial markets. Risk is an inherent feature of all financial markets, and risk-pricing thus provides an almost universal benchmark for the comparison of pricing operations in different markets. Derivatives provide a universal language which allows for easy translation or conversion between different markets. The crucial function of derivatives, according to Bryan and Rafferty, is to provide 'financial market commensuration' through the fulfilment of two interrelated roles:

> Binding: derivatives, through options and futures, establish pricing relationships that 'bind' the future to the present or one place to another.
> Blending: derivatives, especially through swaps, establish pricing relationships that readily convert between ('commensurate') different forms of asset.[58]

As I have already mentioned, the simplest form of arbitrage occurs when the same commodity is traded at different prices in different markets – for instance, if gold is traded at different prices in LBMA (London) and NYMEX (New York). When financial markets evolve and become more complex, so do forms of arbitrage. As derivatives provide commensuration to financial market, they facilitate almost infinite possibilities for price comparison, with the purpose of spotting arbitrage opportunities. Bryan and Rafferty elaborate on derivatives' capacity for commensuration:

> Each derivative product is a package of conversion of one form of capital to another – whether this is a simple commodity futures contract or a complex conversion of a particular currency index to a particular stock market index. When all these products are taken together, they form a complex web of conversions, a *system of derivatives*, in which any 'bit' of capital, anywhere and with any time or spatial profile, can be measured against any other 'bit' of capital, and on an on-going basis.[59]

---

58 Bryan and Rafferty, 'Financial Derivatives and the Theory of Money', 140.
59 Ibid., 141.

If financial markets have an inherent tendency to automatically gravitate towards a state of equilibrium and efficiency, this 'complex web of conversions' is merely a speculative infrastructure that allows arbitrage traders to function very efficiently as janitors of the system, constantly surveying the state of the markets, making sure that price discrepancies are immediately closed, and taking a minor speculative profit for their benign effort. However, if market efficiency is an ideological veil covering up the perpetual production of price gaps that are nurtured by ever increasing volatility in the markets, the 'system of derivatives' as a 'complex web of conversions' comes to benefit speculative spiders that can use it to capture their share of a continuous stream of profits.

While Bryan and Rafferty seem to lean towards the first of these scenarios, they provide very accurate observations of the functioning of derivatives that are valid regardless of the viewer's normative and ideological inclinations on the issue of derivatives:

> Derivatives are, in this sense, 'behind the scenes' money, ensuring that different forms of asset (and money) are commensurated not by state decree (e.g. fixed exchange rates) but by competitive force. In this sense, the effect of derivatives is to merge the categories of capital and money: to bring liquidity to the market for financial assets, making all assets more like money, and to bring capital-like attributes to money – at the extreme, presenting money as itself capital. The effect is to break down the differentiation between the spheres of production of commodities (the so-called 'real' economy) and the money economy.[60]

Since money circulates not only in financial markets but also in all other sectors of the economy, the commensuration between money and capital and the eventual capitalization of all forms of money which is facilitated by the proliferation of financial derivatives allows the rationality (or lack thereof) of financial markets to pervade all of those spheres of life that are structured by money. Derivatives become vehicles for the financialization of money itself.

The capacity of derivatives to make 'all assets more like money' means that in today's financial capitalism, an increasing array of assets

60 Ibid., 153.

become the object of speculation. It's not only the usual suspects of stocks, government bonds and currencies that are traded in financial markets. The prices of real estate, energy, food and a number of other mundane assets are also determined in financial markets, thus causing the volatility of these markets to reverberate far into the intimate sphere of private homeowners, consumers and ordinary families.

Perhaps the most significant consequence of the emergence of financial derivatives and the exponential development in the volume of trading in derivatives markets is the increasing decoupling of trading in financial markets from ownership of the underlying assets. While a stock in GM represents a fraction of the collective ownership of the company, the holder of a call option on the same stock does not own any part of GM. The same holds for derivatives on bonds, currencies, commodities and especially derivatives tied to various indexes, where even the underlier is nothing but an abstract figure.

The increasing decoupling of financial trading from ownership of the underlying assets means that financial profits also become increasingly decoupled from profits in the underlying economy. While profits in the stock market are highly correlated with the profitability of the underlying companies to which the stocks refer, the same does not hold for derivatives on stocks. While holders of stock call options will generally profit when there is growth in the general economy and stock prices increase, holders of put options and sellers of call options will profit when there is a downturn in the general economy and stock prices decline. In brief, derivatives enable traders to make money not only when the market goes up but also when it goes down. Indeed, short selling, which is the selling of a security that the seller does not have but merely 'borrows' until it is repurchased again, made this possible even before the invention of financial derivatives, but the proliferation of these instruments have multiplied the opportunities. The growth in financial derivatives trading thus signifies the emergence of an increasing number of agents in financial markets whose interests are not aligned with those of the general economy. This class of agents profit when individual businesses or entire economies crash.

The concept of financialization does not simply imply that the financial and the productive spheres of the economy are wholly decoupled. We have seen how price fluctuations in derivatives markets may have significant effects not only on the determination of prices in the underlying markets, but even on the operation of the actual productive economy. There is reciprocal causality between derivatives markets and the rest of the economy. As the volume of trading in derivatives markets increases, the impact of price fluctuations in these markets on the rest of the economy becomes equally larger. This development signifies, in popular terms, a trend towards a situation where the 'financial' tail is wagging the 'productive' dog.

SUPPLY AND DESIRE FOR POST-CREDIT MONEY

In 1999, a bill called the Gramm-Leach-Bliley Act was passed by the US Congress. The bill was the last stage in a process of deregulating the banking industry that had been taking place since 1980. This process can be seen as a rollback of the 1933 Glass–Steagall Act that was originally passed to separate investment banking from commercial deposit banking. Against the backdrop of the 1929 stock market crash, the idea of the Glass–Steagall Act was to protect the money of 'ordinary people' in the real productive economy from the fluctuations and collapses of financial markets. With the Gramm-Leach-Bliley Act, the final legal obstacles to the merger of commercial banks, investment banks and insurance companies were cleared, thus paving the way for banks such as JP Morgan Chase, Citigroup, Bank of America and HSBC to develop into multiservice financial corporations.

From a monetary perspective, the ultimate repeal of the Glass–Steagall Act meant the opening of the floodgates between, on the one hand, credit money created in commercial banks on the basis of deposits from private individuals and companies, and on the other, the whirlpools of speculative capital floating around in financial markets. We have already seen how the price of money has come to be determined in financial markets rather than by political decisions in nation-states. The merger of commercial banking and investment banking adds yet another element to this development, as it allows banks to create credit money which is then subsequently absorbed by financial markets. This marks a reconfiguration of the desire for post-credit money.

The shift in central bank policy from credit rationing to discount window regulation is sometimes referred to as a shift towards demand-driven credit creation.[61] Instead of controlling the production of credit by determining the supply of money that is lent to

61 Ryan-Collins et al., *Where Does Money Come From?*, 104.

commercial banks, central banks provide whatever amount of credit is demanded by the market at a given price. In other words, the demand for credit in the market determines the supply of credit.

While the notion of demand-driven credit creation is indeed helpful in understanding how the supply of credit money is (not) regulated by central banks, it is perhaps at the same time misleading if we look at it from a philosophical perspective. The notion of demand implies a certain relation between the object in demand and the demanding subject. The demand for an object stems from certain needs in the subject the may be satisfied through the acquisition of the particular object qua inherent qualities of the object. For instance, a person my demand an apple because he is hungry and because the apple satisfies this demand on account of its nutritional qualities.

As we have already seen, Žižek's model of the subject is based on a break with the notion of demand. Instead, Žižek invokes the concept of desire when he insists that 'the subject . . . and the object-cause of its desire . . . are strictly correlative'.[62] This means that the need for an object is not pre-existing in the subject, and nor are the qualities of an object inherent in the object itself. Rather, the object 'causes' the desire in the subject, and at the same time the subject projects a conglomerate of qualities onto the object. The concept of desire enables a different and perhaps more radical understanding of the creation of credit money than the concept of demand. It allows us to unfold the relationship between credit-money creation and financialization. The creation of credit should be understood as desire-driven rather than demand-driven.

Another crucial point in Žižek's thinking about the subject is the idea that desire is always symbolically mediated. This is captured by the Lacanian slogan: 'Man's desire is the Other's desire'.[63] It means that the subject's desire is never just a simple, spontaneous craving for a particular object. The desire of the subject is inevitably mediated by the symbolic order. Žižek identifies two dimensions of the slogan:

> Man's desire is structured by the 'decentred' big Other, the symbolic order: what I desire is predetermined by the big Other, the symbolic

62 Žižek, *The Fragile Absolute*, 28.

63 Lacan, 'The Function and Field of Speech and Language in Psychoanalysis', 312.

> space within which I dwell . . . The subject desires only insofar as it experiences the Other itself as desiring, as the site of an unfathomable desire, as if an opaque desire is emanating from him or her.[64]

The chartalist theory of money which we encountered in chapter three provides an illuminating illustration of how the notion that desire is always the desire of the Other plays out in the constitution of money. This theory claims that money is essentially a creation of the state. The state's creation of money happens through three interconnected movements. First, a particular kind of object (coins, paper notes, etc.) is legally declared to be money. Second, a steady demand for this object is created when the state accepts it for payment of taxes. And third, these two movements automatically cause the particular money object to be generally accepted as a means of exchange and payment within the domain of the state, since everyone knows that everyone else is eventually going to need these objects to pay taxes. In other words, the state's demand for money is generalized to each particular individual within the state. These three movements immediately translate into the concept of desire.

Paraphrasing Žižek, the legal designation of a particular object as money means that 'what the citizen desires is predetermined by the state, the legal and economic space within which he dwells'. This is the first movement of the chartalist creation of money. In the second move, 'the citizen experiences the state itself as desiring' money in the form of taxes. And in the third move, the desire for the particular object designated as money is internalized in the market when it becomes generally accepted as a means of payment and exchange. The role of the big Other (in the form of the state) in the creation of money is effaced when the citizens experience their desire for money as spontaneously emanating from their encounters with the object of money in the market.

We have already seen how financial markets after the Bretton Woods collapse took over the function of governments in setting the price of money. The emergence and proliferation of financial derivatives are central to this development. But financialization pertains not only to the pricing of money. When the volume of financial markets in general and derivatives markets in particular grows beyond a

---

64 Žižek, *How to Read Lacan*, 41–2.

certain threshold, they take over the role of the big Other in structuring the desire for money that was previously played by the state. In other words, financialization plays out not only in the ontic domain of the pricing of money, but even in the ontological domain of the constitution of money. Reflecting on the exponential growth of derivatives trading, LiPuma and Lee note that

> deposits and transfers of that magnitude must be electronic, notional, and virtual because the amounts being circulated exceed the total quantity of the world's physical currencies. A determining feature of derivatives and their circulation is that they do not involve property, either in physical or fetishized form (such as a stock certificate). The purchase of a derivative grants the buyer an electronically registered future claim in trade for the seller's 'right' to electronically transfer and register a notional credit equal to the quantity extinguished in the buyer's account. The trade is mediated by money in a newly created self-mediating form, engendering, as it were, a currency not directly tethered to any national economy or regulatory structures. In contrast to manufactured commodities, human labor and materials are inconsequential in the creation and valuation of derivatives.[65]

Looking at this through the lens of the chartalist theory of money, we can see that financial markets have come to simulate the way nation-states used to make money. 'It is clear that the system of derivative trading generates enormous settlement volumes that need to be financed'.[66] The frantic rhythm of the creation of new derivatives and the expiry of existing derivatives generates a constant demand for money to settle these contracts. The effect of this constant demand for settlement money in financial markets is comparable to the effects of the imposition of taxes by the state. Financial derivatives and the markets in which they are constantly bought, sold and settled play the role of the big Other as they incorporate the desire for a particular kind of money.

In the chartalist account, the constitution of money is determined by the legal declaration of the kind of object that is accepted for the

65 LiPuma and Lee, *Financial Derivatives and the Globalization of Risk*, 48.

66 McKenzie, 'Casino Capitalism with Derivatives', 212.

payment of taxes. If the sovereign of a state were to accept old shoes for tax settlement, old shoes would in principle come to function as a form of money in that state. When financial markets come to be the main driver in the creation of a desire for money, the crucial question is this: what kind of money is accepted as payment in the buying and selling of financial securities and in the settlement of obligations created in financial markets?

In contemporary financial markets, financial products are rarely if ever traded or settled in physical cash. As noted by LiPuma and Lee, financial trading is mediated by electronic transfers of credit between traders' accounts. We have already seen how the evolution of electronic credit payment systems allows bank customers to use credit money for the purchase of commodities. Parallel to these systems, we find sophisticated interbank clearance systems that allow whole transactions to take place with only a minimal need for state money. The same applies to financial markets, since they provide an outlet for the immediate use of credit money.

The kind of credit money desired by the big Other of financial markets is not just any kind of credit money. In the exposition of the credit theory of money in chapter four, we saw how the value of credit money depends on the creditworthiness of the debtor. In the context of a national banking system, access to the interbank money market as well as central bank lending facilities are crucial to the creditworthiness of a bank, and thus also for the circulation of its credit as immediate means of payment and exchange. The whole purpose of the interbank money market and the central bank is to efface differences between the creditworthiness of different commercial banks, and even between commercial banks and the central bank. Effacing these differences allows commercial bank credit money to circulate at the nominal value with little concern on the part of money-users for the condition of the individual bank where the credit is issued.

When a bank provides credit money to facilitate trading, settlement or the provision of collateral in global financial markets, the value of this money depends not only on the bank's relation to national interbank money markets and central bank facilities. The crucial point is the position of the bank in the infrastructure of financial markets. Is the credit of the bank immediately accepted as payment in the buying or selling of financial products or the settlement of derivative contracts? In other words, financial markets determine not only the price of money in terms of interest rates, currency exchange and commodity prices. The value and usefulness of the credit of a particular bank, and thus the bank's capacity for issuing credit which circulates as money, is determined by its position relative to the financial centres of global capitalism. If the credit issued by a particular bank is readily accepted in the trading and settlement of financial securities and contracts in major financial markets, this gives the bank considerable – and potentially very lucrative – potential for the production of moneIn the discussion of the money multiplier, we saw how the idea of banks as merely mediators between depositors and borrowers is erroneous. In the age of post-credit money, banks do not need to wait for new depositors to deposit money in the bank before they can issue new loans. Deposits can be created in the same move as the loan is issued. The loan is paid out in the form of a credit in a deposit account. The efficient interbank clearance system enables the credit to circulate as money with only a minimal recourse to central bank money. With the merger between investment banks and deposit banks, the money-making mechanics are taken one step further. Not only do banks no longer have to wait for depositors with excess capital. They hardly even have to wait for borrowers to come with a request for extra capital. The combination of the two kinds of banking business allows the banks to trade in financial markets using their own credit as money. In other words, they make money with one hand and immediately put it into circulation in financial markets with the other.

Hedge funds often act as intermediaries when credit money is put into circulation in financial markets. As we have already noted, hedge funds operate by raising a certain amount of start capital, which is then used as collateral to borrow more money, thus raising working capital several times greater than the initial investment. Hedge funds can be set up by independent investors, by investment banks, or by both in collaboration. Besides providing investors with opportunities for large speculative profits, hedge funds facilitate the issuance of new interest-bearing credit money by banks, money that is put into circulation in financial markets.

In the above passage, LiPuma and Lee note an important quality that sets financial markets apart from markets in the productive economy. While the volume of markets for 'manufactured commodities' is limited by the availability of 'human labor and materials', the creation and circulation of financial products, and of derivatives in particular, is not limited by such finite resources. If the 'demand' for credit in the economy was created only by agents in the productive economy wanting to expand their businesses through investments in new machinery, research and development, marketing, etc., this demand would be limited by the availability of profitable investment opportunities and, ultimately, by the availability of 'human labor and materials'. However, when credit money is used to buy financial assets and securities for speculative purposes rather than to make investments in the productive economy, these limits do not exist. Rather than expending existing opportunities, speculation may even have the effect of creating more new opportunities for the use of credit money. The infusion of money into financial markets causes prices to inflate, which in turn creates demand for even more money as even more agents see new possibilities for profit. And when banks accept financial assets as collateral against new loans, the process comes full circle. The price of these assets is determined in the very same markets where the new credit money is put to use. This means that the issuance of new credit helps to inflate the price of the underlying assets that serve as collateral for this very same credit. Rather than financial markets providing a finite demand for credit money that can be satisfied with a certain amount of money, it seems more appropriate to think of financial markets as generating a self-propelling desire for credit money that is inherently insatiable.

Of course, the desire for credit money this is used for trading in financial markets is contingent on the direction of general price movements in the market. As prices increase, more agents are attracted by the prospect of speculative profits. The increasing prices of financial assets also lead banks to accept these assets as collateral against which new credit is issued. When prices come down, financial speculation seems less profitable, and decreasing asset prices prohibit borrowers from raising new credit, perhaps even causing default. However, when we look at the markets for derivatives rather than simple stocks or commodities, another pattern emerges. The price of derivatives is not a linear function of the price of the underlying assets. The price of derivatives is a function of the volatility of the underlier. This means that even when prices in stock markets and commodity markets generally decrease, trading volumes and prices may still increase in derivatives markets. In other words, derivatives markets may function to maintain the desire for credit money even when the rest of the financial markets are in crisis. This desire can be generated through agents seeking a speculative profit, or through agents wanting to insure their positions in the face of uncertainty.

As long as the desire for credit money issued by certain banks with key positions in global financial markets is sustained, this money can circulate as post-credit money that does not need to be redeemed in other forms of money. These banks can profit from their exclusive credit-worthiness either by charging interest on the money they have issued as credit, or simply by investing it in the market, where it can generate a profit. When these banks engage in financial trading – either through propriety trading or through the establishment of hedge funds – they have an advantage relative to other agents in the market through their capacity to raise large amounts of credit. As we saw in the preceding chapter, the command of large amounts of capital allows these agents to move prices in the market by trading large volumes of particular assets.

The situation created through mergers between deposit banks and investment banks, together with the collaboration with hedge funds, is comparable to a situation where a casino owner merges with a loan shark and then collaborates with a skilled poker player. The casino owner hosts a game of poker. He provides the venue, the dealer, the cards, the chips, etc., and he makes money by charging a fee (a rake) for players to participate in the game. This is comparable to the fees charged by investment banks when they provide investors with access to financial markets. The loan shark provides loans to players who want to participate in the poker game hosted by the casino owner. He makes money by charging interest on these loans. This is comparable to the interest charged by ordinary deposit banks. The merger between the two affords new profit opportunities. The loan shark no longer has to pay out the loan in cash. It can be paid out directly in chips provided by the casino owner. This allows the loan shark to service many more players, since he is no longer limited by his cash holdings. The trick works as long as the game continues and the players do not come back to the casino to redeem their chips. Furthermore, the liberal issuance of credit generates many more participants in the poker game. Not only do the loan shark's revenues from interest increase, but the casino owner also makes more money from participation fees. This is comparable to the synergy effects created by mergers between investment banks and deposit banks.

But in order to increase profits, the loan shark and the casino owner choose to stake a player in the game. The loan shark and the casino owner provide the player with free credit against a share of his possible winnings. Even if this player is not better than his opponents, his access to almost unlimited chips gives him an advantage. He can play with the largest stack of chips, allowing him to 'bully' his opponents and 'dominate' the table. This is comparable to the hedge fund that has the capacity to move prices through large volume trading. Not only does the loan-shark-casino-owner corporation make money from interest and fees, but it even has a stake in the winnings of the chosen poker player. This is casino capitalism in the age of post-credit money.

Another way to think about the desire for post-credit money in financial markets is through the concept of liquidity. This concept is readily used in financial and economic terminology, yet it is a highly elusive phenomenon. Mishkin defines liquidity as 'the ease and speed with which an asset can be turned into cash'. He states that 'the more liquid an asset is relative to alternative assets . . . the more desirable it is, and the greater will be the quantity demanded'.[67] Translating this definition into the psychoanalytic framework proposed above, it is crucial to note that the causality at play works both ways. It is true that a high degree of liquidity makes an asset more desirable, but we must add that the degree of liquidity is itself also a function of the desire for the asset. The market and the liquid asset as object-cause of the desire in the market are 'strictly correlative'. This also means that liquidity is not an inherent quality of the asset-object itself. It is a quality that is projected onto the object when it is desired. When an asset is desired on account of its liquidity, it is desired on account of the belief that someone else desires the object to an extent that he is willing to exchange it for cash. Ultimately, the asset is desired because there is a general belief that the market itself desires the object. Liquidity is a fantasmatic quality of the object. We encounter here again the dictum that desire is always the desire of the other. In this case, liquidity is the desire for an asset based on the fantasy that the big Other of the market itself desires the asset. When agents in the market share this fantasy, their collective action does indeed generate this desire of the Other. Even though the big Other does not actually

---

67 Mishkin, *The Economics of Money, Banking, and Financial Markets*, 86–7.

exist, the big Other is nevertheless capable of having an effect when each of the individuals in the system act according to the fantasy of the big Other.

In Mishkin, we also find the following proposition: 'Money is the most liquid asset of all because it is the medium of exchange; it does not have to be converted into anything else in order to make purchases'.[68] In this proposition, money becomes the sublime object of the fantasy of liquidity. Money is the perfectly liquid asset, and it is the asset against which the liquidity of all other assets is measured. Conversion into money is the ultimate redemption of the liquidity of an asset. The elusiveness of the concept of liquidity becomes obvious when it is applied not only to non-money assets, but also to money itself. The problem with Mishkin's proposition that money is the most liquid asset of all is that it veils the fact that, as we have seen, money does not exist. The gist of the analysis of money in part two of this book is precisely that money is never just money. Money is characterized by ontological indeterminacy. Any monetary system is characterized by the interaction, interplay and metamorphosis among different forms of money. Therefore, we cannot say that money itself is the most liquid asset of all. First of all, different kinds of money have different degrees of liquidity under different circumstances. Second, the liquidity of money itself is not an inherent quality of money. It is rather a fantasmatic quality that is projected onto money as the result of a particular economic configuration of desire. Therefore, we may sum up the analysis by saying that the contemporary monetary system is characterized by a configuration where there is a sustained desire for post-credit money, thus conferring onto this money the quality of liquidity that allows it to circulate as if it were money. The liquidity of post-credit money is not an a priori quality of the object, but a contingent function of the system.

The continuous desire for credit money which is sustained by the big Other of the financial market allows for certain banks to generate a continuous supply of this kind of money. As long as the desire is steady or increasing, the credit money does not come back to the bank for redemption in other forms of money. At worst, the credit comes back as a demand for the transfer of money to another bank.

68 Ibid., 47.

But as long as this bank is part of the same settlement network, the transfer can be made without recourse to other forms of money. In other words, financial markets serve as repositories for the circulation of post-credit money issued by certain multinational banks. If global financial markets were a casino, the gamblers would be playing with chips issued by JP Morgan Chase, Barclays and other multinational banking corporations. The age of post-credit money affords these corporations the opportunity to make money by making money.

'KEYNESIANISM OR MONETARISM? YES, PLEASE!'

A fundamental point throughout this book has been that the contemporary paradigm of money marks a shift from state-based money to bank-issued money sustained by financial markets. However, this argument should not lead to the conclusion that the state is insignificant or powerless in the constitution of post-credit money. During the recent years of financial and monetary crisis, it has become increasingly obvious that the state plays a crucial role in sustaining our contemporary monetary paradigm. However, state interventions in monetary affairs today are highly paradoxical. It seems that the ultimate goal of these interventions is the maintenance of a monetary order that excludes the state from control over the supply and the price of money.

As the consequences of the financial crisis were rapidly unfolding in September 2008, an emergency meeting was held in Washington, DC between key officials from the US government and representatives from major financial corporations. At the meeting, Ben Bernanke, chairman of the Federal Reserve, strongly urged the US government to provide a $700 billion bailout package to rescue major banks from bankruptcy and inject liquidity into the credit markets. As part of his argument, Bernanke is reported to have presented the following apocalyptic vision: 'If we don't do this tomorrow, we won't have an economy on Monday'. Not only is the bailout itself, which was subsequently approved by the government, exemplary of the way states today intervene in credit markets and banking affairs only to sustain the existing system. But Bernanke's vision is symptomatic of the kind of post-ideological thinking that surrounds the role of the state in contemporary monetary affairs.

What Bernanke should have said was this: 'If we don't do this tomorrow, we won't have an economy based on post-credit money on Monday'. When Bernanke equates the collapse of major financial institutions with the disappearance of the economy as such, he performs the kind of ideological naturalization we touched upon in the introduction. Let us look at Žižek's elaboration of the concept:

> In contemporary global capitalism, ideological naturalization has reached an unprecedented level: rare are those who dare even to *dream* utopian dreams about possible alternatives . . . Far from proving that the era of ideological utopias is behind us, this uncontested hegemony of capitalism is sustained by the properly utopian core of capitalist ideology. Utopias of alternative worlds have been exorcized by the utopia in power, masking itself as pragmatic realism.[69]

Utopian ideas of alternative monetary systems are emphatically absent from contemporary mainstream politics. We seem to have reached the end of history when it comes to developing ways to make money and put it into circulation. Since few governments are inclined to imagine other monetary orders beyond the current one, questions of monetary issues are quickly reduced to a pragmatic realism where the existing order is granted the right to define the conditions for its own maintenance, and politicians willingly reduce themselves to mere administrators working to facilitate the system within these conditions.

The key condition for the contemporary system of post-credit money is the capacity of private banks to issue debt that is liquid and thus capable of circulating as money. The system functions smoothly as long as demands for the redemption of debt come back to the bank only in the form of demands for credit transfers to other banks. As noted above, this kind of transfer can be carried out with minimal recourse to state-created fiat money. However, when crisis in the system emerges in the form of liquidity crisis, the dependence on state-created money is unveiled. When credit-money-users start doubting the credit worthiness of banks, or when banks start doubting each other's credit worthiness, credit money loses its capacity to circulate as money. It loses its liquidity. This is when the state steps

69 Žižek, *First as Tragedy, Then as Farce*, 77.

in as the believer of last resort. By providing credit to commercial deposit banks or even investment banks, the central bank demonstrates its sustained belief in the moneyness of the credit issued by these banks. In other words, the central bank uses its own position as the issuer of credit on behalf of the populace to confer credibility onto agents in the private banking system, thus conferring liquidity onto the credit money issued by these banks. This is essentially what the state-sponsored bailout packages offered by the US Federal Reserve, the European Central Bank and a number of other central banks in the past few years have been about. In the age of post-credit money, control over the supply as well as the pricing of money may be in the hands of privately owned banks and financial institutions, but the powerful and profitable position of these agents ultimately depends on an umbilical cord connecting them to the placenta of the state, from which liquidity flows whenever it is needed.

The political options for responding to the economic problems exposed by the financial/debt crisis are typically reduced to a choice between two positions: Keynesianism and monetarism. The former recommends that the state stimulate growth through expansive fiscal measures, even if this means running state deficits. The latter, by contrast, prescribes fiscal austerity, as potential benefits from excessive government spending are believed to be more than counteracted by increasing inflation. The choice between Keynesianism and monetarism is a false choice for two reasons. In addition, the debate between the two options functions to conceal the underlying fundamental problem.

It should be noted that both Keynesianism and monetarism in their *realpolitische* form have as little to do with the original writings of John Maynard Keynes and Milton Friedman as the policies of the Soviet Union had to do with the writings of Karl Marx. Using the terms in the present context, I am thus referring to the way that Keynesianism and monetarism appear as ideas in actual political practice and rhetoric.

In a Marx Brothers joke which is quoted several times by Žižek, Groucho is in a restaurant. When the waiter approaches him with the standard question, 'Tea or coffee?', he replies 'Yes, please!'[70] The joke

---

70 Žižek, *Contingency, Hegemony, Universality*, 90.

illustrates how a seemingly neutral choice between two alternatives contains an inherent logic with certain presuppositions. Groucho's reply undercuts this logic, and may thus serve as a vantage point for uncovering the presuppositions of a false choice. A similar logic is at play in the choice between Keynesianism and monetarism.

First of all, the choice between Keynesian fiscal expansionism or monetarist austerity poses the two measures as mutually exclusive in the same way that the waiter poses the choice between tea or coffee as an either-or decision. Curiously, the US government as well as the EU and many nation-state governments have in fact responded to the financial/debt crisis in the style of Groucho Marx. Their immediate response to the crisis when it emerged as a liquidity crisis in financial and money markets was to inject liquidity into these markets in the form of central bank credits. This was an eminently Keynesian response, although perhaps not in the form originally envisioned by Keynes himself. Instead of stimulating the real productive economy directly by providing additional fiat money through government spending, the money provided by government-sponsored bailouts was primarily channelled into the financial system.

Following this Keynesian stimulus of the financial and credit markets, a second wave of political interventions in the general economy seem to be unfolding. These interventions concern the fiscal policies of governments. While Keynesian stimulus seemed to be the obvious choice in the case of the financial and credit markets, monetarist austerity in government spending is now being propagated as the only sensible way out of the crisis. At least in Europe, this is a very obvious trend. In 2012, EU nation-state governments signed a financial treaty committing themselves to keeping their individual national budget deficits and debts within strict predefined limits. Meanwhile, the policies of the Obama administration in the US have been less clear cut, to the point that the traditional balance between Keynesian Europe and neoliberal America seems to have tipped some. Here is how one commentator sums up the two waves in the case of Europe:

> Fearing a financial Armageddon, governments transformed private bank debt into public debt via bailouts, lost revenues, lower growth, higher transfers, and yawning deficits. The unavoidable result across the European continent was a massive increase in government debt. While painting this as a story of fiscal irresponsibility has some

> plausibility in the Greek case, it simply isn't true for anyone else. The Irish and the Spanish, I and S in the eponymous 'PIGS', were, for example, considered 'best in neoliberal class' in terms of debts and deficits until the crisis hit. Public debt is a consequence of the financial crisis, not its cause.[71]

We see here how governments, most clearly in the European case, have responded to the question posed by the financial crisis – 'Keynesianism or monetarism?' – with the (Groucho) Marxist answer: 'Yes, please!' When it comes to banks and financial markets, states apply Keynesianism. When it comes to citizens and ordinary money-users, the states apply monetarism. The situation here is more intricate than just a simple case of hypocrisy and double standards. It is not just that first the state chooses Keynesianism, and second it chooses monetarism. There is a dialectical logic at play whereby the first choice brings about a set of circumstances that condition the second choice. Government intervention in the banking system and the financial markets created the massive public debt which was then subsequently posed as the very cause requiring governments to cut spending.

The logic is only reinforced by the fact that government deficits are being financed through lending in banks and financial markets. This means that fiscal balances become increasingly vulnerable to price fluctuations in these markets, especially with regard to interest rates. Due to this vulnerability, governments must choose a fiscal policy which they believe is the one preferred by 'the Market'. Prior to the signing of the EU financial treaty of 2012, Helle Thorning-Schmidt, the Danish Prime Minister from the Social Democratic Party, announced:

> Denmark is sending a crystal clear signal to the financial markets that we are conducting a responsible economic policy by joining the EU financial treaty. There is no doubt that the new discipline regarding European economic policy is also beneficial to Denmark. It is good for Danish economy to signal that we too are living up to the new discipline.

---

71 Blyth, 'How to Turn a Continent into a Subprime CDO'.

There is a kind of displacement at play in this quote. The main argument is not that this new and disciplined fiscal policy is necessarily good for the Danish economy as such. It is rather that this is what the Prime Minister believes the financial markets want Denmark to do. In Lacanian terms, the Prime Minister's reason for signing the treaty is not a desire for fiscal discipline as such (although we cannot rule out the possibility that there is a certain amount of surplus-enjoyment attached to letting oneself become reduced to merely an instrument of the will of the financial markets) but a desire for being desired by the big Other of the financial markets. And the possible reward for compliance with the demands of the financial markets is that Denmark and the rest of the treaty-countries become the object of desire of these markets, thus preventing an increase in the interest rates on government debt.

While at first glance the financial crisis in 2007–8 looked as if it were the beginning of the end of financial capitalism, it seems that the crisis, including the response to the crisis by the governments of the US and the EU, has ultimately served to propagate the tendency towards financialization of ever larger domains of life. We have already explored the tendency towards the de-politicization of the monetary policies of most nation-states, whereby the issue is reduced to a matter of administration according to predefined policy goals (primarily low inflation) that is undertaken largely by technocrats in semi-independent central banks. The signing of the EU financial treaty may be taken as a symptom that this de-politicization is now extending even into the domain of fiscal policy.

The choice between Keynesianism and neoliberal monetarism is also a false choice for a second and more profound reason. When economic policy is framed a choice between raising taxes or lowering taxes, raising social benefits or lowering social benefits, raising government spending or lowering government spending, this is at the same time a narrowing of the field of politics. The economic questions debated in contemporary mainstream politics have the form: How should the state spend its money? With Heidegger, we can say that this type of question operates in the domain of the ontic. The question merely invokes money as a being when it asks: What do we want to do with money as a particular being? While this question is indeed an important political issue, it has the tendency to cover up the fundamental ontological questioning of money. The reduction of economic policy to a choice between Keynesianism and monetarism is a symptom of *Seinsvergessenheit* concerning the question of money within the domain of politics. The ontological question that needs to be posed is this: How do we want money to be? In more profane terms, we might pose this question as: What kinds of money do we want in the world today?

Conclusion: Life after Debt – Revolution in the Age of Financial Capitalism

> The modern bourgeois society that has sprouted from the ruins of feudal society has not done away with class antagonisms. It has but established new classes, new conditions of oppression, new forms of struggle in place of the old ones. Our epoch, the epoch of the bourgeoisie, possesses, however, this distinct feature: it has simplified class antagonisms. Society as a whole is more and more splitting up into two great hostile camps, into two great classes directly facing each other – Bourgeoisie and Proletariat.[1]

When Marx and Engels wrote their Communist Manifesto, they identified the bourgeoisie and the proletariat as the two opposing classes in society. The bourgeoisie was the ruling class, living at the expense of the rest of society. The proletariat, in turn, was the potentially revolutionary class. The identification of these two classes was of course built on Marx's analysis of society. This was an analysis of industrial capitalism.

Today, the Marxist analysis of class struggle and revolution is both timely and untimely. The analysis of industrial capitalism does not seem to fit the current structure of our economy. We do not live in industrial capitalism any longer. That is not to say that industrial production has vanished from the face of the earth. Quite the contrary, the amount of industrial production at the time when Marx wrote *Capital* was only a fraction of what it is today. However, the distribution of wealth between different classes in society today does not seem to be determined primarily by the logic of industrial exploitation. A key, defining characteristic of contemporary capitalism is the logic of finance, which enables class dominance on the basis of what we might call monetary exploitation.

As we have already explored in the introduction, the title of this book plays on the double meaning of the phrase 'making money'. The

1 Engels and Marx, *The Communist Manifesto*, 2.

standard Marxist account of exploitation and class struggle is primarily based on the first and most immediate meaning of the term. Through the classic analysis of the relations between labour, commodities and capital, Marx shows how the capitalist is able to make money through the accumulation of surplus-value extracted at the expense of the worker. However, this notion of making money merely refers to the uneven distribution of existing money in circulation. Marx is concerned with the production and appropriation of value rather than the production of money. In fairness to Marx, it should be noted that he does provide some ideas about the role of credit and finance within the system of capitalist production and accumulation. However, these ideas do not amount to a coherent theory and their importance in relation to the overall analysis of money and capital is unclear.[2]

The argument of the current book is built around the exploration of the ontological question of money, which is concerned with the second meaning of the phrase. This is the question: How *is* money today? We have seen how the Being of money is constituted by the interrelations among three different ontological dimensions: the real, the symbolic and the imaginary. These three dimensions enable three different forms in which money may emerge as distinct beings: commodity money, fiat money and credit money. Yet, these forms should be regarded as ideal types since specific historical monies are always impure in the sense that they are constituted in the interplay among all three dimensions.

The dominant form of money today is post-credit money. This kind of money is created by private commercial banks when they issue credit circulating in an extensive and efficient credit payment system. The credit payment system together with the interbank system of mutual credit clearance allows private bank credit to function immediately as a means of payment – that is, as money. The issuance and circulation of private bank credit money is supported by states and their central banks through a number of measures. First of all, the state has allowed and endorsed the emergence of the electronic credit payments system, thus outsourcing control over the monetary infrastructure of the economy to private agents with special privileges. As an increasingly smaller

2 Harvey, *The Limits to Capital*, 239.

proportion of financial transactions are carried out in cash fiat money relative to bank credit money, the once sovereign privilege of states to create money has been handed over to private agents operating primarily to make profits. Secondly, central banks throughout the Western world have adopted policies to intervene in interbank money markets and other sectors of the private banking system only to support the maintenance of this system. The creation of credit and money in this system is largely regarded as a matter that is ultimately beyond the scope of political control, unless of course the system is in crisis, in which case the rescue of the system is a political responsibility. The age of post-credit money is marked by a post-political approach to monetary policy. Finally, even though fiat cash money constitutes only a fraction of all money in circulation, it still plays the crucial ideological role of providing the ideal fantasmatic image of money as such. It allows the users of money and as well as government officers to still entertain the belief that all money is ultimately created by the state and that banks are merely a financial intermediary between lenders and borrowers. This serves to veil the role of banks in the creation of money and the self-imposed impotence of the state in monetary matters.

A key purpose of the exploration of the ontology of money is to reclaim the constitution of money as a political question. The evolution of different forms of money is not merely a matter of convenience and efficiency. Money is not merely a practical solution to a practical issue. The particular constitution of money in a society lays bare important premises for the distribution of power and profit in that society. The nineteenth century British banker Amsel B. M. Rothschild was quoted as stating: 'Let me issue and control a Nation's money and I care not who makes its laws.' As we have established throughout the book, the paradigm of post-credit money enables exploitation through the simple procedure of making money. Private banks are given the privilege of creating the vast majority of the money in our economies. When this money is sent into circulation as interest-bearing debt or financial capital, it earns vast profits for the creators of the money. The paradigm of post-credit money enables a specific class within the network of international banking and financial markets to simply make money by making money. Even though the exploitation of labour as identified by Marx truly still exists, the distribution of the wealth appropriated through industrial exploitation may itself become the object of this kind of monetary exploitation. As Marx points out, money in the form of capital is a crucial element in the exploitation of labour. But today the functioning of this capital is also subject to the conditions of global financial markets and international banking. In the age of post-credit financial capitalism, even good old-fashioned industrial capitalists may become the subject of exploitation.

The *Seinsvergessenheit* regarding the question of money, which we also touched upon in the introduction, is not merely a phenomenon that pertains to mainstream economics. It is also very much a feature of our public debate and common political thinking about money. Most people today have a sense that there is something fundamentally wrong with our banking and financial system. While the general economy is still suffering from layoffs and cutbacks after the crisis of 2008, major banks and financial institutions seem to have already bounced back with profits, salaries and bonuses restored to pre-crisis levels. We are experiencing rising levels of economic inequality, and this is not only due to the lower and middle classes becoming poorer, but also to the really rich becoming even wealthier. Yet, few people have any idea how to fundamentally change this system. The most radical proposal to find its way into mainstream political debates seems to be the introduction of the so-called Tobin tax on financial transactions, which will at best cause a minor ripple in the flows of financial capital, and at worst provide just another opportunity for smart traders to make money on arbitrage. The idea of a Tobin tax stays well within the ontic domain of thinking that is concerned merely with the way money circulates as a being. Even when central banks apply unconventional monetary policies, such as quantitative easing, that do in fact go beyond the ways that money typically comes into being in the paradigm of post-credit money, this is done to conserve the existing state of affairs rather than bring about changes to the system. Ideas that intervene in the ontological constitution of money to fundamentally change the way we make money are found only at the margins of public and political debate, where they are typically dismissed as being merely figments of 'gold nuts', 'nostalgics', 'utopians', 'radicals' or other figures beyond reason. The political *Seinsvergessenheit* pertaining to money takes the form of a naturalization of money, where it becomes impossible to imagine ways of making money other than the ones that currently prevail.

In a similar vein as the Rothschild statement above, twentieth century industrial magnate Henry Ford was quoted as saying: 'It is well enough that people of the nation do not understand our banking and monetary system, for if they did, I believe there would be a revolution before tomorrow morning'. The shift from industrial to financial capitalism is not merely a shift in the way that profit is generated and exploitation is imposed. This shift also has profound implications for the way we can imagine a revolution. It is beyond the scope of this book to decide whether revolution is in and of itself a good thing. It is easy to demonstrate that the financialization of capitalism and the dominance of post-credit money have created a wide range of problems all over the world. Yet, it is less easy to demonstrate that revolution is necessarily the best solution to these problems. Revolutions can be beautiful, but they are most often very ugly at the same time. But regardless of whether we think revolution is a good thing or a bad thing, it is worth thinking about and imagining what a contemporary revolution might look like.

The shift from industrial to financial capitalism does not mean that class opposition disappears. In Marx's analysis, class position is determined by the subject's position relative to the means of production. The capitalist class is defined as the owners and controllers of the means of production, while the subjects of the labouring class own nothing but their own labour-power, which they are forced to sell to the capitalist. In financial capitalism, the appropriation of wealth and profit is not only and sometimes not even primarily mediated through the production and selling of commodities. With the paradigm of post-credit money, the very production and circulation of money has become one of the most profitable and influential enterprises of our time. This creates a second axis of class opposition supplementing the classic Marxist distinction between worker and capitalist. The evolution of an economy largely based on credit money has gradually outsourced the privilege to create money to private banking agents. When this money is sent into circulation in financial markets, it serves to redistribute and appropriate the profits generated in the productive sphere of the economy for the benefit of those agents that are in an advantaged position relative to these markets. In contemporary financial capitalism, class position is thus determined by the subject's position relative to the network in which credit money is created and circulated. Ultimately, this criterion renders two opposing classes: debtors and creditors. The creditors are the ruling class while the debtors are the potentially revolutionary class.

The identification and mobilization of the revolutionary class of debtors is of course made very difficult by the fact that most people are simultaneously debtors and creditors. It is not uncommon for someone to be a debtor by having a mortgage and a bank loan, while at the same time being a creditor on account of having bank deposits or savings in a pension plan that are invested in bonds or stocks. Furthermore, the role of states as major debtors blurs the picture, as it is unclear who is actually liable to repay the huge debts accumulated by nation-states such as the US, Italy, Greece, etc. At this point Marx would of course have argued that this blurring of the class boundaries is merely temporary and that the opposing class interests shall become more and more distinct as history approaches the climactic point of revolution.

The capacity not only to make money but to make money simply by making money is the defining privilege of the ruling class of creditors. Most money today is issued as debt. But that is not to say that all debt is money. Many people today are in a position where they can take out a loan and thus create debt. But few people are in a position where they can create a debt that functions as money. In fact, this is the special capacity of banks. In a religious society, priests have a privileged position because their words coincide with the words of God. In post-credit capitalism, banks have a similar position because their debt coincides with money. Their credit is generally accepted by the whole of the economic community and thus functions immediately as money. The fundamental difference between the two classes of debtors and creditors revolves around this capacity to create money. Creditors are in a position where they can make their own money, or at least they are in a privileged position to benefit from the creation of money. Debtors, on the contrary, cannot make their own money. Therefore they have to pay money to use money. In the simplest form, this money is paid as interest. We can think of interest as a kind of tax which is paid by the debtor for his participation in the money system. Today, even many nation-states are net-debtors, and interest payments on loans to banks and private investors constitute major items in their budgets. Some of the ordinary taxes paid by citizens are thus converted into the government's payment of 'tax' on the money they use.

In Marx's analysis, surplus-value emerges as the worker produces use-value in excess of the amount of money she is paid for his labour. Exploitation occurs as this surplus-value is appropriated by the capitalist. The worker is forced to participate in this exchange of labour for money since he does not have the means for valorizing labour himself. In a similar fashion, we can think of interest as a kind of monetary surplus-value that is emblematic of contemporary post-credit capitalism. Credit money generates this surplus-value, as it must be repaid with an amount of money exceeding the principal. Money-users have to engage in this kind of transaction since they do not have the capacity to create their own money. Even if a particular money-user is able to stay out of debt by saving up the money he needs, interest on this money is still paid by someone else in the system who has taken out the loan through which the money was originally created. Even if individual money-users stay out of debt, the class of debtors as a collective is still subject to monetary exploitation insofar as monetary surplus-value is appropriated by the class of creditors who are the ultimate source of the issuance of credit money.

This way of thinking about interest as the source of monetary exploitation and as a kind of tax paid by money-users is of course in contradiction to the way we normally think about interest. It is certainly in contradiction to the way interest is conceived in mainstream economic discourse. Interest is typically conceived as a kind of rent that the borrower pays to the lender for the right to dispose of the money for a particular period of time. Along these lines, interest compensates the lender for not being able to use the borrowed money for other purposes and for taking the risk that the borrower might default on the loan. Although the preceding analyses of post-credit money certainly makes it relevant to revisit the idea of interest, the point at this stage is not to refute conventional notions of interest but merely to disclose another aspect of money that is veiled by the typical conception. We shall unfold this point through a small analogy.

Imagine that words came into the world with certain ownership rights attached. Every time a language user wanted to use a particular word, he would have to pay a small fee to the original 'owner' who first coined the word. Such a scenario is very foreign to the way we normally think about language, and most people would be appalled by such a capitalization of language itself. We do not think of the words of a language as someone's property, but rather as components of a collective system of meaning that is common and shared by everyone who has invested the time and effort in learning the language. The creation of a new word is dependent on the existing reservoir of words. We can credit someone for the idea of coming up with a new word, but at the same time it is generally accepted that the creation is indebted to the whole of the language system. Therefore it makes no sense to tax the use of words.

Contrary to language, we tend to think about money as the property of the individual. Money is a system for keeping track of the purchasing power that each individual in the system is entitled to command. While money certainly has this capacity, it is at the same time also a collective system that is common and shared by every member of the collective. Just like language, the money system of an economic community works only because the members of the community have structured their social interactions around this money system. In this sense, the beggar and the billionaire contribute equally to the system insofar as both act as if the token circulating as money in the community is in fact money. The beggar and the billionaire may differ in the amount of money they own as individuals, but they have an equal share in money as the system which structures their economic interaction. 'Most things in life – automobiles, mistresses, cancer', says John Kenneth Galbraith, 'are important only to those who have them. Money, in contrast, is equally important to those who have it and those who don't'.[3] The point here is that the opposite is equally true: People who have it and people who do not are equally important to money. The money of rich people has value only insofar as even poor people accept this money as money.

Once we start thinking about money in these terms, the inevitability with which we accept a money system based largely on interest-bearing credit money seems to disappear. Why must money-users put themselves in debt to become part of the monetary system? Why should money-users in an economic community pay a fee to particular agents in the money system to be allowed to participate in a system

3 Galbraith, *Money, Whence It Came, Where It Went*, 5.

that is only maintained through the common effort and investment of all the members of the community? And what is the moral obligation of debtors to repay their debts, if this debt has been imposed upon them by a system that inevitably creates more debt than what can possibly be repaid? These questions may be summed up by the following point made by David Graeber: 'Money has no essence. It's not "really" anything; therefore, its nature has always been and presumably always will be a matter of political contention'.[4] We need to counter the prevailing *Seinsvergessenheit* in monetary matters and insist on posing the question of the Being of money as a political question. It is crucial to unveil the political nature of money because it gives every citizen the right to question every aspect of that particular monetary system to which he is subject. If democracy is to mean anything in capitalism, it must include the right of citizens to have an influence not only on *how* the government spends the money of the community but also on *which kind* of money should be circulating in the community. If this question is not included in the formal framework of democracy, it forces people to go beyond this framework to exert their democratic influence.

In industrial capitalism, the ultimate political weapon of the working class is the strike. Collective refusal to work not only applies immediate pressure on the capitalist class of factory owners when it puts an immediate halt to the production of value and the accumulation of profit. It also serves to demonstrate how labour is the ultimate source of value without which no value is created. The displacement of class division from industrial to financial capitalism means that also the revolutionary potential of the suppressed class changes. The strike is not an appropriate means of resistance against the class of creditors. First, the class of creditors does not derive profits immediately from the material production of goods. As we have seen, investors in financial markets are able to make profits when the market goes up as well as when it goes down. Second, the class of debtors is not identical to the class of workers. In fact, one of the consequences of the financialization and globalization of the monetary system is the outsourcing of labour to low-wage countries in Asia, South America and Africa, which means that many people of the traditional working class in the West are put out of a job. These people do not even have a

4 Graeber, *Debt*, 372.

job that they can refuse to do. Still, this does not mean that they do not have revolutionary potential. What the collective strike is to the class of workers in industrial capitalism, collective default is to the class of debtors in financial capitalism. In an economy where most money is ultimately debt, this money not only relies on money-users accepting and believing in this money. It also relies on them paying back their debts. But if large numbers of people were to collectively refuse to pay their debts, this would effectively prevent the system from functioning.

In the immediate wake of the so-called financial crisis of 2008, for a few weeks there was a brief moment when there was talk of a collapse of capitalism itself. Experts were saying that the economy was finally adjusting itself to the 'real values' of the underlying assets, and even Marx was quoted in mainstream newspapers. Allegedly, publishing houses experienced a sudden rise in the sales of *Capital*. Yet this general scepticism about the sustainability of capitalism itself was short lived, and public focus soon narrowed into a polemic about the pros and cons of stricter regulation of financial markets. I think this brief moment of collective doubt about the basics of capitalism was a revolutionary moment. However, it was a moment of a revolution that did not happen. A revolution that evaporated before it even got under way. Still, this moment may be used as an occasion to pose the conterfactual question: what did it look like, this revolution that did not happen?

Even though the underlying causes of the crisis may be traced back several years and even decades to the continuous deregulation of financial institutions and the evolution of increasingly complex financial instruments, the onset of the crisis was sparked by a rapidly rising number of defaults of American homeowners. Default on a mortgage and perhaps a resulting eviction is most often experienced as a personal failure. In itself, a default hardly seems like a revolutionary act. Nevertheless, I think these defaults were precisely elements of a revolution that did not happen. There are three major reasons why these defaults did not lead to revolution.

The first reason why default on a mortgage is not a revolutionary act is that it does not even qualify as an act. Default is not an intentional result of the will of the defaulter. Instead, a default is usually something that is brought upon the defaulter by outside forces. The second reason is that the defaults of American homeowners were merely a series of individual events. The defaults did not cause a collective mobilization of the debtors. In Marxist terminology, defaulting American homeowners remained a class *an sich* rather than mobilizing themselves into a class of debtors *für sich*. For the default of the American homeowners to have metamorphosed into an act of revolution, the debtors would have taken their defaults upon themselves as intentional political acts rather than the result of unfortunate circumstance, and they would have used the occasion to realize their collective interest as a class of debtors *für sich*. The third reason is that the US government stepped in to remedy the consequences of the default. Instead of letting the banks and the financial system take the losses, the government essentially took over some of the debt and hence also bore the consequences of the defaults.

If we take the amount of bonuses paid out to banking executives as a sign of the general health of banks, most of them seem to have recovered pretty quickly from the 2007–8 financial crisis. However, no sooner did economic commentators start to turn off the alarm of financial crisis than economic emergency reemerged in the form of a public debt crisis. Having compensated for the loss of productive jobs to China and other non-Western countries through infusions of cheap credit money into their economies, many countries in the West were now suffering as the air went out of the inflated prices of real estate and other kinds of assets that were believed to justify the value of this credit money. And having to foot the bill for private banks struck by the effects of the financial crisis obviously did not improve the solvency of these countries either.

When countries like Spain and Greece announced severe cuts in public spending to accommodate the demands of Germany and other creditors which came to the rescue to prevent national default, this was met by public protest. Contrary to the aforementioned events in the US, the response to the effects of the crisis was indeed a collective mobilization. This was especially the case in Greece, where thousands joined in collective strikes and demonstrations. Indeed, the protest had the contours of the formation of a class *für sich*.

The problem with the protests in Southern Europe was their target. Since the immediate problems experienced by the people took the form of public spending cuts, their revolt was directed at their governments. This means that the Greeks and the Spanish were mobilizing as a collective of dissatisfied citizens, not as a class of debtors.

The protests have failed to identify the other class which is the true opponent in the class struggle. This is of course the class of creditors. The state comes to function as a buffer between the two classes, which veils the real underlying class antagonism. The problem is not that the state imposes the consequences of its indebtedness onto the people. The problem is that the state has allowed private agents to profit by flooding the economy with credit money of their own making in the first place.

Marx was sceptical about the state. In his analysis, the state merely serves to enforce the interests of the ruling class. Formulated thus, this is of course a very crude claim. It does not seem to immediately correspond with the functioning of contemporary states, particularly those that like to think of themselves as welfare states. Still, when we look at the way that Western governments have responded to the financial/debt crisis, it is difficult not to see their initiatives as so many attempts to protect the position and the interests of the class of creditors. In the preceding chapter, we saw how governments and central banks have gradually outsourced control over the pricing and supply of money to private banks and financial markets over the course of the past four decades. Given this role of the state in the evolution of the paradigm of post-credit money, it seems difficult to imagine a monetary revolution in the age of financial capitalism without also a struggle between the class of debtors and the state.

In an ideal form, the monopoly of the state to coin money is a monopoly of the people to make their own money. But as we have seen, in the age of post-credit money, the state's monopoly on creating fiat money is primarily used to support the creation of credit money by private banks. The situation is comparable to a situation where the state monopoly on violence enjoyed by the police and the military would be used merely to protect and maintain the power of private cartels of gangsters to collect bribes and protection money from ordinary citizens. A popular revolution in financial capitalism would not only imply collective default by the class of debtors. It would also require the people to reclaim the right to make their own money. This is equivalent to Marx's call to the workers to reclaim control over the productive capacity of their own labour power. Of course, it is an open question as to which constitution of money would be ideal today and which institutions would be most adequate to make this money come into being. Ultimately, the answer to this question depends on the kind of society and the kind of life one holds as ideal. It is beyond the scope of this book to review all of the ideas of alternative monetary systems, such as local currencies, public banking, free banking, negative interest money, barter circles, international currency, Bitcoin, etc. that are fortunately already in circulation even though they are struggling to find their way into the mainstream.

However, I do want to end by pointing to one particular proposal for reform. This proposal is particularly interesting because it reconfigures the usual coordinates of political thinking by short circuiting the relationship between the revolutionary and the conservative. In the context of the UK, the proposal has first been put forward by Joseph Huber and James Robertson of the New Economics Foundation as a 'seigniorage reform', and subsequently by the movement for monetary reform known as PositiveMoney.[5] In the context of the US, a proposal along the same lines has been suggested by Jaromir Benes and Michael Kumhof of the International Monetary Fund as a revitalization of Henry Simon's and Irving Fisher's original Chicago Plan of 100 percent reserve banking from the 1930s.[6] In the non-English speaking world, similar proposals for reform have been launched under the headlines of 'Vollgeldreform' and 'bankvæsen med fuld reserve'.[7]

The aim of all of these proposals is a banking reform that would restore the prerogative of the state to issue money and also extend it to include non-cash credit money. Such a reform would require private commercial banks to back all outstanding credit with an equivalent deposit of government-issued fiat money in the form of cash or credit with the central bank. This means that private banks would be prevented from creating new credit money that is merely backed by the corresponding debt of money-users or by the debt of other agents in the private banking system. Private banks would no longer be allowed to create new deposits that are nothing but the outstanding debt of the bank itself. Instead, they would only be able to lend out money that they had subsequently retained, earned or

---

5 Huber and Robertson, *Creating New Money*; Jackson and Dyson, *Modernising Money*.

6 Benes and Kumhof, *The Chicago Plan Revisited*.

7 Binswanger, Huber, and Mastronardi, *Die Vollgeld-Reform*; Bjerg, *Gode penge: Et kontant svar på gældskrisen*.

borrowed in the form of central bank money. In the same way that a person can only lend out a bicycle, a wrench or a cup of salt if he is already in possession of a bicycle, a wrench or a cup of salt, private banks can now only lend out money that they already possess.

The potential effects of such a seemingly simple reform should not be underestimated. It is fair to say that they might even be revolutionary. First, control of the money supply would be shifted from commercial banks and credit markets to the central bank and the government, which would restore the government's capacity to apply measures of monetary policy in order to stabilize the economy or perhaps even steer economic development towards specific societal goals such as equality or sustainability. Second, the profits from issuing new money (seigniorage) would be reclaimed by the central bank and made available to the government for public spending rather than being appropriated by for-profit private banks and distributed to shareholders, managers, speculators or other members of the current monetary aristocracy. Rather than borrowing from private banks and investors in international capital markets at variable interest rates, the state would be able to borrow at zero interest from its own central bank, thus reducing or even eliminating the growing volume of debt that is currently burdening many national economies. And third, the risk of bank runs and monetary collapse would be eliminated as banks would have no other liabilities than what is immediately covered by their reserves of central bank money.

As the balance of power and profit is shifted from private banks and financial markets to nation-state governments, the outcome of the proposed reform would be only as good as the political institutions governing the creation of money. There are no guarantees that the economic forces reclaimed by the government would not be channelled into useless warfare, reckless deficit spending, corruption, suppression of political opponents, preferential treatment of political allies or other stupidities. This would depend on the quality and strength of the political community supporting the monetary system. Yet, we do not need our governments to be perfect for the proposed reform to be a success. It is enough for them to be just marginally better than the bankers and traders that are currently running things.

As much as this revolutionary potential may spark the dream of a better, more equal and more sustainable world to emerge from out of our current times of crisis, the true beauty of the reform lies in its utter conservatism. What is being proposed is not a new and weird utopia about money, government and banking. The restoration of the state's prerogative to make new money and the reduction of banks into mere financial intermediaries that lend rather than create money would do nothing but make both parties conform to the idea of what most people already erroneously believe they are doing.

Glossary of Financial Terms

arbitrage Profits made from speculation that takes advantage of similar assets being priced differently in different markets at the same time.

bank run A situation where more bank customers demand to get their deposits paid out in cash than the bank has cash reserves. Unless the bank is able to borrow additional cash from other banks or from the central bank, the bank run may result in the collapse of the bank.

Black and Scholes options pricing model An algorithm for the calculation of the theoretically correct price of an option on the basis of the historic *volatility* of the asset underlying the option. The algorithm was developed by Fisher Black and Myron Scholes in 1973, and the techniques behind it were subsequently used to develop models for the pricing of other kinds of derivatives.

bond A tradable form of debt that gives the holder the right to receive interest and repayments of the principal sum according to specified conditions. Typical forms include government bonds issued by states and company bonds issued by private companies.

Bretton Woods An international agreement pegging the exchange rate of all the major Western currencies including the Japanese Yen to the US dollar, while at the same time obliging the US treasury to ensure convertibility of the US dollar to gold at a fixed price. The system was founded in 1944 and ultimately terminated as President Nixon abandoned convertibility of US dollars into gold in 1971.

call See *option*

chartalism or chartalist theory of money See *state theory of money*

chartism See *technical analysis*

collateral Assets put up as security against a loan.

commodity theory of money A theory of money stating that the value of money is ultimately derived from the value inherent in commodities. According to the theory, money emerges as a particular commodity – for instance, gold – and is then elevated to the status of a general medium of exchange.

credit theory of money A theory of money stating that money is ultimately debt. According to the theory, money emerges as the credit of a creditor against a debtor is transferred to a third party in payment for commodities or services.

derivative The generic term for *options*, *forwards*, *futures*, *swaps* and other financial instruments that do not imply direct ownership of any underlying asset such as a company, a debt or a commodity, but derives its value from the price at which such a corresponding underlying asset is traded.

discount rate The interest rate at which commercial banks may borrow funds from the central bank. The discount rate is determined by the central bank.

E-V rule Expected returns – variance of returns rule assuming that in an *efficient market* there is inevitably a trade-off between the possible profits of an investment and the risk of the investment. If two *securities* trade at the same price, while one holds the possibility of high returns and the other holds only the possibility of modest returns, it is to be expected that the former is also a riskier investment with a higher probability than the latter of no returns at all.

Efficient Market Hypothesis (EMH) The theoretical assumption that markets have always already incorporated all relevant information into the pricing of the assets traded in the market. Under this assumption, the prices in the market always provide the best possible evaluation of the value of the assets traded, and it is impossible for individual traders to outsmart the market.

fiat money See *state theory of money*

forward or forward contract A particular kind of *derivative* that obliges both buyer and seller to execute the trade of a specific asset at a specified price at some specified time in the future. If the forward is traded on an organized exchange, it is also referred to as a *future*.

fractional reserve banking A system where banks are capable of issuing credit in excess of their reserves of liquid money.

fundamental analysis A kind of analysis that aims to estimate the actual value of a financial asset based on relevant economic fundamentals beyond the financial market in which the asset is traded. A fundamental analysis of a stock looks into the conditions of the underlying corporation and tries to project its future earnings by taking into consideration the state of the markets in which the corporation operates, the state of the corporations competitors and other relevant factors in the actual economy. Fundamental analysis may be opposed to *technical analysis*.

future see *forward*.

gold standard A monetary system in which the convertibility of money into gold at a fixed rate is guaranteed by a bank or government entity.

hedge fund A particular kind of investment fund that is characterized by engaging in highly speculative investment strategies, using *leverage* to increase potential return on investment, allowing only a limited number of participants able to invest large amounts, and sometimes taking advantage of off-shore locations to circumvent national regulations and taxes.

interbank money market The market where commercial banks borrow money from each other in order to settle temporary deficits in their balance of payments.

leverage The level at which an investment offers potential profits and losses that are large relative to the capital staked in the investment. A high level of leverage may be achieved by using an initial investment as *collateral* for borrowing even more capital that is then also used in the investment. Leverage often plays a key role in the investment strategies used by *hedge funds.*

liquidity The extent to which an asset is easily converted into money. The most liquid kind of assets is money itself.

option A particular kind of *derivative* that gives the owner the right but not the obligation to trade a specific asset, such as a stock or commodity, at a specified price at some specified time in the future. *Put* options give the owner the right to sell and *call* options give the owner the right to buy.

portfolio The collection of financial assets held by an investor.

put See *option.*

Random Walk Hypothesis The assumption that the direction of future price movements in a market is wholly unpredictable, which allows for the treatment of such movements as purely random events. The significance of the assumption is that it enables analysts to use probability theory to estimate the probability of future price trajectories. The Random Walk Hypothesis is closely connected with the *Efficient Market Hypothesis.*

repo or **repurchase agreement** A contract where a financial asset is sold with the agreement that the seller buys back the asset after a certain period of time. This creates, effectively, a collateralized loan from the buyer to the seller of the asset that is repaid when the contract expires.

security The generic term for tradable financial assets and instruments such as *stocks*, *bonds*, *forwards*, or *options*

short selling or **shorting** A trading technique whereby a trader sells a financial asset that he or she does not own, or owns only temporarily. The trader may have borrowed the asset from a broker or another trader, who in turn receives a fee. Short selling typically serves the purpose of making a profit on the expectation that the price of the asset is going to fall. The falling price allows the seller to recover the asset at a price lower than when it was sold short.

state theory of money A theory of money viewing money as ultimately being a creation of the state or another government entity. State money is created as a sovereign power declares certain objects to be legal tender and thus acceptable for payment of taxes, customs, fines and other debts. The sovereign power is at the same time also in a position to impose these taxes, fines and debts onto its subjects. Money emerging out of this system is also referred to as *fiat money* or *chartal money* and the state theory of money is also referred to as *chartalism.*

stock A security that offers co-ownership of a corporation and the right to a share of the dividends from the corporation.

swap A particular kind of *derivative* where two parties agree to swap the income stream from an underlying asset. A common example is the interest rate swap, where two parties exchange a fixed rate interest stream and a floating rate interest stream on the same principal sum.

technical analysis A kind of analysis that aims to predict future price movements in financial markets based on patterns of past price movements. Technical analysis is also sometimes referred to as *chartism* because it relies on charts of historic price movements. Technical analysis may be opposed to *fundamental analysis.*

volatility The extent to which the price of an asset fluctuates.

Bibliography

Agamben, Giorgio. *Homo Sacer: Sovereign Power and Bare Life*. Palo Alto: Stanford University Press, 1998.

———. *State of Exception*. Chicago: University of Chicago Press, 2003.

Alexander, Sidney S. 'Price Movements in Speculative Markets: Trends or Random Walks'. *Industrial Management Review* 2, No. 2 (1961): 7–26.

———. 'Price Movements in Speculative Markets: Trends or Random Walks', *Industrial Management Review* 5, No. 2 (1964): 25–46.

Bachelier, Louis. *Louis Bacheliers Theory of Speculation: The Origins of Modern Finance*. Princeton: Princeton University Press, 1900.

Bell, Stephanie. 'Do Taxes and Bonds Finance Government Spending?' *Journal of Economic Issues* 34, No. 3 (2000): 603–620.

Benes, Jaromir, and Michael Kumhof. *The Chicago Plan Revisited*. IMF Working Paper, 12/202, 2012.

Bennet, Rick. *King of a Small World*. New York: Arcade Publishing, 1995.

Bernstein, Peter L. *Capital Ideas Evolving*. New Jersey: John Wiley and Sons, 2007.

———. *Capital Ideas: The Improbable Origins of Modern Wall Street*. New Jersey: John Wiley and Sons, 1993.

Beunza, Daniel, and Daniel Stark. 'How to Recognize Opportunities: Heterarchical Search in a Trading Room'. In *The Sociology of Financial Markets*, edited by Karin Knorr-Cetina and Alex Preda, 84–101. Oxford: Oxford University Press, 2005.

Binswanger, Hans Christoph, Joseph Huber, and Philippe Mastronardi. *Die Vollgeld-Reform – wie Staatsschulden abgebaut und Finanzkrisen verhindert werden können*. Solothurn: Ed. Zeitpunkt, 2012.

BIS. *Semiannual OTC derivatives statistics at end-December 2012*. Basel: Bank for International Settlements, 2013.

Bjerg, Ole. 'Drug Addiction and Capitalism: Too Close to the Body'. *Body & Society* 14, No. 2 (2008): 1 –22.

———. *Gode penge: Et kontant svar på gældskrisen*. København: Informations Forlag, 2013.

———. *Poker – The Parody of Capitalism*. Ann Arbor: University of Michigan Press, 2011.

Black, Fischer, and Myron Scholes. 'The Pricing of Options and Corporate Liabilities'. *The Journal of Political Economy* 81, No. 3 (1973): 637–654.

Blyth, Mark. 'How to Turn a Continent into A Subprime CDO'. *TripleCrisis.com*, 2011.

Board of Governors of the Federal Reserve System. 'FRB: Who owns the Federal Reserve?' *federalreserve.gov*, 2012.

Bondt, Werner F. M. De, and Richard H. Thaler. 'Further Evidence on Investor Overreaction and Stock Market Seasonality'. *Journal of Finance* 42, No. 3 (1987): 557–581.

Bryan, Dick, and Michael Rafferty. 'Financial Derivatives and the Theory of Money'. *Economy and Society* 36, No. 1 (2007): 134–158.

———. 'Money in Capitalism or Capitalist Money?' *Historical Materialism* 14, No. 1 (2006): 75–95.

Buffett, Warren. 'Chairman's Letter'. *Berkshire Hathaway 2002 Annual Report* (2002).

Callon, Michel. *The Laws of the Markets*. Oxford: Blackwell, 1998.

Chicago Board of Trade. *Action in the Marketplace*. Chicago: Chicago Board of Trade Publications Department, 2000.

Christiano, Lawrence, Roberto Motto, and Massimo Rostagno. *Financial Factors in Economic Fluctuations*. Working Paper Series. European Central Bank, 2010.

Cootner, Paul H., *The Random Character of Stock Market Prices*. Cambridge MA: MIT Press, 1964.

Cowles, Alfred. 'Can stock market forecasters forecast?' *Econometrica: Journal of the Econometric Society* 1, No. 3 (1933): 309–324.

DailyFinance. 'Big Risk: $1.2 Quadrillion Derivatives Market Dwarfs World GDP'. *DailyFinance.com*, 2011.

Das, Satyajit. *Traders, Guns, and Money*. London: FT Prentice Hall, 2006.

Davies, Howard, and David Green. *Banking on the Future: The Fall and Rise of Central Banking*. Princeton: Princeton University Press, 2010.

Davies, Richard, and Peter Richardson. 'Evolution of the UK banking system'. *Bank of England Quarterly Bulletin* 4 (2010): 321–332.

Davis, John B. 'The Nature of Heterodox Economics'. *Post-Autistic Economics Review* 40 (2006): 23–30.

Eichengreen, Barry J. *Exorbitant Privilege: The Rise and Fall of the Dollar and the Future of the International Monetary System*. New York: Oxford University Press, 2011.

———. *Globalizing Capital: A History of the International Monetary System*. Princeton: Princeton University Press, 1998.

Engels, Freidrich, and Karl Marx. *The Communist Manifesto*. Whitefish: Kessinger Publishing, 1848.

Epstein, G.A. *Financialization and the World Economy*. Cheltenham: Edward Elgar Publishing, 2005.

Fama, Eugene F. 'Efficient Capital Markets: A Review of Theory and Empirical Work'. *Journal of Finance* 25, No. 2 (1970): 383–417.

———. 'Market Efficiency, Long-Term Returns, and Behavioral Finance'. *Journal of Financial Economics* 49, No. 3 (1998): 283–306.

Federal Reserve Bank of Chicago. *Modern Money Mechanics: A Workbook on Bank Reserves and Deposit Expansion*. Chicago: CreateSpace, 1994.

Ferguson, Niall. *The Ascent of Money: A Financial History of the World*. New York: The Penguin Press, 2008.
Fisher, Irving. *The Purchasing Power of Money: Its Determination And Relation to Credit Interest and Crises*. New York: Cosimo, 1911.
Fox, Justin. *The Myth of the Rational Market: A History of Risk, Reward, and Delusion on Wall Street*. New York: HarperCollins, 2009.
Friedman, Milton. 'A Theoretical Framework for Monetary Analysis'. *Journal of Political Economy* 78, No. 2 (1970): 193–238.
———. *The Optimum Quantity of Money*. Piscataway: Aldine Transaction, 2005.
Galbraith, John Kenneth. *Money, Whence It Came, Where It Went*. Boston: Houghton Mifflin, 1975.
Gervais, Simon, and Terrance Odean. 'Learning to Be Overconfident'. *Review of Financial Studies* 14, No. 1 (2001): 1 –27.
Gnedenko, Boris V., and Andrei N. Kolmogorov. *Limit Distributions for Sums of Independent Random Variables*. Reading MA: Addison-Wesley, 1954.
Graeber, David. *Debt: The First 5,000 Years*. New York: Melville House, 2011.
Greenspan, Alan. 'Corporate Governance – At the 2003 Conference on Bank Structure and Competition, Chicago, Illinois'. The Federal Reserve Board, 2003.
Grossman, Sanford J., and Joseph E. Stiglitz. 'On the Impossibility of Informationally Efficient Markets'. *The American Economic Review* 70, No. 3 (1980): 393–408.
Hacking, Ian. *The Taming of Chance*. Cambridge: Cambridge University Press, 1990.
Hamilton, William Peter. *The Stock Market Barometer: A Study of its Forecast Value Based on Charles H. Dows Theory of the Price Movement*. New York: Harper & Brothers Publishers, 1922.
Harvey, David. *The Limits to Capital*. London: Verso, 1982.
Hassoun, Jean-Pierre. 'Emotions on the Trading Floor: Social and Symbolic Expressions'. In *The Sociology of Financial Markets*, edited by Karin Knorr-Cetina and Alex Preda, 102–20. Oxford: Oxford University Press, 2005.
Heidegger, Martin. *Being and Time*. London: Wiley-Blackwell, 1927.
———. *Introduction to Metaphysics*. New Haven: Yale University Press, 1935.
———. *The Fundamental Concepts of Metaphysics: World, Finitude, Solitude*. Bloomington: Indiana University Press, 1938.
———. *The Principle of Reason*. Bloomington: Indiana University Press, 1956.
Ho, Karen. *Liquidated: An Ethnography of Wall Street*. Durham: Duke University Press Books, 2009.
Horgan, John. *The End of Science: Facing the Limits of Knowledge in the Twilight of the Scientific Age*. London: Abacus, Little, Brown and Company, 1996.
Huber, Joseph, and James Robertson. *Creating New Money: A Monetary Reform for the Information Age*. London: New Economics Foundation, 2000.

Hudson, Michael. 'The Archaeology of Money: Debt Versus Barter Theories of Money's Origins'. In *Credit and State Theories of Money: The Contributions of A. Mitchell Innes*, edited by L. Randall Wray, 99–127. Cheltenham: Edward Elgar Publishing, 2004.

Humphrey, Caroline. 'Barter and Economic Disintegration'. *Man* 20, No. 1 (1985): 48–72.

Ingham, Geoffrey. '"Babylonian Madness": On the Historical and Sociological Origins of Money'. In *What Is Money?*, edited by John Smithin, 16–41. London: Routledge, 2000.

———. 'The Emergence of Capitalist Credit Money'. In *Credit and State Theories of Money: The Contributions of A. Mitchell Innes*, edited by L. Randall Wray, 173–222. Cheltenham: Edward Elgar Publishing, 2004.

———. *The Nature of Money*. Cambridge: Polity, 2004.

Innes, A. Mitchell. 'Credit Theory of Money'. *The Banking Law Journal* 31 (1914): 151.

———. 'What Is Money'. *The Banking Law Journal* 30 (1913): 377.

Jackson, Andrew, and Ben Dyson. *Modernising Money: Why Our Monetary System Is Broken and How It Can Be Fixed*. London: PositiveMoney, 2013.

Jevons, William Stanley. *Money and the Mechanism of Exchange*. Charleston: Forgotten Books, 1875.

Kahneman, Daniel, and Amos Tversky. 'Prospect Theory: An Analysis of Decision under Risk'. *Econometrica* 47, No. 2 (1979): 263–291.

Kant, Immanuel. *Critique of Pure Reason*. Cambridge: Cambridge University Press, 1787.

Kaufman, George G., and Kenneth E. Scott. 'What Is Systemic Risk, and Do Bank Regulators Retard or Contribute to It?' *Independent Review* 7, No. 3 (2003): 371–391.

Kavanagh, Thomas M. *Enlightenment and the Shadows of Chance: The Novel and the Culture of Gambling in Eighteenth-century France*. Baltimore: The Johns Hopkins University Press, 1993.

Keynes, John M. *A Treatise on Money*. London: Macmillan, 1930.

———. 'Review'. *The Economic Journal* 24, No. 95 (1914): 417–419.

Kinsella, N. Stephan. 'Funny Money'. *Liberty* 7, No. 2 (1994): 12.

Klein, Naomi. *The Shock Doctrine: The Rise of Disaster Capitalism*. New York: Picador, 2008.

Knapp, Georg Friedrich. *The State Theory of Money*. London: Macmillan and Company, 1924.

Knorr-Cetina, Karin, and Alex Preda. *The Sociology of Financial Markets*. Oxford: Oxford University Press, 2005.

Lacan, Jacques. *Television: A Challenge to the Psychoanalytic Establishment*. London: W. W. Norton & Company, 1990.

———. *The Four Fundamental Concepts of Psychoanalysis*. London: W. W. Norton & Company, 1973.

———. 'The Function and Field of Speech and Language in Psychoanalysis'. In *Écrits*. London: W. W. Norton & Company, 1966.

Lawson, Tony. 'The Current Economic Crisis: Its Nature and the Course of Academic Economics'. *Cambridge Journal of Economics* 33, No. 4 (2009): 759–777.

———. 'The Nature of Heterodox Economics'. *Cambridge Journal of Economics* 30, No. 4 (2006): 483–505.

Leeson, Nick. *Rogue Trader*. New York: Warner, 2001.

Lerner, Abba P. 'Money as a Creature of the State'. *The American Economic Review* 37, No. 2 (1947): 312–317.

LiPuma, Edward, and Benjamin Lee. *Financial Derivatives and the Globalization of Risk*. Durham: Duke University Press, 2004.

MacKenzie, Donald A. *An Engine, Not a Camera: How Financial Models Shape Markets*. Cambridge MA: MIT Press, 2006.

Malkiel, Burton G. *A Random Walk Down Wall Street*. New York: W. W. Norton & Company, 1973.

Mallaby, Sebastian. *More Money Than God: Hedge Funds and the Making of a New Elite*. New York: Penguin, 2011.

Mandelbrot, Benoit, and Richard Hudson. *The (Mis)Behaviour of Markets*. New York: Basic Books, 2004.

Mankiw, N. Gregory, and Mark P. Taylor. *Macroeconomics*. 6th edition. New York: Worth Publishers, 2007.

Markowitz, Harry. 'Portfolio Selection'. *Journal of Finance* 7, No. 1 (1952): 77–91.

Marx, Karl. *A Contribution to the Critique of Political Economy*. New York: C.H. Kerr, 1859.

———. *Capital – Volume 1*. London: Dent, 1867.

Marx, Karl, and Friedrich Engels. *Karl Marx and Frederick Engels: Selected Works in One Volume*. New York: International Publishers, 1865.

McKenzie, Rex A. 'Casino Capitalism with Derivatives: Fragility and Instability in Contemporary Finance'. *Review of Radical Political Economics* 43, No. 2 (2011): 198 –215.

Merton, Robert C. 'Theory of Rational Option Pricing'. *The Bell Journal of Economics and Management Science* 4, No. 1 (1973): 141–183.

Mirowski, Philip. *More Heat than Light: Economics as Social Physics, Physics as Nature's Economics*. Cambridge: Cambridge University Press, 1989.

Mishkin, Frederic. *The Economics of Money, Banking, and Financial Markets*. Upper Saddle River: Prentice Hall, 2004.

Mosler, Warren. 'Full Employment and Price Stability'. *Journal of Post Keynesian Economics* 20, No. 2 (1997): 167–182.

Neumann, John, and Oskar Morgenstern. *Theory of Games and Economic Behavior*. Princeton: Princeton University Press, 1944.

Nørretranders, Tor. *Det udelelige: Niels Bohrs aktualitet i fysik, mystik og politik*. Copenhagen: Gyldendal, 1985.

Parguez, A., and M. Seccareccia. 'The Credit Theory of Money: The Monetary Circuit Approach'. In *What Is Money?*, edited by John Smithin, 101–123. London: Routledge, 2000.

Pryke, Michael, and John Allen. 'Monetized time-space: derivatives – money's 'new imaginary'?' *Economy and Society* 29, No. 2 (2000): 264–284.

Rhea, Robert. *The Dow theory: an explanation of its development and an attempt to define its usefulness as an aid in speculation*. Flint Hill: Fraser, 1932.

Ryan-Collins, Josh, Tony Greenham, Richard Werner, and Andrew Jackson. *Where Does Money Come From?: A Guide to the UK Monetary and Banking System*. London: New Economics Foundation, 2011.

Samuelson, Paul. 'Proof that Properly Anticipated Prices Fluctuate Randomly'. *Management Review* 6, No. 2 (1965): 41–49.

Schumpeter, Joseph Alois. *History of Economic Analysis*. London: Routledge, 1954.

Seaford, Richard. *Money and the Early Greek Mind: Homer, Philosophy, Tragedy*. Cambridge: Cambridge University Press, 2004.

Sharpe, William F. 'Capital Asset Prices: A Theory of Market Equilibrium under Conditions of Risk'. *Journal of finance* 19, No. 3 (1964): 425–442.

Shaxson, Nicholas. *Treasure Islands: Uncovering the Damage of Offshore Banking and Tax Havens*. London: Palgrave Macmillan, 2011.

Shiller, Robert J. 'From Efficient Market Theory to Behavioral Finance'. *Cowles Foundation Discussion Paper No 1385* (2002).

———. 'Tools for Financial Innovation: Neoclassical Versus Behavioral Finance'. *Financial Review* 41, No. 1. Financial Review (2006): 1–8.

Simmel, Georg. *The Philosophy of Money*. London: Routledge, 1900.

Smith, Adam. *The Wealth of Nations*. New York: The Modern Library, 1776.

Smithin, John N. *Controversies in Monetary Economics*. Cheltenham: Edward Elgar Publishing, 2004.

Tobin, James. 'Money'. In *The New Palgrave Dictionary of Money and Finance*, edited by Peter Newman, Murray Milgate, and John Eatwell, 770–779, 1992.

Weintraub, E. Roy. 'Neoclassical Economics'. *The Concise Encyclopedia of Economics* (1993).

Werner, Richard. *New Paradigm in Macroeconomics: Solving the Riddle of Japanese Macroeconomic Performance*. Basingstoke: Palgrave Macmillan, 2005.

Williams, John Burr. *The Theory of Investment Value*. Cambridge MA: Harvard University Press, 1938.

Wittgenstein, Ludwig. *Philosophical Investigations*. Malden MA: Wiley-Blackwell, 1945.

Wolfe, Tom. *The Bonfire of the Vanities*. New York: Random House, 1987.

Wray, L. Randall. *Understanding Modern Money: The Key to Full Employment and Price Stability*. Cheltenham: Edward Elgar Publishing, 1998.

Zaloom, Caitlin. *Out of the Pits: Traders and Technology from Chicago to London*. University of Chicago Press, 2006.

Zelizer, Viviana A. *The Social Meaning of Money*. New York: Basic Books, 1994.

Žižek, Slavoj. *Contingency, Hegemony, Universality: Contemporary Dialogues on the Left*. London: Verso, 2000.

———. *First as Tragedy, Then as Farce*. London: Verso, 2009.

———. *How to Read Lacan*. London: W. W. Norton & Company, 2006.

———. *In Defense of Lost Causes*. London: Verso, 2009.

———. *Living in the End Times*. London: Verso, 2010.

———. *Looking Awry: An Introduction to Jacques Lacan through Popular Culture*. Cambridge MA: The MIT Press, 1991.

———. 'Philosophy, the 'unknown knowns', and the public use of reason'. *Topoi* 25, No. 1–2 (2006): 137–142.

———. *The Fragile Absolute or, Why Is the Christian Legacy Worth Fighting For?* London: Verso, 2000.

———. *The Parallax View*. Cambridge MA: MIT Press, 2006.

———. *The Plague of Fantasies*. London: Verso, 1997.

———. *The Sublime Object of Ideology*. London: Verso, 1989.

———. *The Ticklish Subject: the absent centre of political ontology*. London: Verso, 1999.

———. *Violence: six sideways reflections*. London: Profile Books, 2009.

Žižek, Slavoj, and Glyn Daly. *Conversations with Žižek*. Cambridge: Polity, 2004.

Zupančič, Alenka. 'Reversals of Nothing: The Case of the Sneezing Corpse'. *Filozofski Vestnik* 26, No. 2 (2005): 173–186.

Index

Page numbers in **bold** refer to figures.

On the Typeface

This book is set in Minion, a typeface designed by Robert Slimbach for Adobe Systems in 1990, which has become one of the few contemporary book faces to rival the classic types of Caslon, Bembo and Garamond. Though it has no obvious precursor, it retains a calligraphic sentiment that Robert Bringhurst dubs 'neohumanist' in his *Elements of Typographic Style.*

Telltale features of Minion include the subtle cant in the bar of the 'e', the angular bowl of the 'a', and the tapered bulbs that terminate the head of the 'a' and the tails of the 'y' and 'j'.

Minion's restrained personality and even colour have made it a popular workhorse type, the narrow set width of which provides economy yet does not detract from its suitability for book settings.